The first edition of this book was dedicated to my wife. Now–and at her suggestion–I want to re-dedicate it to one of its heroes, Airey Neave, who was murdered on Friday, 30 March 1979.

The reader will find, in chapter two, an appreciation of Airey written while he was alive. Of necessity it concentrated on his skills as a party politician. There is much, much more to be said about his heroism in war and under Gestapo torture, his dedication in peace and his–in my experience–unique generosity of spirit. Organizer of the European resistance to Nazism, Nuremberg lawyer, campaigner for the aged, chairman of the Commons Committee on Science and Technology, and the man who made Margaret Thatcher Leader of the Conservative Party and Prime Minister– he was all these things. And just when he seemed to be about to achieve this, his greatest triumph, he was struck down by cowards. 'If they come for me,' he once said, when asked if he feared assassination, 'the one thing we can be sure of is that they will not face me. They're not soldier enough for that.' Thus it was.

For four years this hero of mine was my friend. In that I was very lucky.

Patrick Cosgrave is uniquely qualified to write this book. A distinguished Cambridge historian – author of a much acclaimed volume on Winston Churchill and the war, the second part of which is to appear later this year – he has also a remarkable record as a political columnist.

For this special post-election edition, Patrick Cosgrave has written an extra chapter, telling how the election battle was waged, discussing its major issues and describing how Mrs Thatcher's historic victory occurred.

Margaret Thatcher
PRIME MINISTER

Patrick Cosgrave

Arrow Books

The widespread enthusiasm which her election
aroused was partly due to her novelty and partly
to her striking looks, but more than all else, it
was due to her being the embodiment of many
hopes.

RUSSELL LEWIS, *Margaret Thatcher:*
a personal and political biography,
London, 1975

Socialism [is] fatal to the Parliamentary system.

WINSTON CHURCHILL

Arrow Books Ltd
3 Fitzroy Square, London W1P 6JD

An imprint of the Hutchinson Publishing Group

London Melbourne Sydney Auckland
Wellington Johannesburg and agencies throughout
the world

First published by Hutchinson 1978 as
Margaret Thatcher: A Tory and her Party
Arrow edition 1979

© Patrick Cosgrave 1978

Made and printed in Great Britain by
The Anchor Press Ltd, Tiptree, Essex

ISBN 0 09 918430 3

Chapter one
The woman

A few days after Margaret Thatcher was elected to lead the Conservative Party, the literary editor of the *Spectator* had occasion to ring Norman St John Stevas. The Shadow Education Minister was one of the few senior Tories genuinely torn by conflict during the often bitter and never less than acrimonious events of the preceding weeks. Edward Heath was his friend, and had given him his first major political break. St John Stevas, so unlike the former Prime Minister in almost every aspect of his personality, outgoing and extravagant and emotional where Heath was angular, tense and buttoned-down, nonetheless had great fondness for his Leader. On the other hand, the Ministry where Heath had given him a job was that headed by Margaret Thatcher. Again, there had been a potential clash of personalities, and few thought the highly coloured St John Stevas was likely to get on with the (as she seemed then) sharp, precise, disciplined and combative Secretary of State. In fact, their necessary alliance turned quickly into friendship. A romantic, St John Stevas found it not only easy, but highly agreeable to work for a woman. He drew out her own often concealed sense of humour, and was licensed in a way no colleague had been previously to make elaborate and ironical jokes about her. When Heath was eliminated in the first ballot for the leadership, St John Stevas became an enthusiastic Thatcher partisan, and when Peter Ackroyd offered conventional congratulations on her success he replied, 'It wasn't an election. It was an assumption.'

There is always acuity even in St John Stevas's most random or jesting observations. On this occasion he put his finger on one important part of the somewhat stunned feeling with which the Conservative Party lived for some weeks after Margaret Thatcher had polled 146 votes (to William Whitelaw's 79, James Prior's and Geoffrey Howe's 19 apiece, and John Peyton's 11) in the second ballot of the leadership election. To be sure, the Party was stunned partly because it had overthrown, in its first-ever open leadership election, the most dominant and (in the way he organized his own grip on its organization) most efficient Leader it had ever had. Partly, too, they were stunned because they had chosen a woman, and a woman who had been the most un-fancied of outsiders when she declared her intention of entering the contest. But most of all, as St John Stevas saw, they were disconcerted by the growing awareness that the new Leader was not at all what she had seemed to be, either earlier in her career when she was embattled in support of unpopular policies against a press and a teaching profession both adamantly hostile to her, or later when, after the débâcle of February 1974, she emerged as what most opinion regarded as a somewhat strident right-wing critic of the policies of the previous decade and longer.

A number of Tory backbenchers had begun to gain some insight into her private character when they had sipped claret with her in the Westminster room of Robin Cooke, the Member for Bristol West, in the weeks of the leadership campaign. During this period, of course, Margaret Thatcher was leading for the Opposition on the Finance Bill, and these committee sessions gave ample opportunity for the display of her better known talents – mastery of the most complicated and recondite information; an aggressive but not displeasing style; a ready, if acid, wit; and a capacity to remain unruffled and elegant whatever the pressures of the day. In Cooke's room, though, she expounded neither philosophy nor policy at any length (something which surprised those who had been led by Heath's campaign managers to believe that her contributions to Cabinet discussions had invariably taken the form of harangues); instead she created an impression of gentleness and concern.

The two defeats of 1974 had delivered a deep shock to Tory self-esteem and self-confidence. They also released for public airing a number of misgivings about Heath's style of leadership which the tight discipline he imposed, and the natural instinct of the Party to rally behind its leadership in times of crisis, had kept under wraps. To all the worries, complaints, doubts, hesitations and even fears expressed in these sessions the hitherto distant and icy Mrs Thatcher lent a sympathetic and somehow encouraging ear. Once the great stride of actually putting her in Heath's place had been taken, there was time, as there had not been before, to reflect on the two personalities, to absorb something of the contrasts and contradictions in her nature which had emerged, and to speculate on what life with her was going to be like. Though the acrid taste of intra-Party conflict was to continue for some months, most backbenchers liked what they saw, and began to preen themselves on the wisdom of their choice as though it had been a considered affair, whereas in fact it had been the most improbable compound of her own reckless courage, the exceptional tactical skill of a handful of hitherto obscure advisers, the blundering of Heath's managers, and the deep, inchoate but desperate and powerful wish of the Parliamentary Party for a change. Before matters settled down, however, one of the tougher characters among those who had voted for her on the second ballot called on her in the long, drab room that was then the Leader of the Opposition's office in the Palace of Westminster, and was moved to tears by the sight of a small, slight, fair and rather vulnerable woman getting down to her first day of work in what had always seemed to him to be a place reserved for the experienced, dominating, and sometimes even great, male.

Just before the first ballot Bernard Levin wrote an article in *The Times* encouraging the Tories to choose Margaret Thatcher over the other contestants. He addressed himself particularly to any reservations they might have on account of her sex. While it might seem an enormous leap in the dark to choose a woman – the first woman to lead a Western political party – Levin argued, once they had done it, the Conservatives might well find that it had been a natural thing to do, and would almost certainly find the experience of being led by a woman who was able no different from being led by a man with similar qualities. While the article was of real assistance and comfort to her supporters, particularly at a time when almost the whole of the press was overtly for Heath, with Whitelaw the majority choice as an alternative (Derek Marks of the *Daily Express* had thundered that she was 'totally out of touch with anybody but carefully corseted, middle-class, middle-aged ladies . . .'), it was wholly wrong in its prediction. The Party quickly found that being led by a woman was in fact a very different experience from being led by a man.

Discussion of her sex appeal – even of her sex – is not something that particularly pleases Margaret Thatcher. To the inevitable question, at her first press conference as Leader, on what she thought about Women's Lib, she snapped, 'What has it ever done for me?' In her speeches, broadcasts, and off-the-cuff replies to questions, she regularly invokes, and identifies with, the image of the housewife. The family and family life is another recurring theme. The genuineness of her identification is not in question, but its expression is somewhat ritualized. About her own personal status as middle-aged housewife she is even prepared to joke. For example, at a large discussion lunch at the Institute of Economic Affairs in Lord North Street (from the IEA there has emerged most of the intellectual thrust behind the phenomenon called monetarism which has greatly influenced her section of the Party) just after the defeat of February 1974 Christopher Tugendhat, then Member for the City of London and Westminster, was foolish enough to assert that the more abstruse conclusions of economic liberalism simply could not be explained to constituency parties dominated by middle-aged ladies in flowered hats. 'Speaking,' Margaret Thatcher began, 'as a middle-aged lady who likes hats . . .' and she went on to a withering critique of the Tugendhat view. Open references to her sex are, however, generally avoided.

Consciously or unconsciously, however, her femininity, even her sex appeal, frequently affects those who meet or work with her. Sometimes it is a matter of more than masculine consideration for others. On one occasion when a speech drafted for her by a colleague was to be rewritten at her instructions, and when she had painstakingly gone over the new structure with one of her aides, she admonished him to the effect that any consultations with the original author which proved to be necessary should be handled with great tact. Assuming that she was referring to no more than the danger of damaging an author's normal *amour propre*, the aide offered perfunctory reassurance. 'No,' she said, 'you don't understand. His marriage has just broken up. He is not to be upset.' Since the speech was an important one, requiring substantial emendation and due for delivery the following day, her concern was exceptional and of a kind not normally to be found in a senior politician.

More striking and – if audience reaction is anything to go by – much more unexpected was her behaviour on a visit to Cambridge early in 1976. She did not have to make a speech. Rather, the highlight of the engagement was a question and answer session with an audience drawn from town and gown. Though such occasions tire her, she enjoys them and seems to profit from even the most banal and trivial questions. She invariably, however, betrays a flutter of concern and nervousness beforehand, and this time, in the car taking her from London, questioned her companion closely on the likely character of the audience. His only response was the quotation of a frivolous judgement from an eminent Cambridge don to the effect that whereas *his* place of learning was a university Oxford was no more than a night club.

That evening she first attended a buffet supper given by the Master of Peterhouse, the college she was visiting. Afterwards, wearing a long black velvet skirt, white silk blouse and black velvet jacket, she repaired to the Peterhouse Senior Combination Room. It was already crammed, but lit by only two table lamps, one on each side of the speaker. In a few sentences the Master explained that she was not going to make a speech, that she would answer questions on anything the guests wished to raise, and that she would say a few words of introduction.

At large public gatherings, and on television, Margaret Thatcher's voice often seems both sharp and high. Within smaller confines, and in more relaxed situations, its natural softness asserts itself. Pointing to each of the lamps in turn, she said, 'I was told on the way here that Cambridge was a real university, while my Oxford was only a night club. But I've never seen anything more like a night club than this.' She took off her jacket and made as though to throw it over her shoulder. 'If it is a night club,' she added, 'you'd better have my cabaret. Questions?' For nearly two hours she answered a great variety of them, but the battle for the heart and attention of a highly critical audience had been won with her first sentences.

Informality of that kind is relatively rare – unfortunately, in the opinion of many of her staff. She tends to be stiff and aggressive on television, having no love for the appurtenances of studios. Press interviews do not delight her, and though she has a high regard and a genuine friendliness for a number of journalists (a file of Bernard Levin's articles is kept in her office) she does not love the press as a whole. Occasionally, she can delight a Fleet Street audience, as she often does at her weekly sessions with the parliamentary press lobby. When this happens, however, her performance, even at its best, is inclined to seem prepared, polished, somewhat artificial. Her wit then is often cruel and she is inclined, if not exactly to be overbearing, to make some of her questioners the butts of her jokes and her briskness. This tendency, which journalists naturally find irritating and, occasionally, humiliating, has been noticeable for some time. There was the occasion (when she was Secretary of State for Education) when the slightly overweight Ivan Rowan of the *Sunday Telegraph* interviewed her in her office in Curzon Street: at the end of their talk, when Rowan was preparing to wait for the lift to take him to the ground floor, she instructed him rather peremptorily to walk, adding that his waistline required exercise. But while she held that office, she determined to make a major effort to repair her bad relations with the (almost invariably critical) educational correspondents. She gave a party for them and lavished on each of her guests a somewhat seigneurial charm. Afterwards she sat down and invited questions, subsequently sending the great majority away annoyed if not angry that she had displayed what they regarded as contempt for questions which betrayed a less complete grasp of all the facts about education than she had herself. Few disputed her greater knowledge or command (though many would dispute the conclusions she drew) but nearly all felt that she had been wantonly rude. The difficulty, as one well-disposed adviser present saw it, was that she did not seem even to realize that she had given offence.

It is at home that she is most clearly seen without the armour the successful politician wears at Westminster. A woman visitor who had not seen her in person for some months, but who had watched several television performances she had given in the meantime – performances exhibiting the strength rather than the pleasantness of her character – was surprised to be reminded by confrontation of how small, how youthful and how transparent (the visitor's word) she looked. Her skin is, of course, very pale, and her hair very fine, requiring constant attention to keep it in the order she prefers: some months after her election, she took to wearing it shorter and looser, a style which emphasized the slenderness rather than the aquilinity of her features. She is fortunate, too, in that her skin is remarkably unlined: even around the neck – the most tell-tale of places for a woman in middle age – there are few of the channels that usually arrive with fifty, if not earlier. For all this, however, there is the sharpest possible contrast between Thatcher on television and Thatcher in the flesh. If the contrast has made her less sympathetic on television than her supporters would wish there is some compensation in the delighted surprise which leads quickly to devotion of supporters in the constituencies who meet her for the first time. Realizing this, she travels a great deal, and already rivals for mileage Edward Heath, the most travelled Leader in the Party's history.

It is when she is tired that her frailty, a frailty which calls forth a protective instinct in women as well as men, becomes

exceptionally apparent. She is unfortunate in being of that
fairly rare group who sound a great deal worse after they have
more or less recovered from a cold than while they are suffering
from it. At times when her voice has been reduced to a croak a
sort of hush descends on her Private Office, however excellent
her spirits, and secretaries, aides and colleagues go about with
frowns on their faces as though she were seriously ill: this
phenomenon has led to a number of quite unfounded rumours
in the press about her ability to bear the physical strain of
leadership. In fact, as her career testifies, she possesses quite
remarkable powers of physical endurance. From the beginning
of her parliamentary career she coped as efficiently with the
duties of a housewife and mother as with those of a politician –
she did not stand in the 1955 election because she thought her
children were too young to leave alone.

On one occasion, however, a combination of fatigue and
distress seemed almost to overwhelm her. This was at the outset
of her campaign against Heath. Not long after the February
defeat she had come to the conclusion that the Party needed a
new Leader. Given her judgement that the collectivism in
economic policy – and particularly the determination to con-
struct and make permanent a complicated statutory incomes
policy – which Heath had espoused had led the 1970 government to disaster and represented a betrayal of the essential
philosophy of Toryism, it was logical for her to support her
friend Sir Keith Joseph for the leadership. Joseph's formal campaign opened in September 1974 with a speech at Preston highly
critical of the late government's general economic policy, and
he was the only member of the Shadow Cabinet who shared
Mrs Thatcher's own views. To the very few who suggested that
she herself should run she replied that she had had too little
experience, and that the Party would never choose a woman:
this judgement she put on record in several newspaper interviews. Only when Joseph, who had never been personally
ambitious, and who was modest about himself to an excessive
degree, withdrew did she determine to put herself forward. She
assumed the mantle of challenger in no vainglorious spirit but

because, as she put it, 'somebody from our lot had to stand', and she was the only one.

She was not prepared for the storm that broke about her head. Heath had a capacity unusual in a man so apparently remote and often disagreeable to excite fervent devotion in friends and colleagues, and throughout the period from his February defeat to his final overthrow, many of his supporters fought the roughest battle the Tories, no slouches at party in-fighting, could recall. In November every effort was made to draw public attention to an interview she had given to the magazine *Pre-Retirement Choice* the previous summer. She had advised pensioners and those about to retire to hedge against inflation by building up stocks of high-protein long-life foods. She was accused of encouraging hoarding and, because of the foods she had recommended, of betraying ignorance of the desperate financial plight of pensioners. Sometimes, as every student of Fleet Street knows, insignificant stories like this blow up into a major sensation, and so it proved on this occasion.

The whole affair rapidly got out of hand, and Margaret Thatcher quickly realized the truth of Winston Churchill's dictum that there is no difference in politics greater than that between being number one and not being number one. As the only challenger to Heath, and an unusual and unexpected one at that, her every action was subject to close and overblown scrutiny. Every paper paraded the 'hoarding' story and most used it to express doubt about her capacity and judgement. One reporter attempted to bribe her cleaning woman to provide useful details about life at home with the Thatchers. On an LBC phone-in conducted by George Gale a caller – a 'Mr Tallis' – claimed that he had frequently seen her in his shop in Finchley High Road, and that she had tried to exploit her position to get special treatment during the sugar shortage. She was out of town on that day, but her constituency secretary, Alison Ward, heard the broadcast. A telephone call confirmed that she never shopped in Finchley High Road; a further check revealed that the shop named did not exist; and LBC broadcast an apology. But, of course, some damage had been done and the surprise and hurt of the Thatcher family – even if some more experienced politicians could have told them they were being naive – was considerable.

Matters were at this stage when she came to lunch at the *Spectator* in Gower Street on 6 December. From late 1973 the *Spectator* had from time to time canvassed her as a possible Leader of the Party; from the moment of Keith Joseph's withdrawal the enthusiasm of the editorial staff for her cause had known no bounds. All of us were distressed by the fact that she seemed both disturbed and tired. There was talk at the time that she was allowing herself to be used merely as a stalking horse for Edward Du Cann, the chairman of the backbenchers' 1922 Committee. Our advice was strongly against even a tentative alliance with Du Cann before the first ballot decisively tested her strength, and we mistakenly assumed that her hurt anger with the press, her evident tiredness, and her helplessness in the face of the grossest misrepresentation all suggested a weakening of resolution. Harry Creighton, the proprietor and editor, put our question to her bluntly. The quality of her will showed in her reply. 'Don't misunderstand me,' she said. 'I saw how they broke Keith, but they won't break me.'

Once the battle for the leadership was over, however, a whole series of different problems developed. Some of these, including that of rebuilding Party morale, will be discussed in later chapters. For the moment, however, it is the impact of the new responsibility on her personality that concerns us.

Although Margaret Thatcher was throughout her career more interested in matters of general policy and political philosophy than was fashionable (especially in the Heath years when Ministers and Shadow Ministers were expected to keep strictly within their ministerial briefs) the exercise of will and the expenditure of time that were required to bring her into the front rank of politics and yet maintain a normal family life, left her little leisure or opportunity for philosophizing. A serious candidate for the leadership of a major party is generally expected to have held one or more of the major offices of state (that is, a major economic ministry, the Foreign Office or the Home

Office) partly because of the technical experience such a job gives and especially because the top posts offer an individual the opportunity of familiarizing himself with the wider as well as the narrower problems of government. A Chancellor or a Foreign Secretary will generally have sat on the more important Cabinet committees dealing with overall policy, and is likely to have enjoyed membership of the so-called inner cabinet, a shifting body, consisting of those who at any one moment particularly enjoy the confidence of the Prime Minister of the day, or on whose ministerial performance he is particularly dependent.

Margaret Thatcher had enjoyed none of this invaluable experience. Despite her professional ability, there was a sense in which, in 1970, she was the statutory woman in the Cabinet and, of course, her portfolio of Education was one thought to be particularly a woman's: the first woman to hold high office in Britain, Ellen Wilkinson, was herself Minister for Education though she was not a member of the Cabinet. Nor had Mrs Thatcher ever enjoyed a particularly close relationship with Heath. There is, indeed, some evidence that he regarded her, especially during the intense Cabinet debates of 1972 when the great change of direction in economic policy and management was under discussion, as something of a nag. He certainly felt that when many problems of greater immediacy and importance (in his view) were pressing upon him her inability to run the Department of Education and Science without exciting damaging controversy was a considerable handicap. Though he never failed to back her in public there were rumours, when Reginald Maudling resigned from the Cabinet in July 1972, that she would lose her place in the consequent reshuffle. All of these past events, and the nature of her own senior experience, conspired to ensure that the early stages of her leadership would be marked by some uncertainty, and some fumbling which greater expertise might have avoided.

The leadership is a job requiring a generalizing mind. Previous experience as, say, Foreign Secretary or Chancellor of the Exchequer can be so useful as to enable a man to avoid, without too much criticism, the tiresome job of becoming knowledgeable over a wide range of subjects. The Department of Education, however, and some facility in economics, were insufficient background for a new Leader in the spring of 1975. Moreover, as Education Secretary and subsequently as Shadow spokesman on the environment and then on finance, she had applied her formidable intellectual energy to acquiring complete technical mastery of her subjects. All her earlier activity had encouraged the side of her mind – first given shape and discipline by her studies as a chemist and as a lawyer – that preferred to concentrate information and put it in order. Her working habits of an early morning start and a finish late at night likewise cut down the time available for reflection, brooding, and even daydreaming. All this led some who favoured the candidacy for the leadership of Whitelaw or Du Cann to suggest that in choosing her the Party would merely be acquiring a female Heath, a gifted technician, but one without general vision or human sympathies.

From excessive intellectual austerity she was saved principally by her love of poetry – and particularly Kipling – her studies in political philosophy, and her fervent patriotism. But such reading had been less a part of her day-to-day life than the preoccupation of rest periods and holidays. One of her inclinations was to run the Leader's office on a basis of insufficient delegation and over-anxiety to keep up her personal work rate. Even now there is some criticism of her attention to detail: it is useless to present her with a draft speech, article or letter which contains an unfamiliar allusion, quotation or piece of information which does not have attached to it documentation giving necessary supporting detail, or the context of a quotation used.

A certain unwillingness to delegate, and a finicky approach to detail, extend even into mundane aspects of her life. Rather than send to the House of Commons Library for a book or a reference, she will go herself, though this tendency, it is fair to add, is as likely to indicate that she has turned the whole of her mind to the preparation of a speech as it shows a characteristic desire to do all things for herself. A missing document, even one of no particular significance, can create a flap of some proportions. Even when she is in a difficult mood, however, this is not resented by her staff for, however hard she works them, her consideration on other occasions more than makes up for spells of hard labour. Small parties on festive occasions are the order of the day, and her attitude to them is nicely indicated by the occasion on which at her insistence, and at some inconvenience to senior colleagues, a farewell party for a junior member of her Private Office was moved from a tiny unoccupied office to the more commodious surroundings of the Shadow Cabinet room.

A readiness to dare is likewise one of the features of her personality which saves it from any tendency to aridity. Her most notable apparent deficiency when she became Leader was a complete lack of any background in foreign policy, a lack of which Sir Harold Wilson made much during their early exchanges at Prime Minister's Question Time on Tuesdays and Thursdays. Yet the biggest impact she has made – and it has been a world-wide impact – as Leader of the Opposition has been in foreign policy, in her critique of the policy of *détente* with the Soviet Union, a critique now supported by President Carter. Her willingness to take the high ground, against the advice both of the Shadow Foreign Secretary, Reginald Maudling, and some of her more timorous advisers who felt she might come a cropper, was first made apparent in a Question Time challenge to Wilson on the subject of a trade deal with Russia which he had just negotiated and of which he was particularly proud. Afterwards, of course, she sought and received expert advice in her preparation of three major speeches, before, just after, and on the first anniversary of, the Helsinki Declaration. But the initial risk, the initial instinct, was her own.

A particular habit of her own and of Conservative Central Office prevents the exceptional coherence and moral power of some of her speeches in the country becoming generally known. A number of speeches into which a great deal of thought and preparation (on a level a great deal higher than is common in modern politics) have gone are not reported at all, because she chooses to treat the occasion of their delivery as a rehearsal. In the case of others – particularly of a very powerful speech on

economic policy delivered to a banking audience in London in
January 1977 – only a truncated version is issued from Smith
Square. Sometimes it seems that she and her advisers do not
realize that, in the age of radio and television, a great deal of
political reporting is not done by journalists on the spot, but by
desk-bound writers working from press releases. Sometimes, it
seems that there is simply a lack of awareness of how much has
to be done to draw the full attention of the press even to a
speech by a potential Prime Minister. There is, too, a desire –
in my view mistaken – to make speeches excessively simple on
the assumption that only such are really attended to in the era
of the visual media.

For example, when on 31 July 1976 (the anniversary of the
Helsinki Agreement) she made the third of her speeches critical
of those accommodations between the West and the Soviet
Union normally brought together under the heading *détente*, she
deliberately quoted and reapplied to herself the description
'Iron Lady', given to her by the Russian press. As anybody
watching them could see, the television cameras in the hall were
switched on only as the sentence containing that description
came in view of the cameramen – who had advance texts. Four
Sunday newspapers the following day used the words 'Iron
Lady' in their headlines; as did a great many other papers in
the course of the following week. Several journalists, of whom
Adam Raphael of the *Observer* was the most inaccurate, specu-
lated about the origins and preparation of the speech. Save in
the leader columns of *The Times* and the *Daily Telegraph* there
was no considered or informed discussion of her analysis – which
seemed then so unfashionable – and none which did not assume
that the argument of the whole speech was not accurately sum-
marized by the self-accepted description 'Iron Lady'. But then,
not a single political correspondent of a national newspaper
made the – perhaps outrageously lengthy – trek from London
to Dorking in Surrey to hear the speech; and from the quality
of their comments it would be difficult to believe that they
had read the full text either. They were as selective as the
cameramen. Yet her arguments were reported and discussed

around the world, and the first three pages of the speech are now President Carter's foreign policy.

Given such treatment it is hardly surprising that, when she spoke to the Zurich Economic Society at the University of Zurich on 14 March 1977 – in effect, to a meeting of Britain's creditors – she and Conservative Central Office had arranged for no more than a two-page press release summarizing what was certainly her most important speech since becoming Leader of her Party. The British press, it seemed, could be expected to digest no more than a few quick phrases. Yet, and perhaps to her surprise, the *Daily Express* and one or two others discussed her argument in some detail. The fact remains that there is something of a tussle between those of her advisers who believe that the press will refuse to absorb more than the barest and most hatchet-carved outlines of policy and those who believe that, even before journalists again read speeches, or even go to hear them, it is desirable to circulate full texts, though with guidance as to points of emphasis added for the unwitting or unwilling.*

Her preparation for an important speech, and indeed for the whole business of speech-writing, is both idiosyncratic and revealing. Quite apart from the intensive work that goes into an individual speech, she indulges in informal seminars on general subjects which have as their end a speech rather than a policy document or decision. The distinguished American political philosopher Shirley Letwin and her lawyer husband were surprised and gratified by the fact that in one such session several lengthy papers they had prepared were analysed and criticized at considerable length, and attention was drawn to the fact that there were failures in philosophical logic at several points. In no case, and whatever the pressures of the day, will Margaret Thatcher allow a draft to pass muster if she is doubt-ful, not so much about its technical detail or conformity with policy, as about its inner philosophical coherence.

Wisely or not, today's politicians make a great many more

* The argument about *détente*, and the significance of Mrs Thatcher's Zurich speech, are discussed below, in chapter 7.

speeches than did those of earlier generations. In addition, there
are thousands of letters to be dealt with – she receives an
average of 400 a day – and hundreds of messages to be sent to
constituency organizations for fêtes, dances, yearbooks and
other occasions. For Margaret Thatcher, as for anybody else in
her position, the greater part of this output must be drafted by
others. But, from her regular general sessions and from views
that filter down rapidly from her through what is, by, say,
American standards, a very small private office, the impress of
her ideas and personality is given to everything that goes out.
A typical period of speech preparation begins with a long conversation with her in which she explains the destination she
wants the argument to reach and the track along which it is to
go. After the first draft there will be another such session.
Frequently she will prepare the second draft herself. At whatever inconvenience to herself and others further changes will
continually be made until she is satisfied. And even when the
aide has departed she may well have another go at the text
herself. Indeed, if she is still not satisfied she is likely to jettison
the text and speak off the cuff, not always with the happiest of
results.

The evening of a day when she is obliged by whipping arrangements to remain in her suite at the House is a favourite time for
the dissection and preparation of speeches. An offer to feed anybody whose presence is required cannot, however, be taken as
an invitation to a square meal. Her appetite is often birdlike
and, for a woman who is an excellent, sometimes even a brilliant,
cook, her tolerance for seedy House of Commons salads, a yog-
hurt and a tomato is remarkable. Her favourite drink is whisky,
her taste for which greatly surprised the formidable journalist
George Gale who, for his first meeting with her had laid in a
bottle of dry sherry, on the supposition that it was the only
tipple favoured by ladies so recognizably Tory as herself.

Of course, in addition to the ordinary and predictable burdens
of her job, there are certain extra problems which being constantly in the public eye imposes on a woman naturally fastidi-
ous in dress. Parliament has not yet really adjusted to the

presence of women and, until the Christmas of 1976, when she acquired a suite, the single large room available to her as Leader of the Opposition provided few facilities for changing and repairing make-up in advance of an evening engagement. On one occasion, it is related, Norman St John Stevas announced that he was leaving a Shadow Cabinet meeting earlier than usual because he had to go home to change for dinner. She protested, observing that she was attending the same dinner, and had no intention of cutting the meeting short. 'Yes, Margaret,' he replied, 'but it takes me much longer to change than it does you.'

Indeed, especially given the fact that she never appears in the casual, comfortable, easy to wear and hard to rumple clothes available to and thought suitable for modern women, the simplicity and modesty of her retinue is remarkable. Again, it reflects a simplicity of personality, and a lack of interest in the parades of modern political leadership. Her wardrobe for travel is prepared and supervised by Guinevere Tilney, wife of a Tory backbencher of distinction, who makes certain that the Leader is amply provided with suitable clothes and gadgets (including, for her difficult hair, a set of Carmen rollers) for engagements away from London. But the speed and efficiency with which an appearance is prepared owes much, not merely to habits built up over an adult lifetime, but to a preference for neatness over display and plainness over decoration. Almost all of her jewellery, including the distinctive bracelet to be seen in every photograph which shows her hands, is inexpensive and was given to her by her husband, Denis.

These personal tastes are reflected in public conduct. To the amazement and even the horror of some of her advisers she announced, on becoming Leader, that she would fulfil all the engagements previously entered into in her ministerial and Shadow capacities. One such was an undertaking to open a school in Horncastle. She arrived at the school alone, on a wet day, and in advance of the local party and was not at all put out either by her own discomfort or their embarrassment. The small size of her travelling parties abroad is a wonder to foreign politicians, accustomed to advance guards as well as large staffs. And she never exploits her office to make people wait on her if it is reasonable to wait on them.

Much of this simplicity is concealed, however, by a frequent peremptoriness of manner. She is given to personal remarks, even to slight acquaintances, which are often thought rude. She can be cutting with opponents, especially within her own party, as when she asked a young member of the left-wing Tory Reform Group, with an icy sweetness, exactly what it was he wanted to reform. Though humour enters into such exchanges it is usually more apparent to her than to the victim, and they reinforce the superficial impression of a tough and even hardened lady.

So do various of her policy positions, perhaps especially her support for capital punishment, the only political subject on which she and her husband are known to disagree. On the other hand, she has few of the conventional prejudices of what might be thought of as her type. The morning after the resignation of Jeremy Thorpe (whom she scarcely knew) as Leader of the Liberal Party she surprised a friend whose line on the Thorpe affair was a stern and harsh one, with a passionate defence of Thorpe and his right to privacy, as well as a warm expression of sympathy and understanding. After an uneasy lunch at which a rather drunk young politician whose acquaintance with her was slight confessed that he was in difficulties with Central Office over a speaking engagement which he had failed to keep because a crisis in his marriage had arisen only a few days before, she made it her business to sort out his difficulties at Smith Square. And throughout her career, she has shown a warm personal preference for the more extrovert rather than the more staid of her acquaintances.

With children she has a magic touch. It is, perhaps, her one similarity with Edward Heath. Their company immediately cheers her, whatever her previous mood. She has that rare facility for entering immediately into their world and speaking to them directly on their own terms. A child may be allowed to keep a politician waiting, but the reverse never occurs. She is endlessly tolerant of their foibles and eternally preoccupied, not with the future just of children she knows, but of whole generations: she has never forgotten and frequently refers to a remark I once made, in the bliss that attends recent parenthood, about the effect the birth of my daughter had on my whole conception of life; and she has more than once used it as the starting-point of a wide-ranging discussion on political and public affairs, for she almost invariably proceeds from the particular to the general, rather than the other way round.

No political leader that I have known has ever been less dependent on the advantages and trappings that attend high office for the impact she makes; and none more dependent on the force of her own character and mind. Naturally, having come so far and having triumphed without the aid of particular social or political advantage, she has an unforced faith in herself. Real gloom descends on her only when she contemplates the decline of her country, and the grim prospects the future holds for it. She understands, some believe she exaggerates, the difficulties she will face if she wins a general election. Certainly, she believes that the electoral contest at which she will lead her Party is perhaps the most crucial of the century, and for her kind of party and her kind of nation a last chance. This conviction, which is deep and not conventional nor egotistical, gives drive and urgency to everything she does, lends her the strength to overcome the doubts and hesitancies of more experienced colleagues and advisers, and gives her the power with which, on her day in the House of Commons or on a platform, she sweeps all before her. Just as Thatcher the Leader has been a surprise and a revelation even to those who thought they knew her, so Thatcher the Prime Minister would be a surprise and a revelation to the country that elected her.

Chapter two
The battle

Margaret Thatcher had a busy day on Thursday, 21 November 1974. Apart from her routine duties as an MP and as the leading Opposition spokesman on the Finance Bill, she had in her diary engagements with a Portuguese businessman, a journalist who was also a Tory candidate, one of the authors of what would become the Nuffield College book on the general election of the previous October, and a representative of a women's teaching organization – for she had not yet detached herself from the interests and responsibilities in the field of education that she had acquired in the years before the defeat of February 1974. She also had to lunch with, and make a speech to, the National Council of Women, attend a Young Conservative reception, and dine with the members of the Chartered Institute of Public Finance and Accountancy. It was a typically full day, but it became marked, not for any of her scheduled arrangements, but because of an interruption.

After the lunch, which was held in the House of Commons, she returned to her tiny, Spartan room on the so-called Shadow Cabinet corridor – one floor above the Chamber of the House and the room of the Leader of the Opposition. There Keith Joseph called on her a little later. He wanted to tell her that he was no longer a candidate for the leadership of the Party. His was not the call of one relay runner to another, to whom he was about to pass the torch, but the act of a candidate for a job telling his best and most loyal supporter that he was no longer in the contest, and that he hoped she would not be upset or damaged by his decision to withdraw. He had been greatly wounded, he told her, by public and political reactions to a speech on social policy which he had made at Edgbaston on 19 October in which, by an unfortunate reference to deprived children born 'in socio-economic classes four and five', he had conveyed an impression both of callousness and of unimaginable political ineptitude. He had suddenly been given a bitter taste of what it was like being out in front in a political struggle, especially against a campaign team as hardened and ruthless as that supporting Heath and, after talking the matter over with his wife, had decided he wanted no part of it. His withdrawal was not unexpected, and she had had time to consider what her own course of action would be in that event for, as she always insisted, 'the one person I knew I would never stand against was Keith'.

Now she offered her sympathy, assured herself that his new resolution was unshakeable, and telephoned to Heath's room. He was free to see her and she went downstairs to tell him that she would be a candidate whenever the leadership election, which he had promised to the 1922 Committee of Tory backbenchers the previous week, took place. According to her recollection she did not sit down, and the interview lasted about a minute and a half. Beset as he was at the time by a multitude of problems, of which the challenge to his authority within the Party was merely the most prominent, Heath does not seem to have taken her offer of battle very seriously. Like herself, like Joseph, and like many of their supporters, he may well have imagined that her declaration would merely precipitate several – perhaps many – other candidacies.

Edward Du Cann, the chairman of the 1922 Committee, would have been a more formidable challenger than Mrs Thatcher. Appointed chairman of the Conservative Party Organization by Sir Alec Douglas-Home he had resigned the post shortly after Heath became Leader, and after a number of disagreeable exchanges between them. He had never been preferred again, but the fact that he had been left out in the cold after 1970 also meant that he was untainted by association with any of the failures of the Heath government. To be sure, the scandal sheet *Private Eye* and one or two newspapers had made the completely unfounded suggestion that his record in the City would not bear overmuch scrutiny and since there had been a great many City collapses and scandals in recent years this was a subject on which backbenchers were unusually nervous. On the evening of 14 November, however, after Heath had told the 1922 Committee that he had asked a committee sitting under Lord Home to make recommendations on how an election fo the leadership should be conducted, and that an election would be held on some date after they had reported, one private gathering of backbenchers who were determined that the Heath era should be brought to a close found that a majority of their number favoured Du Cann. In his favour were his detachment from the Heath government, his record as chairman of the House Public Expenditure Committee, where he had done remarkable work, dark good looks, considerable oratorical skill, and his ability at political manoeuvre. Against him were his City connections, a plummy manner which seemed out of keeping with the time, and what some felt to be an evasiveness of character and a temperamental inability to take big decisions almost as marked as that of Keith Joseph.

Among those who attended the meeting on 14 November were Airey Neave, later to be manager of the Thatcher campaign, who continued until the Christmas recess to keep in intimate touch with the unofficial Du Cann group, and Peter Tapsell, the brave and independent Member for Horncastle. Tapsell, like Du Cann, had been cold-shouldered during Heath's years in power. He had never supported the seemingly tough and resolute economic policies associated with the famous Shadow Cabinet seminar at the Selsdon Park Hotel, but when Heath himself abandoned those policies in 1972 Tapsell was rewarded neither for his courage nor for his consistency. Treatment of this kind, so markedly unlike the generosity of Harold Macmillan to even his strongest critics (for Macmillan believed that all strands of Party opinion should be represented in its higher reaches) ensured a plentiful supply of enemies for Heath in the winter of 1974.

More important than his political record for the purposes of the meeting of the 14th, however, was Tapsell's other life as a distinguished stockbroker with several foreign governments among his clients. In the following weeks he took soundings in the City which convinced him that there was nothing to fear from any investigation of Du Cann's business affairs. Tapsell reported all this not only to his parliamentary colleagues, but also to his numerous friends and admirers in Fleet Street; such is his reputation that nobody could doubt his assurances. The rumour-mongers in the press and in the Heath camp were not silenced, but they were rendered ineffective. As the Christmas recess approached Du Cann was completely free to decide, according to his personal inclination and that alone, whether he would enter the lists or not. Certainly, during this time, the overlap of potential support between the Du Cann and Thatcher camps ensured that serious consideration was being given to whether she should stand down if he came in, so that the opposition to Heath would not be divided.

More formidable as a candidate even than Du Cann, and much more formidable than the untried Mrs Thatcher, would have been William Whitelaw. Of Whitelaw it could be said with absolute assurance that he had no enemies. Only certain members of the radical right, where keen Joseph supporters were to be found, despised him as a bluff squire, a waffler, and a man quite ignorant on economic policies. But they feared him: they feared his genuine popularity, and especially his popularity in the Parliamentary Party and the Party organization. He had been Heath's Chief Whip for five years, and he knew every backbencher intimately. Though he had left Northern Ireland in worse case than he found it he had managed, unlike any other British politician since Arthur Balfour in the nineteenth century (and Balfour had gone on to be Leader of the Party and Prime Minister), to enhance his reputation as a result of his involvement in the affairs of that unhappy island. He was, finally, bang in the centre of the paternalist Tory tradition made triumphant in the 1950s by Harold Macmillan; and the right, convinced that that tradition had had its day, and that it led ultimately both to economic failure and creeping socialism, feared him for that as well. And, finally, he had a case against Heath: it was widely believed that if there had not been a general election in February 1974 his Northern Ireland 'power-sharing' executive would have worked.

There was one moment when, it was rumoured, Whitelaw could have had the leadership merely by stretching out his hand for it. On the Sunday following the October general election defeat a number of the more radically minded Tory back-benchers, as well as some defeated candidates who were likewise partial to the libertarian philosophy once expounded, then abandoned, by Heath, gathered at the London flat of Nicholas Ridley, the Member for Cirencester and Tewkesbury. Ridley, tall, fair, charming and a distinguished painter, had been something of a favourite of Heath's in the 1960s. Enjoying great skill both as a speaker and a writer, and with a facility for ruthlessly logical economic analysis that recalled his great friend Enoch Powell, Ridley had entered the 1970 government as a junior industry minister. His brief, and the brief of the political team at the giant new Department of Trade and Industry, was to implement the drastic Conservative policy of cutting subsidies to failing industry and ensuring that those firms who could not swim in highly competitive modern markets sank without benefit of government-financed resuscitation. The death of Iain Macleod, however, brought in as the new head of the Department the untried businessman John Davies. Adept on the public platform and on television, though wretchedly inferior in the House of Commons, Davies talked very tough indeed on industrial policy. However, he acted very soft and, as the pressures on the Heath government mounted, its industrial policy was reversed; subsidization on a hitherto undreamt-of scale became the order of the day along with huge public investment in business in order to reach the growth targets that had eluded every British government for more than a decade. There was no place in the new Department for Ridley or his fellow junior minister, Sir John Eden. Eden was offered and accepted an alternative job, as Minister of Post and Telecommunications. Ridley was, probably because of his artistic leanings, offered the Ministry of the Arts which, of course, included presiding over the spending programme of the Arts Council. He refused. 'Ted didn't seem to realize,' he said, 'that I was *against* public spending, not for it.'

In the following years Ridley's reputation as a trenchant and often brilliant critic of the Heath government from a standpoint on the right continued to grow. Only an apparent lack of broader sympathies, a determination, it seemed, to see every human activity only in the light of free market economics, an outrageous frankness of speech, and quite unfounded rumours about his lack of technical competence as a Minister, held him back. Nonetheless, with Powell out of the Party and out of Parliament, with Joseph given neither to socializing nor to intriguing, Ridley was an ideal host for a get-together of Heath's critics on the right. And, while all present sensed an opportunity was to hand, they were also extremely worried.

For them, on Sunday 13 October 1974, Joseph was the only conceivable candidate. Thatcher they scarcely thought of. Powell, whom some would certainly have supported, was, in the most emphatic way, unavailable. And they all knew that in other London drawing rooms plans were being discussed if not hatched to replace Heath by Whitelaw at speed, so as to ensure at least the continued dominance of the Party by its centre and left. The curious thing here is that while, as the story of the battle for the leadership unfolds, it will become apparent that ideological considerations of the kind dominant in the minds of Nick Ridley and his friends had little influence among the generality of Tory MPs, the campaigners for Heath and Whitelaw focused from the very beginning on the threat from the right. Peter Walker, who was to become Heath's campaign manager, Ian Gilmour, who is certainly the most intellectually distinguished of Conservative centrists, and the dominant factions in Conservative Central Office and the Party's Research Department, all thought in this way. Moreover, the language some used in describing the adherents of Keith Joseph and, later, of Margaret Thatcher to their contacts in the press became, as the weeks went by, increasingly strong, strident, and abusive. Dislike and contempt was returned in full measure from the numerically much smaller ranks of the right, though in fact the Thatcher campaign was not run by any recognizable right-wing ideologue.

The division engendered at this stage of the battle remained to plague the Party afterwards: at the Party conference of 1975, when the new Leader presented herself for the first time to the massed ranks of her supporters, some indiscreet and widely publicized remarks made by Heath late at night to some journalists created a furore and revealed that he still considered his defeat as essentially in the nature of a take-over of the Party by right-wing extremists, though nothing could, in fact, have been farther from the truth. In the long run, indeed, it may well prove that the partisans of both the so-called right and the so-called left were acute in their instincts. For, to the outside observer, it is clear that the struggle between Edward Heath and Margaret Thatcher was not merely a struggle between proved defeat and possible success, but between two wholly different visions of the future, for country as well as Party.

Nonetheless, the almost fierce attachment to Joseph of many of those who gathered at Ridley's flat (and others of their friends who were not there) implied some detachment on their part from Margaret Thatcher, and this may be one of the reasons for a quite extraordinary lack of energy in her campaign organization between 21 November and the end of the year. Anyway, those who feared, on 13 October, that Whitelaw might steal a march on Joseph were reassured. First, in the course of a telephone call to Joseph that evening he said categorically, 'I am a candidate for the leadership, and will be a candidate whenever the election takes place. You have my authority to tell that to anybody who asks.' This assurance was of great importance because it immediately scotched any attempt – and some at least of those accused of organizing such an attempt now deny that they did any such thing – to replace Heath by Whitelaw

without a contest. Secondly the friends of Joseph were reassured
when, over the next few days, it became abundantly apparent
that Heath had no intention of standing down; and that Whitelaw was not prepared to push him.

It was subsequently said of Whitelaw – and particularly in
the interval between the first and the second ballots – that in
those few days he displayed an utter lack of the ruthlessness and
resolution that is required in moments of crisis from anybody
who wants to lead a great political party. Margaret Thatcher,
by contrast, though she did not have the means to display ruthlessness, increasingly demonstrated her resolution as the weeks
went by, resolution which in the end brought her a huge – indeed the biggest possible – bonus. But to make such a judgement on Whitelaw without qualification is to fail to take account
either of the strength of Heath's will, or the difficulties of
Whitelaw's position.

The comparison most frequently made when it was all over
– and by some of Whitelaw's friends as well as his critics – was
between Willie Whitelaw in the autumn of 1974 and R. A. Butler
in the winter of 1963. It seems now fairly clear that Butler's
campaign train was hijacked by those who wanted to replace
Macmillan by Lord Home. But it was still possible for Butler,
who enjoyed considerable support in Parliament and wide
support in the country, to upset the plans of his opponents by
refusing to serve under Home. Had he done this, it is also clear,
Home would have withdrawn from the race and Butler would
have entered into his inheritance, albeit as Leader of a very
divided Party. Subsequently, in a vivid television performance,
Enoch Powell compared Butler's inaction to that of a man in
possession of a loaded pistol pointed at his deadliest enemy, who
is unwilling to fire because guns make a noise, and because
guns hurt those at whom they are discharged. In the weeks and
even months following the October 1974 election the back
benches and the Westminster press corps spawned dozens of
mimics who regaled audiences with imitations of the Powell
broadcast, and followed up with an application of the moral to
Whitelaw.

But the cases were not at all similar. Butler confronted a man who was as yet neither Prime Minister nor Leader of his Party. Indeed, contrary to all recent precedent, Home had not, on visiting the Queen, kissed hands, which would have made him Prime Minister immediately, but undertook merely to take soundings to see if he could form a government. He was at all times until Butler agreed to serve under him open to a coup and, indeed, by all his words and actions demonstrated that he would not resist one if it was staffed by sufficiently senior officers.

Heath was a very different man and in a very different position. He was the Leader of the Party and there was, at that time, no mechanism for getting rid of a Leader of whom the Party had tired. There was no weapon for use against him, indeed, save that of attrition. His stubbornness, moreover, was legendary. He was utterly convinced that the events of the next couple of years would vindicate the account he had given, in both the February and October general elections, of the challenges facing Britain and the measures government would have to take. And he had the advantage of a small, but utterly devoted and highly organized, group of friends who now closed ranks about him: interestingly, they were allies whose allegiance had been gained less through the domestic policies that had brought him to defeat than through fidelity to the policy of EEC membership for Britain, with which he was identified more than any other senior politician. As became almost immediately clear through a long series of lunches and dinners to which Heath and his allies invited new, wavering or critical backbenchers and peers, there was no disposition on Heath's part to leave the field, and the palm, to Whitelaw.

In such circumstances a ruthless, hard-headed, ambitious course was still open to Whitelaw. But a declaration of his candidacy would have been but the prelude to a long and bruising battle, which would almost certainly have produced much greater division in the Party than was occasioned by the battle that actually occurred. Politicians are either warriors or healers. Margaret Thatcher is a warrior. Edward Heath is a warrior.

Enoch Powell is a warrior. But William Whitelaw and R. A. Butler are healers. Whitelaw was neither built for nor ambitious enough to seek the kind of struggle on which he would have had to embark to gain the leadership.

There is evidence, too, that he knew exactly how rough it would be. Though he supported Heath – as did every member of the Shadow Cabinet except Keith Joseph – up to the débâcle of the first ballot, he was not intimately involved in the mechanics of the Heath campaign: that was for stronger stomachs. But when at last he did become a candidate he withdrew immediately from Conservative Central Office where, because of his chairmanship of the Party, manifold personal facilities were available to him. Moreover, he sought Mrs Thatcher's permission (which was immediately granted) to use, between the first and second ballots, the services of his Central Office-paid secretary, since his personal secretary was on holiday. It is clear that this remarkable scrupulousness was the product not merely of an inherently decent and honourable nature, but of some real unease at the way in which the Party organization had been mobilized in the fight to keep the Heath leadership alive.

Finally – as was not the case with Margaret Thatcher – the potential supporters of William Whitelaw were more or less the same as the potential supporters of Edward Heath. Among them were many who felt Heath should go because he had failed in three general elections out of four; because they were alarmed at the extent of his unpopularity; or for other reasons – but not because they thought he was wrong. Indeed, the vast majority of them would, if they had had the choice in their own hands, have preferred Heath as Prime Minister to Whitelaw. They knew, as Whitelaw did himself, of the long years of his intimacy with Heath both as Chief Whip and subsequently. They knew, and he knew himself, that he had always been, in a way none of the so far canvassed challengers had been, an intimate member of the higher directorate of the Heath government. That he had counselled against calling the general election of February 1974 which had brought calamity on Heath was not enough to make him a strong and distinctive candidate. Not of such stuff were the members of a conquering army capable of overthrowing an entrenched and doughty rival made. So Whitelaw did not move until it was far, far too late.

In the second half of October, therefore, three replacements for Heath were being openly canvassed – Du Cann, Joseph and Whitelaw. Other names appeared from time to time, perhaps the most bizarre being that of the legless war hero Richard Wood, a good and honourable man who had been Minister of Overseas Development in the 1970 government, but who was, to say the least of it, rather obscure. Most of the Shadow Cabinet having rallied around Heath, it seems clear that Du Cann enjoyed more than anybody else of that support which might, in terms of years and seniority, be called substantial. But while Joseph was off and running, gaining mixed plaudits and brickbats from the press and in the country for a series of revisionist policy speeches, Du Cann's attitude was ambiguous and uncertain.

In the House, though, Joseph had energetic supporters, particularly David Mitchell, young, hard-working and enthusiastic, who had been his Parliamentary Private Secretary at the Department of Health and Social Services, and Sir Frederic Bennett, *bon viveur* and chairman of the Commons catering committee. Airey Neave moved quietly between all these groups, leaning distinctly towards Du Cann, but uneasy about the evasiveness of that candidate and suspicious of Keith Joseph's resolution under fire. At that time, indeed, Joseph wrote to a journalist who had praised him in somewhat extravagant terms, thanking him and adding, 'But don't expect too much. The tasks ahead are for giants, and I am no giant.' The modesty, straightforwardness and moral integrity of Joseph are precisely the qualities that have won him so many devoted friends and supporters; but that letter was not the stuff to give the troops.

There were also a few supporters for Margaret Thatcher, notably her ex-PPS Fergus Montgomery, who, having lost his seat in February, had returned to the Commons in October, representing Anthony Barber's old constituency of Altrincham. The difficulty faced by all the supporters of Thatcher, Du Cann and Whitelaw was quite simply that their horses had not declared. It was at Margaret Thatcher's suggestion – virtually, indeed, at her instruction – that the *Spectator* came out so solidly for Joseph. We would have supported either of them, but distinctly preferred her. However, she made it clear more than once that in her view she was unlikely to be a successful candidate, but that, in any event, she would never enter the lists while Joseph was there. Her partisans therefore went about their business brandishing swords for Keith Joseph, but, like Airey Neave, preserving in their hearts a certain suspicion of his staying power.

The result of all these absences of commitment and overlapping of friendships, however, was that after the first flurry of bitterness following the election, and with the onset of winter, many of Heath's partisans began to breathe more easily, thinking that although discontent with their man remained rife, and though he would sooner or later face an intense challenge, he probably had a guaranteed life of another year or so. The same view generally prevailed in the world of political reporters and analysts: the weakness and divisions of the contestants was the topic of the day. Thus matters stood when the backbenchers and the executive of the 1922 Committee took action. From the moment of his defeat Heath underestimated the strength of back-bench feeling against him, perhaps because it had not coalesced around any alternative candidate.

From the moment Parliament returned after the October election the possibility, even the very nature, of a Du Cann candidacy was defined and limited by his chairmanship of the 1922 Committee. It was clear to himself and his supporters that he could not become candidate for the leadership while remaining as chairman, since the chairman is obliged to be neutral in interpreting the feelings and opinions of backbenchers to the Leader of the Party. On the other hand, everybody who wanted a thorough ventilation of the question of leadership – including all those who were determined that Heath should go, but including some others as well – knew that the chance of achieving their ambition was greatly increased by the presence at the head of their affairs of a chairman at once skilful, popular, and in no way committed to Heath. Du Cann's supporters, every one of whom was certain that Heath had to go, were thus much less hard on their champion for his refusal to say whether he would be a candidate or not than they might have been, since they recognized the importance of the work he already had in hand. It should be added that, though Heath remains convinced to this day that Du Cann set himself, from the morning of 11 October, to end a leadership that had lasted nearly a decade, there is no indication whatsoever that at any time between the general election and the victory of Margaret Thatcher Du Cann behaved otherwise than with the utmost propriety as the conduit of back-bench feeling.

When Parliament reassembled, however, one very simple technical difficulty confronted Du Cann and his colleagues on the executive, and it was the manner in which they resolved it that initially gave birth to Heath's suspicions. The 1922 Committee has an automatic membership of all Conservative backbenchers. It derives ultimately from a meeting of the Parliamentary Party in the Carlton Club in 1922 which overthrew the Liberal–Conservative coalition headed by Lloyd George and precipitated a general election in which the Tories, under Andrew Bonar Law, enjoyed a spectacular victory. In the present formal sense, however, it began merely as a gathering of MPs first elected in the 1922 general election: its membership became broader as the usefulness of a forum in which backbenchers could speak their minds became apparent. At the beginning of each parliamentary year, in October, the backbenchers elect a chairman and an executive of eight. Among their various activities are large meetings addressed by the Leader of the Party, at which he answers often harsh and critical questions and, apart from such sessions, the chairman is supposed regularly to keep the Leader in touch with what backbenchers are thinking and saying. Of course, the Chief Whip has a similar task; but while it is the job of the Chief Whip to persuade members to do what the leadership wants, it is the job of the chairman rather to persuade the leadership to do what the backbenchers want. The difference is crucial.

In the opinion of a great many experts whom I have consulted and, perhaps most importantly, in the opinion (expressed in a letter to *The Times* in November 1974) of the historian of the Committee, Philip Goodhart, the Member for Beckenham, the writ of a 1922 executive and chairman runs from election to election: it is not in abeyance either during a recess or after a general election. Like a government, it governs until its electorate replaces it. This, however, is not now, and was not in the autumn of 1974, the opinion of Edward Heath.

With the October returns in, it was the view of Du Cann, and of every member of his executive, that a discussion of the leadership question was urgent; and that it would be best if Heath himself invited such a discussion. So far as I can judge, it was also the private view of each member of the executive that Heath should be replaced: his knowledge that this was the case very naturally increased Heath's suspicion of the executive as a whole. On 14 October, then, the executive met in Du Cann's house in Lord North Street and quickly arrived at a consensus that there should be an early leadership election with Heath as a candidate. Ordinary good manners required that Heath should be informed immediately of this view, but there was also the problem that only he could set in motion the machinery required to stage such a ballot. Du Cann therefore went to see him at his new house in Wilton Street.

It is clear that their discussion was not an amicable one. More to the point, however, was Heath's view that Du Cann's mandate (and that of the executive) had run out with the calling of the October general election; that only a freshly elected chairman had the right to address the Leader on this subject; and that Du Cann had betrayed a disagreeable relish in thus putting pressure on the man who, nearly ten years before, had terminated his chairmanship of the Party. Du Cann, it appears, had not expected the interview to be a particularly pleasant one: neither did he expect to be confronted with what was to him a novel doctrine about the Party's constitution. Clearly, he would have to consult the executive again.

As any long-lived leadership runs its course – and this is all the more true of a highly domineering tenure like that of Heath – it is in no way surprising that backbenchers should assert reservations, criticisms and alternative choices wherever they continue to exercise free preferences. It does not even follow that such assertions imply hostility to the leadership: it is simply the exercise of a balancing instinct in human nature. Be that as it may, however, Heath certainly regarded the executive of the 1922 Committee, as constituted in October, as a club for his critics. Du Cann had no cause to love him, and he was perhaps particularly suspicious of John Biffen, the Member for Oswestry – a friend of Enoch Powell, and perhaps even more effective as a right-wing critic of the 1970 government than Nicholas Ridley – and of Neil Marten, a senior backbencher famous for his knowledge of parliamentary procedure, and the longest standing of all Heath's opponents on the issue of membership of the Common Market. It is hardly surprising, therefore, that as soon as Du Cann had left him Heath set in train a campaign to replace such dissidents by loyalists in the forthcoming elections to the 1922 executive. It proved, in the event, to be the most disastrous evidence of how far out of touch with back-bench opinion he was; for the old executive were returned to a man.

Meanwhile, Du Cann and his colleagues were concerned both by Heath's attitude and by the natural and pressing curiosity of newspaper reporters about what was going to happen in the Tory Party. They were not, at this stage, anxious to parade Party differences, so their meeting the following day (15 October) was arranged for Du Cann's City offices in Milk Street. Unfortunately for them, united though they might have been about what should be done, their families did not always share their views. The wife of one member of the executive allowed both the venue and the confidentiality of the next meeting to become known. Conservative Central Office was then used to make sure that the press knew as well, and were briefed to expect a plot against the leadership.

When the executives met at Milk Street they decided to put in a letter to Heath their view of what should be done. Leaving the building they were confronted by reporters and cameramen and, panicking, several sought to leave quietly by the back door. This undignified and embarrassing performance gave birth to the legend of the 'Milk Street Mafia', of a devious plot against Heath, and of the ruthlessness of the Tory Party with failed leaders. It also made clear to Edward Du Cann, if he had not already realized it, that he could not be both chairman of the 1922 Committee and a candidate for the leadership.

The whole affair was widely regarded as an important, and perhaps decisive, blow in Heath's battle for survival. Fury, scorn and threats now became the weapons of his supporters. They were, they claimed, enraged by Du Cann's plotting. They were, they said, scornful of Joseph – the only declared candidate – after his social policy speech of 19 October. And they did threaten members of the executive of the 1922 with humiliating defeat in the forthcoming elections if they continued on a course judged by the Leader to be both obdurate and disloyal. For his part Heath replied curtly and formally to the letter drafted by the executive at Milk Street, saying that he would enter discussions on his leadership, but only with a freshly elected executive. Thus matters stood on 29 October when Parliament reconvened. Heath and his friends, in better shape than they had been for some time, had reckoned – like others – without the backbenchers, and in this respect the situation was extraordinarily like that in 1922, when Stanley Baldwin gave tongue to a great many scarcely articulated but profoundly felt reservations about the Lloyd George leadership and thus brought the government crashing down around the ears of a Prime Minister regarded until that moment as, if not beyond reproach, then at least beyond attack.

The Baldwin of the day was Kenneth Lewis. The stage was set for his powerful intervention by the re-election of the entire 1922 executive and its chairman, a bad blow to Heath's friends and one which, it seems, they did not anticipate: already what was to prove a fatal inability to understand the thoughts and feelings of backbenchers was apparent. At the full meeting of the 1922 on 1 November Lewis, the first of more than twenty speakers, asked a question which gave the most felicitous verbal expression to the commonsense question in nearly everybody's mind. Was the leadership, he asked, which had now been in one man's hands for a decade, to be regarded as a freehold or a leasehold? The question transcended the developing personal antagonisms of recent days and months.

Once the matter was put like that it was immediately clear that, in the hard modern world, the Conservative Party would be foolish to rely for its fortune on leaders who would behave with the gentlemanly forbearance of Lord Home, who so readily gave up the leadership after his defeat in 1964. No: some mechanism had to be provided for passing interim judgement on a Leader, and this proposition the committee whole-heartedly supported. Even the most enthusiastic supporters of Heath, strenuously though they were to argue against the seeking of too early a verdict on the stewardship of their hero, could not, in plain commonsense, resist the general application of the view put forward by Lewis and supported by most of the others who spoke at the meeting. Most important of all, the meeting of 1 November enabled Edward Du Cann to write to Heath with enhanced authority as the representative of back-bench opinion. It is important to add that his authority was as much enhanced by his conduct of the 1 November meeting as by his re-election. After that meeting it was impossible for even the most vehement supporter of Heath to sustain the charges that had seemed so plausible after the Milk Street episode.

In response to the 1 November meeting Edward Heath made two moves, one of which was the most damaging of his career and proved fatal to his hopes for the future. He agreed to meet the whole 1922 Committee in full session, undertaking at the same time to provide means for a review of his leadership; and he reshuffled his Shadow Cabinet, making Margaret Thatcher second spokesman on Treasury matters, supporting Robert Carr. In the matter of the first move Heath had really no choice – in the long history of politics it is remarkable how rarely politicians do have a choice between courses – but in the matter of the second he was being obtuse.

It seems that at this moment Heath, like his supporters, did see a serious doctrinal challenge coming from the right, but he identified it solely with Keith Joseph. In September Joseph had made a speech at Preston apologizing for his role in supporting the economic policies of the latter phase of the Heath government and in particular questioning the wisdom of the long-term statutory incomes policy on which, more than anything else, Heath's policy and government depended in 1973 and 1974. Clearly, therefore, Joseph could not be Shadow Chancellor. It seemed wiser by far to appoint to that position somebody who could be totally trusted to support the collective and interventionist policies of the second half of the 1970 government. The man chosen was Robert Carr. But Carr, who had presided over the introduction of the Conservative Party's legislation on industrial relations and subsequently been a markedly liberal Home Secretary, had neither economic nor forensic skill – certainly not enough to stand up to Denis Healey, who had worsted every Conservative spokesman sent against him including, in the 1964 Parliament, Enoch Powell.

In the first week of November invitations to join the Shadow Cabinet were refused both by Reginald Maudling, an ex-Chancellor, and by Du Cann, often considered to be a possible future Chancellor. Now, if throughout her career Margaret Thatcher had demonstrated anything to friend and enemy alike it was an ability quickly to master subjects, together with considerable skill in House of Commons debates. For some reason Heath seems to have regarded her alliance with Joseph as unimportant: he gave her to Carr as an assistant to provide extra muscle for the Treasury team on the front bench. Since the following weeks revealed how ill-equipped with knowledge of and contacts with the broad membership of the Party on the back benches she was, the opportunity thus given to her to shine as a Party gladiator in the Chamber and in committee was vital to her prospects. It would have been more in Heath's own interests to have kept her confined within her original Shadow brief of the Environment. However, apart from his other preoccupations, Heath could have been forgiven for failing to take his new challenger seriously. For one thing, immediately after their first conversation, she did precisely nothing to advance her case. For another, she had – in an interview with the *Liverpool Daily Post* the previous June – given voice to the prevailing view that a woman could not be expected to gain the leadership of a major party, when she said, 'It will be years before a woman either leads the Party or becomes Prime Minister. I don't see it happening in my time.' At the time of Heath's battles with the executive of the 1922 Committee, moreover, the only senior political figures who had ventured the opinion that she would prove to be a better stayer in the race than Keith Joseph was Angus Maude, the Member for Stratford (who had once been dismissed from the Opposition front bench by Heath, following an indiscreet magazine article).

Against the tendency to dismiss Margaret Thatcher's claims, however, there were one or two other objections. During the October campaign she had been spectacularly successful, and had given life to a battle universally judged dull. Her weapon had been a Tory undertaking to guarantee mortgage rates at $9\frac{1}{2}$ per cent, to which commitment was added sundry other bonuses designed to appeal to the first-time home buyer. The scheme had been devised by a committee under her chairmanship which had reported towards the end of June. In Shadow Cabinet Heath had tried to persuade her to lower the rate to 8 per cent; but she had refused, arguing both that the money was not available and that the complicated package of guarantees and incentives that she had drawn up would not allow of any adjustment to the rate. Even so, various of those who might have been her allies in a leadership campaign – and who were certainly sympathetic to Joseph – were highly suspicious of the whole idea: the element of subsidization in it, they believed, smacked altogether too much either of socialism or of the kind of collectivism to which Heath had given his support. Anthony Crosland, the Secretary of State for the Environment, dubbed the whole scheme 'midsummer madness'. She was attacked both from the left and the right, but her performance at a press conference on 28 August – when the plan was unveiled – and her subsequent defence of it during the campaign, demonstrated yet again her ability to present a brief with panache and skill. For all that, she had few friends who mattered at the end of November.

But there was a hint or two that a new political star was in the making. There was no denying that the Heath Cabinet before the February election – and the Shadow Cabinet after it – lacked glamour; nor that, having emerged from her rough period at the Department of Education, Mrs Thatcher was well placed to provide it. Her gradual emergence as one of the more entertaining figures in the Tory firmament was noted by the *Daily Mirror* at the end of May 1974. It was known, of course, that she was a great favourite at the annual Conservative conference, and at Party meetings around the country. In consequence of this popularity, William Wolfe reported, Heath was contemplating her appointment as chairman of the Party organization.

Nothing came of this rumour but, a day or two later, on 2 June, Crossbencher of the *Sunday Express* envisaged even grander things for her. It was widely accepted, of course, that after February the Conservative Opposition was in state of shock. Just after the February defeat for example, they had decided to oppose Labour's Queen's Speech. On reflection it appeared that even if they won, another general election, for which they were singularly unprepared, would be precipitated; and that it might lead to destruction. As many as forty Tory backbenchers were prepared to refuse their support on the grounds that the Opposition motion referred to the usefulness of incomes policy. With division in the ranks and the prospect of catastrophe ahead, the leadership decided not to risk a vote, and were promptly and effectively denounced by the Liberal Party – then riding high on their own general election success – as alternatively 'thundering' and 'funking'.

There was thus an unhappy combination of depression, indecision and false aggression in the Opposition stance which lent point to Crossbencher's judgement on the Shadow Secretary of State for the Environment that 'She is the one Opposition spokesman who carries real conviction in attack'. The writer predicted that she had an excellent chance of being, at some later date, Chancellor in a Tory government. Greatly daring, he added that she might even aspire to the leadership on some future occasion. Perhaps most significantly, he concluded that 'Mrs Thatcher, once dismissed as cold and imperious, has impressed by the kindliness she has shown.'

Straws in the wind such observations might be; but they were nonetheless of consequence. The sheer amateurishness of her initial challenge, after her visit to Heath on 21 November, was shown by the fact that the press only gradually woke up to the fact that she *was* a challenger. On Monday the 25th, it is true, the *Daily Mail* carried an interview with her announcing her determination to enter the lists. But there had been no statement through the normal channels of the Press Association and James Margach, the political correspondent of the *Sunday Times*, who reported her decision on the 24th, has since said that he made his story firm rather than tentative because one of her admirers had persuaded him to do so: if the story was less than categorical, Margach's informant said, she would still have a way out. If not a wholly correct account of her state of mind this was at least a shrewd appreciation of her inability to lay down a gage she had publicly picked up.

But she made no move to set up an organization to campaign for her. Various bees were still buzzing around the hive of Edward Du Cann. Joseph still had a number of somewhat dispirited admirers. Even the Whitelaw men were not without their hopes. Mrs Thatcher, while confiding her ambitions, reasons and principles to anybody who asked her, got on with the business of studying the Finance Bill: her evenings were spent going through economic papers, not plotting her takeover bid. As a woman, of course, she was the reverse of familiar with the Members' smoking room; and so the swirl of gossip and cogitation passed her by.

That was until 28 November. On that day the morning papers carried accounts of her interview, given the previous summer, to *Pre-Retirement Choice*: 'The Thatcher Hoard,' screamed the

Daily Mail. Lord Redmayne, a former Tory Chief Whip and a director of Harrods, gravely denounced her advice, suggesting that to encourage panic buying at a time of inflation was the height of irresponsibility: he did not, however, subsequently discourage the sale of deep freezers in any of the stores in which he had an interest. The following day the *Daily Express* – which was to remain enthusiastically in support of Heath throughout the campaign and even after – suggested that there must be 'weeping, wailing and gnashing of teeth among those who want Mrs Thatcher to lead the Tory Party . . .' 'Alas poor Margaret,' sang the *Sun*, and went on to describe the interview as 'a political suicide note'. Hysteria was already in the air, and the *Express* reported that a certain Mrs Sandra Brooke, chairman of the National Housewives' Association, was setting out for London with a delegation to demand that Mrs Thatcher hand over to them, for distribution to pensioners, the contents of her own larder. The intervention of the fictional 'Mr Tallis' has already been noted. Seldom, it may be said, has even Fleet Street plumbed such depths of nonsense as on this occasion; and never can there have been anything as silly as the *Express* interview with Mrs Brooke. The disgusting absurdity of the behaviour of the press, however, was little consolation to a badly shaken candidate.

It took a week for the whole business to die down. During that week, however, the initial depression of her handful of supporters in the House of Commons turned quickly to anger as, in Annie's Bar (that reserved for the use of Members of both Houses and selected pressmen), the Stranger's (where MPs may entertain their guests), the tea-room and the smoking room, they saw and heard Edward Heath's campaign team. It could be argued that it was understandable that Heath's supporters, with their man under such pressure from events and the dissatisfaction of the backbenchers, should smirk a little as the second declared opponent appeared to bite the dust. But if it was understandable, it was certainly unwise.

Nor was this all. Normally, when even a quite junior Tory politician is traduced in the press, Conservative Central Office is ready with soothing advice, balm for the nerves, and stout support through its Fleet Street contacts. This time, at first, there was silence. Then it emerged – largely from pressmen who, even if they were not commending her for the leadership, were at least personally well-disposed towards her – that the Smith Square machine was being used against her. The feeling that the whole weight of the Party establishment was being brought to bear against the only declared opponent of the Leader became widespread, and if it strengthened the resolve of her supporters – who had little to lose anyway – it had the additional and useful effect of upsetting the sense of propriety of a great many other Members. After all, they seemed to be saying, if this is what he is doing now, what would he do if he got back?

The week or ten days following Margaret Thatcher's declaration of candidacy served, in this respect, to remind many of the way in which Central Office had been run since 1970 and the uses to which its influence had been put during that time. It should be remembered – indeed stressed – that, in theory at least, Conservative Central Office is the private office of the Leader of the Party. It is not (like, say, Labour's HQ at Transport House) the possession or instrument of the Party as a whole. Only its size and the manifold duties it sustains (from giving advice and succour at every occasion from a local government by-election to an area office ball, to supervising the printing and distribution of the Conservative Party's many publications) have given it the appearance of an autonomous body. The fact that it is a large and expensive bureaucracy has, however, made it highly unwieldy as a private office, and Leaders have therefore invariably had a separate staff with a base in the House of Commons. Furthermore, the Conservative Research Department – the body devoted to policy study – is physically separate from Central Office (it has premises in Old Queen Street) and, in a period of intense policy-making, such as Heath favoured between 1965 and 1970, the tendency was for CRD to become an extension of the Private Office, to the exclusion of Smith Square. In the years before the 1970 election Heath's economic adviser, Brian Reading (the author of the famous 'at a stroke' commitment to curtail the rise in prices) and Michael Wolff, Heath's chief speech-writer, had rooms in Old Queen Street. When the election was lost in February Wolff was made Director General of Central Office both, it was thought, to repair what appeared to be a lamentable decline from its legendary standards of efficiency and, in a dangerous situation, to reassert the control of the Leader over the Party machine.

But it should clearly be understood that Heath was perfectly within his rights in making what use he chose of Central Office in his fight for survival. The trouble was that what (like a defence of Mrs Thatcher) was left undone and what (like the revelation to the press of the meeting at Du Cann's Milk Street offices) was done, was felt to be an offence against customary practice. Heath's rights at Smith Square were not enough to protect him from this accusation.

Many Members who were tempted to be dissident – on any one of a variety of matters – felt a cold wind on their necks in the week following 24 November. In a fashion wholly at variance with the traditional practice of the Party (whose central organization had only once in its history refused recognition to a candidate chosen by a local constituency Party) those who had disagreed with Heath after 1970, particularly on the issue of the Common Market, had been ruthlessly leant on. Neil Marten, Ronald Bell and Richard Body were all senior backbenchers whose constituency executives had been approached by Central Office to compel them to change their anti-Market line. Roger Moate, a much younger backbencher, had been likewise pressed on the same issue, and even physically accosted by a Heath supporter in the House of Commons. Alan Clark (son of Lord Clark, the art historian) had faced steadfast Central Office opposition in his Plymouth constituency for years.

At least two senior backbenchers widely held in regard, Joan Quennell and Simon Wingfield-Digby, had, before their retirement, expressed deep worry about the way the Party was being run. Russell Lewis, the Director of the Conservative Political Centre (founded as a Tory counterpart to the Fabian Society and the source of a series of distinguished and somewhat academic pamphlets) had been peremptorily dismissed by Michael Wolff, apparently because of his intellectual independence. The candidates' advisory committee (which, strictly speaking, has the function merely of ensuring that anybody entered in the Central Office list of candidates, which is circulated to constituency chairmen as soon as a vacancy occurs, is not thoroughly undesirable) had been, over the previous two years, steadily denying recognition to aspirants who dissented from Party policy as laid down by Heath, and even removing from the list already sanctioned candidates who subsequently expressed disagreement on policy. Finally, a move was afoot to ensure that Party agents should in future be employed directly by Central Office rather than by the local organizations. Though this plan commended itself on grounds of efficiency (it would mean that the poorer constituencies would not be in constant danger of losing their abler men to richer areas) it was in the circumstances seen as yet another part of Heath's plan to impose his own dominance on the Party to the exclusion of criticism. It did not help his case that he was widely known as a very expensive Leader.

Discontent, worry and dissatisfaction had not hitherto arisen for several reasons: Heath's early success; the exceptional natural loyalty of the Party; the fact that the issue that occasioned most of what came to be called persecution – that of the EEC – was one in which Heath commanded the backing of an overwhelming majority of the Tory Party. In the troubled days of November it was recalled, however, that Neil Marten, one of the greatest experts on parliamentary procedure in the House, was also widely loved and respected. If Neil could be squeezed, who was immune? Against this background Heath's campaign team made a very bad mistake to let it appear that they were contemptuous of a challenger; and the Central Office machine a worse mistake not to ensure that it was unfailing in defending Mrs Thatcher against the *canards* of the press.

Then all seemed to fall silent. Until the Douglas-Home committee on the way the Party should choose its Leader reported,

the campaign necessarily went into a desultory phase. Still the
challenger made no move to set up a machine of her own. She
was busy with other things. In December it was announced that
she and Joseph had set up an independent research organization
of their own – the Centre for Policy Studies – with the consent,
if without the enthusiasm, of Heath, who nevertheless had a
nominee of his own on the board. The new organization had a
clear ideological purpose: it was to present the case for the free
market and for capitalism. It echoed the Heath programme of
1970 and, in keeping with Joseph's speeches, clearly repudiated
the Heath policies from 1972 onwards. It pointed up the
doctrinal split in the Party between right and left, and was
resented because of that. And, on a more mundane level, being
financed from the City, it reduced funds flowing to the already
straitened official Research Department. It was a clear indication that the right disagreed with the Leader of the Party on
more than the question of who should hold his job; and it was
proof, if proof were needed, that the Thatcher challenge was
about more than personal ambition.

On 11 December Nemesis began to stalk Heath in earnest.
That day he received the report of the Douglas-Home committee.
To his friends – who rapidly dubbed it 'Alec's revenge', remem-
bering the fashion in which Heath had taken advantage of
mounting critical pressure on Sir Alec to begin his own successful bid for the leadership in 1965 – it was a savage blow. The
crucial provision, as they saw it, was that, although three ballots
were allowed for, to be successful on the first ballot a candidate
needed not only to collect an overall majority of all Tory backbenchers (not just those voting) but, in addition, 15 per cent
more votes than his nearest rival. To win a first ballot contest
Heath would thus need not just 140 votes, but 42 more than his
nearest rival. This was a hobble around Heath's ankles,
especially as Douglas-Home stipulated that it should be open
to fresh candidates to enter on the second ballot. This provision
led to the new procedure being dubbed the 'Coward's Charter'.
Peter Walker, Timothy Kitson, Kenneth Baker and Nicholas
Scott (Heath's campaign managers) as well as the Leader

himself immediately saw the possibility that Margaret Thatcher might well cripple Heath on the first ballot, thus denying him a vote of confidence and opening the field to Whitelaw in the second.

Except in the fraught days between 11 and 17 December (when the Home plan was published) nobody has supposed that Lord Home was moved by malice. He was trying to solve three problems, one of which was merely a product of the moment. First, he wanted a system of election which would establish – to use Kenneth Lewis's phrase – that the leadership was a lease-hold, not a freehold. That, in modern times, was vital, and it completed the partial reform of the method of election initiated by him in 1965. Secondly, he wanted to ensure that in this and in any future contests, the winner's moral authority would be unassailable. Hence the stringent requirements for victory. And thirdly, to meet the mood of many backbenchers at the end of 1974, he wanted the first ballot to be, essentially, a test of the incumbent Leader. Thus the provision that fresh candidates could enter on subsequent ballots.

The whole process was then and later described as both excessively complex and excessively lengthy. The first provision was for a ballot for the leadership within twenty-eight days of every new session, or three to six months after the opening of every new Parliament. (This, of course, applied only if there were a challenger to an incumbent.) If there was no clear winner on the first ballot a second ballot should be held a week later: this time, only a simple majority of all Tory Members was required for victory. If, however, nobody came out the winner, a third ballot should be held among the top three contestants. Each Member would be required to give a first and second preference and, should there be no clear winner, second preferences would be distributed until one candidate had the requisite number of votes. With this clause it was the turn of Margaret Thatcher's supporters to complain: they already saw that even if she eliminated Heath, a third ballot with transferable preferences would very likely see the choice of a compromise candidate – probably Whitelaw – for an appeal to cautious opinion was unlikely to be her forte. In the event her supporters were unnecessarily worried.

Of course, the Home proposals were in the nature of a recommendation merely. Heath had no love for them, and it was unlikely that the 1922 Committee would consider them before the Christmas recess. When Parliament broke up for the holidays, everything was still in the air. Only one other thing of note could be chewed over by Members scattering to their constituencies: on 16 December, the day before the publication of the Home report, Margaret Thatcher had destroyed Joel Barnett, the Chief Secretary to the Treasury, in a debate on the Finance Bill. If a champion was what they wanted, the Tories had one to hand. Indeed, the unfortunate Barnett was on several subsequent occasions to be the means by which Mrs Thatcher proved to her own backbenchers that she possessed the qualities they were looking for.

By now a certain disenchantment with Du Cann was becoming apparent, and forces were slowly gathering around Margaret Thatcher. She already had Fergus Montgomery and William Shelton, a backbencher expert in public relations and a superb, though as yet unproven, campaigner. She had, of course, Joseph: their friendship had begun in 1967, when she took over from him as Opposition spokesman on Fuel and Power. His extraordinary consideration for her – he not only briefed her thoroughly on her new responsibilities, but took the trouble to introduce her to all the people relevant to the discharge of her new job – forged an unbreakable friendship. 'Keith and I have no toes,' she says of this alliance, meaning that no disagreement could cause hurt or a breach between them. But Joseph was quite unversed in the subtleties of vote getting in Westminster, and Montgomery and Shelton were junior, almost unnoticed figures.

Five days before Parliament reassembled on 5 January, Margaret Thatcher entertained Airey Neave to dinner. He too was a friend, one of what she calls the 'club of '50' – those who first stood for Parliament in that year. By now Neave was convinced – and this was confirmed on the 13th – that Du Cann, whose wife had no love for political strife, would not stand. As chairman of the Commons Select Committee on Science and Technology – and a most distinguished chairman – he had got to know Mrs Thatcher very well during her time at the Department of Education and Science. Over dinner he satisfied himself of her resolution and emerged, in fact if not yet formally, as her campaign manager.

When it was all over, the press expressed wonderment at the emergence of a figure to them totally obscure, whose only great moment in life appeared to have been his escape from Colditz, as a campaign manager effortlessly superior to the experienced and tough team working for Heath. There are, of course, many elderly backbenchers with distinguished war records – though few as distinguished as Neave's – and they tend to be thought of by the press as rather forgotten, dusty figures, long ago put away on a high parliamentary shelf. Thus was Neave considered.

Certainly his high political experience was brief. He had retired from junior office in Harold Macmillan's government because of a mild heart condition. When his problem was explained to the then Chief Whip, Edward Heath said, in his own special manner, 'Well, that's the end of your political career, then.' By the middle of December his own soundings had convinced Neave that the Heath years were drawing to their close, and he waited on the Leader to tell him so. Surprisingly, their conversation, if not cordial, was well-mannered enough on both sides; but Heath was not open to persuasion.

Neave, however, was no meteor who flashed twice across the sky of public life. A short man with a red face, rather sharp features and an exceptionally broad smile, he carries his head set back between stooping shoulders and seems always to drift along rather than walk. After his escape from Colditz he organized a famous exit route from Occupied Europe for other prisoners. Later, he was a junior prosecutor at Nuremberg, and served arrest warrants on such Nazi war criminals as Hess and Speer. He has written a series of best-selling books about the war, all remarkably vivid, graceful and incisive, in marked contrast to the much rougher and more primitive style of most

war books, even the good ones. He is a lawyer of wide experience, at one time specializing in shoplifting cases. As chairman
of his Select Committee he had produced a number of acclaimed
reports, though his unusual reserve with the press prevented
his gaining that public attention which more extrovert committee chairmen frequently command. In a word, if he had had
fewer opportunities than his talents deserved, he was far from
being the obscure and disgruntled backbencher of Heath's
imagining.

Now events began to move very quickly. On the 13th Nigel
Fisher told his two dozen or so friends that Edward Du Cann
was certainly out of the running; most agreed to support
Margaret Thatcher, under the guidance of Airey Neave. Later
that evening Neave formed his own staff, with Shelton as his
deputy. The following day, after a certain amount of grumbling
– and in spite of the protests of Sir John Taylor, chairman of the
National Union of Conservative Associations whose members,
the voluntary Party workers throughout the country, felt that
they should have a say in the election – the 1922 Committee
accepted the Home proposals. The battle was on and, in spite
of her own inactivity hitherto, Margaret Thatcher found, with
the defection of Du Cann, that she had a nucleus of between
twenty-five and thirty supporters.

From this point onwards the Thatcher campaign operated on
two levels. The challenger's job was to impress in public. A
brilliant and funny speech to the Parliamentary Press Gallery
lunch on 21 January made a beginning, with curious, hostile
and rather baffled reporters looking at her with fresh eyes.
While she made the speeches, Neave and his allies devilled
away. The point of contact was Robin Cooke's room, where
Mrs Thatcher was available, whenever business permitted, to
discuss matters with potential supporters. On the morning of
the 21st Neave's and Shelton's calculations showed that she had
sixty-nine votes to Heath's forty-three. That evening, in a
packed House of Commons, she attacked the Chancellor's proposals for a capital transfer tax. Denis Healey is in every respect
a formidable House of Commons debater. Moreover, he plays

the game very roughly indeed, and no front-bench Tory had so far even troubled him. Margaret Thatcher showed no respect either for him or his reputation and, moreover, revealed that he had an embarrassingly loose grasp of the details of his proposals. On the 22nd, when the debate resumed, he responded viciously, denouncing her as the 'La Pasionaria of Privilege', taking up exactly the note the *Daily Express* had sounded that morning.

Margaret Thatcher rose. She wished, she said, that she could say that the Chancellor had done himself less than justice. In fact, he had done himself justice:

Some Chancellors are micro-economic. Some Chancellors are fiscal. This one is just plain cheap. When he rose to speak yesterday we on this side were amazed how one could possibly get to be the Chancellor of the Exchequer, and speak for his Government, knowing so little about existing taxes, and so little about the proposals which were coming before Parliament.

It seemed to the audience that Mrs Thatcher had lost her cool, but to great effect:

If this Chancellor can be Chancellor, anyone in the House of Commons can be Chancellor. I had hoped that the Rt Hon. Gentleman had learnt a lot from this debate. Clearly he has learnt nothing. . . . He might at least address himself to the practical effects because it will affect . . . everyone, including people born as I was with no privilege at all.

That evening Neave and Shelton again compared figures. They were able to tell her that they reckoned she now – after the debate and perhaps because of it – had ninety-five votes to Heath's sixty-four, with nine for a new and unconsidered candidate, the engaging Scottish aristocrat Hugh Fraser. Already that morning the *Guardian*'s shrewd political editor, Ian Aitken, while admitting that it was still 'a matter of guesswork' how strongly she would poll, reckoned she had a good prospect of between 90 and 100 supporters. The first objective – that of denying Heath a first ballot victory – was within reach. She was astonished.

Her assault on Denis Healey was hardly the stuff of statesmanship. In considering its effect, however, one must remember that Westminster is like a village; and the Tories were only half of that village. She had successfully mixed it with the bully on the other side; and she was 'only a woman'. From first to last none of the national papers really grasped the fact that the opinion of the City, or of the establishment, or of the electorate as recorded in the opinion polls, or of the Tory Party in the country, would in the end matter much less than the opinions and feelings, frustrations and joys of 278 backbenchers who, after all, would have to live and work in close proximity, perhaps for years, with the victor in this contest. She had given them hope, and perhaps even more important, she had given them the kind of cruel but very real satisfaction that comes from seeing an ally cut down a hated enemy. Nobody had ever treated Denis Healey with such convinced disdain: indeed, no other Tory frontbencher had so readily vanquished a government Minister since the disaster of the previous February. For a day or two, Tories in Annie's or the Stranger's or the tea-room or the smoking room were able to observe with rare satisfaction crumpled and irritable Labour faces. As Harold Macmillan once observed – and the pro-Thatcher Tories were quick to trot out the adage of the old master – mastery of the country begins with mastery of the House of Commons. So when, on 23 January, Heath announced to the 1922 Committee that he accepted the Home recommendations, and that the first ballot would take place on 4 February, Neave and his troops were in good heart.

The counter-offensive was not long in coming. It was announced, indeed, by Gordon Greig in the *Daily Mail* on the 24th; a 'Stop Thatcher' movement, he said, had started. In two days – and not forgetting the patient early spadework of Neave and Shelton – she had transformed the situation. 'By God,' Eric Heffer, the left-wing Tribune Group MP, said to me one evening, 'it must be great to have somebody like that to back.' He expressed precisely the feeling of the Thatcher team. Now, though, the guns were brought to bear on her, as one after another Lord Carrington, the chairman of the Party, Robert Carr, her notional superior in the Treasury team, and James Prior,

who had been Heath's Agriculture Minister and, earlier, his
Parliamentary Private Secretary, announced their allegiance
to the besieged Leader. Of all the Shadow Cabinet, it seemed,
only Keith Joseph could be relied on.

The weapon chosen by the Party establishment was that
already employed by Denis Healey – class. The method of its
employment was succinctly conveyed in an article by David
McKie in the *Guardian* on 27 January. According to McKie the
message of those supporting Heath was that, while the Thatcher
style – in dress, manner and deportment, as well as in policy –
was undoubtedly palatable to the Party faithful, it would mean
'electoral death' if it became a badge to be worn by Tories in
an appeal to the country. A subsequent article by McKie (on
31 January) made it clear that this line of argument had the
approval of Heath himself. The argument ran that Margaret
Thatcher's attitudes, policies and instincts were ineradicably
middle-class; that she had no broader view of the national
interest than the assertion of the preferences of her class and –
assiduously conveyed and very likely believed – that a woman
(her sex was relevant to the thesis) with her predispositions
could not conceivably appeal anywhere outside the home
counties. Any danger there may have been in so roundly repudiating the supposed preference of the Party's gut supporters was
ignored.

Nor was this statement of the case against her a hole-in-the-
corner affair. Ian Gilmour (now, having inherited a baronetcy
in 1977, Sir Ian), the Member for Chesham and Amersham, was
and is one of the Party's foremost thinking men. He had owned
the *Spectator* and borne its losses for years. He had published
an arresting book, *The Body Politic*. As Minister of State in the
Department of Defence after the 1970 election he had done
much to streamline the activities of that department, particularly in the intractable field of weapons procurement. He had
been rewarded by promotion to the Secretaryship of State itself.
On 30 January, in a speech in his constituency which was
rightly taken to be a blow for Heath and a blow against the
Thatcher cause, Gilmour warned the Tory Party against

'digging our trenches further to the right'. It was necessary, he said, to be a national party. The Conservatives, he concluded, could not 'retire behind a privet hedge' – this phrase was regarded as being particularly a dig against what was rapidly coming to be thought of as Margaret Thatcher's suburban image. In an interview on LBC radio Heath himself heavily emphasized the dangers of his Party becoming exclusively middle-class, more heavily and more crudely than did any of his supporters.

These were new arguments in the Party battle. Before the advent of Margaret Thatcher no one had been making them: then, the supposedly impending economic crisis and the governability of Britain were the subjects in every Tory mouth. Whether wholly planned, or partly the result of political instinct, it is clear that her initial victories over Barnett and Healey excited Conservatives to attack and denounce a middle-class shibboleth in terms and in language very nearly as violent as those regularly employed against the bourgeoisie by the spokesmen of the far left. Certainly, one can expect almost any excess of argument and language in a political fight as desperate as that going on in January 1975; not all of the Thatcher supporters were restrained in the way they deployed their case against Heath (certainly in the *Spectator*, I was not). It seems to me, however, that there was something extra in the way Ian Gilmour, Edward Heath and others put the case: there was a powerful equation made between the kind of policies – by and large free market and capitalist; by and large the kind of policies Heath had expounded in 1970 – she was supposed to favour and her purported class image. It was as though condemnation of her image (regarded as self-evidently justified) itself disposed of her policies. Lunching at the time with a senior Tory backbencher I was astonished to hear him say of Margaret Thatcher that she was 'insupportable, unspeakably suburban'. There was that much feeling around. This particular backbencher has since changed his position.

And yet, making every allowance for the frantic state of all Tory nerves at the time, there was a good deal of comedy for the detached observer in this counter-offensive. As regards social origins there was little to choose between Margaret Thatcher and Edward Heath: if anything, his family was better off than hers. Certainly, over the years, he had developed a much flashier life-style. Gilmour, the partisan of the classless view, was heir to a baronetcy, and a man of considerable wealth. Of William Whitelaw, a border squire and former Guards officer who was subsequently presented as a worthy successor to Heath on the very grounds that he had wider appeal than Margaret Thatcher, John O'Sullivan of the *Daily Telegraph*, himself a Liverpudlian, observed that 'he may seem a Northerner in Westminster, but in Leeds he's a Southerner'. Moreover – and this proved a crushing argument when made in the lobbies of the House of Commons – the great Tory retreat from the north, the continual loss of seats and decline of votes in the industrial heartland of Britain, had taken place under Heath; it seemed late in the day, and somewhat ineffective, for him to claim that his rival would do even worse than himself.

On the whole, though, the argument of the Heath camp commanded both attention and respect in Fleet Street. Some Thatcher supporters have since suggested that some kind of Fleet Street editorial establishment had simply chosen what seemed a convenient stick with which to beat a candidate to whose views they were opposed and whose parliamentary allies seemed to be the kind of people who had opposed most of those policies introduced by Heath and favoured by fashion – like incomes policy, managerial state capitalism, and entry into the E E C. I myself think it more likely that her personality, and more particularly her sex, made up a phenomenon so unfamiliar that it was hard for our generally uncritical leader-writers and television producers to take it all in. They therefore fell for the obvious – the apparent stereotype of the Tory lady.

It is striking to look back over the newspaper predictions of those days: from the beginning nearly every reporter working out of Westminster, in nearly every article, made a pretty good shot at predicting Margaret Thatcher's real voting strength at 100 or more. Yet nearly every article hedged the judgement;

and nearly every leader-writer who offered a prediction from the comfort of his office, regarded it as inconceivable that she could pull it off. Not for the first time – but particularly on the morning of the first ballot – the press failed to see the political truth staring them in the face. Given the receptions she has since received in the north, and the Tory victories at Stechford and Workington, it is more than faintly ludicrous to read again one of David Watt's long articles (*Financial Times*, 31 January) in which he said, 'To anyone north of the Trent she might as well come from Mars.'

The Heath camp, though, had better material than the class arguments the press were so willing to report. For a start, Heath had the capacious advantage of the Leader of the Opposition's room; and one should never underestimate the psychological advantage of working in comfortable surroundings. As George Gardiner pointed out in his biography of Margaret Thatcher,* her own room was just about large enough to accommodate three people. Her secretary worked in the bowels of the House of Commons, in a typing pool. She was the beneficiary of the voluntary help of Joan Hall, a former M P who drove her hither and thither in a scruffy white Mini and answered the telephone whenever possible. William Shelton made his home in the House of Commons Library – one still point amid chaos. Journalists who knew her home number, however considerate they might be of the pressures on her, were forced to resort to it regularly to check even trivial rumours and stories.

Heath had another advantage, more substantial than even a battery of secretaries. It began to emerge – or perhaps to appear – that the Party in the country was with him. The accuracy of the reports which appeared in the press during the weekend before, and on the morning of, the first ballot can be disputed. After all, one of the strongest points against Edward Heath – though it was not necessarily a point for Margaret Thatcher – among Tory backbenchers from October 1974 onwards was that Conservative candidates in both of the 1974 elections had found

* George Gardiner, *Margaret Thatcher*, Kimber, 1975.

strong doorstep resistance to him, even among traditionally loyal voters. Though the Young Conservative movement, of which he was president, was supposed to be enthusiastically in his support, several YC chairmen subsequently denied that any serious canvass of their members had taken place. The chairman of the Brent East Conservative Association made the same point for the adults.

Yet in the days preceding the first ballot both Sir John Taylor and other equally reputable conduits of constituency opinion made available to Heath's campaign managers – and through them to the press – evidence to the effect that Conservative workers throughout the kingdom were overwhelmingly of the view that Heath should remain their Leader. Guided by Peter Walker, the Heath team released the information about canvass returns to the press in driblets, saving news of the flood-tide until just before the first ballot. Of course, there were reasons other than the dangerous weakness of Heath's parliamentary base for this procedure. Heath had very much hoped that the National Union, as well as the 1922 Committee, would be offered a say in the election by the Home committee: he was very disappointed when no such extension of the electorate took place, and seemed to continue to feel that the leaders of the Party's voluntary workers in the country had a strong moral case. No sovereignty, however, was ever more jealously guarded than that of the Parliamentary Party over its choice of a Leader.

Even in this struggle there was some comedy. The majority of the constituency executive of Sir Timothy Kitson, Heath's close ally, friend and former Parliamentary Private Secretary, in whose home he had stayed for some time after the February defeat, favoured Margaret Thatcher. Kitson did not, however, accept their preference as an instruction. The great majority of MPs did, in fact, take some soundings in their constituencies; most of them made it clear that while they would listen to advice they would in the end make their own choice. So far as I have been able to gather, the investigations of Members produced a far less strikingly pro-Heath return than that undertaken by Central Office and the National Union, whose canvassing was patchy to say the least, and whose judgement was optimistically pro-Heath. Certainly, the Heath view of what the constituencies were thinking was swallowed by the press in a markedly uncritical fashion.

This seems to have been less because of any warmth of feeling for Edward Heath in Fleet Street than because of a distinct animus against Margaret Thatcher, with more than a dash of hope that the end of the struggle would see the triumph of William Whitelaw. The *Daily* and *Sunday Telegraph*s declined on the whole to make recommendations or predictions, but both the *Observer* and the *Sunday Times* recommended Whitelaw on 2 February, the *Sunday Times* being distinctly hostile both to Heath and Thatcher. The *Economist* gave Heath brutally backhanded support, saying that he should be returned provided he undertook to provide a more open style of leadership and hired a competent speech-writer whose advice he then followed: theirs was an extraordinary variety of political logic, suggesting that the Leader should be allowed to continue to lead provided he was led by somebody else. Both the *Sunday* and the *Daily Express* (on Monday) predicted a victory for Heath; nor was this solely an expression of editorial preference, for the polling organization Louis Harris International indicated that the great majority of constituency Parties favoured him. Of the political correspondents Ian Waller of the *Sunday Telegraph* gave Margaret Thatcher ninety votes; James Margach of the *Sunday Times* predicted a victory for Whitelaw in the third ballot, though he assumed that Heath would still be running then; and H. B. Boyne of the *Daily Telegraph* stressed the rising confidence of the Heath camp. Of fifteen national newspapers not one endorsed Margaret Thatcher and three – the *Express*, the *Sunday Telegraph* and *The Times* all came out for Heath. It is perhaps worth adding that on Monday, 3 February, *The Times* diarist, Michael Leapman, announced that he had put a modest £1 on the challenger.

Meanwhile, Margaret Thatcher herself had been taking steps both to counteract the criticisms of her that were being made

and to present a more positive account of her beliefs than
hitherto. Some of this was done in Robin Cooke's room, but
there were three important pronouncements – an article in the
Daily Telegraph, a letter to her constituency chairman released
on the eve of the poll, and a speech in her constituency on
Friday, 31 January.

This last was certainly the most important speech of her
political life. When I dined with her a few days before it was to
be made it was clear that it, more than anything else, was
causing her concern. Her tenseness was evident and, in the
event, she sought to strike both a critical and a positive note.
She repeated, though not in his words, Kenneth Lewis's question
about whether the leadership was a leasehold or a freehold. She
scouted accusations that she was a spokesman for a privileged
class:

You can forget all that nonsense about 'defence of privilege' – I had
precious little 'privilege' in my early years – and the suggestion that
all my supporters are reactionary Right-wingers. . . . This is not a
confrontation between 'Left' and 'Right'. I am trying to represent
the deep feelings of those many rank and file Tories in the country –
and potential Conservative voters too – who feel let down by our
party and find themselves unrepresented in a political vacuum.

And she emphasized what she took to be the traditional Tory
ideals of

compassion and concern for the individual and his freedom; opposition to excessive state power; the right of the enterprising, the hard-
working and the thrifty to succeed and reap the rewards of success
and pass some of them on to their children; encouragement of that
infinite diversity of choice that is an essential of freedom; the defence
of widely distributed private property against the Socialist State;
the right of a man to work without oppression by either employer or
trade union boss.

She was not, then, on the defensive. In the *Telegraph* article she
emphasized above all the fight against inflation: subsequently
the columnist Peregrine Worsthorne justified his support for her
on the grounds that none of the other senior Tory contributors

to the series stressed inflation at all, and Whitelaw never even mentioned the problem. But she wrote also about the criticism of her middle-class image.

If 'middle-class values' include the encouragement of variety and individual choice, the provision of fair incentives and rewards for skill and hard work, the maintenance of effective barriers against the excessive power of the State and a belief in the wide distribution of individual *private* property, then they are certainly what I am trying to defend.

She went to the Finchley meeting in good heart: before she left Westminster Neave and Shelton told her that by their count she had 120 supporters to Heath's 84.

Meanwhile, Heath continued the series of lunch and dinner parties by which he sought to woo the doubters. It cannot be said that these were successful. For instance, assumptions were made about the proclivities of some of the guests which were quite unjustified: one peer found himself expected to defend Heath to two back-bench guests when he had already declared his conviction that there should be a new Leader. Then, Heath was never good at buttering people up: the Prime Minister who at the height of the coal crisis had snapped to a junior minister who, not having seen him for some time, had approached him in a Westminster corridor with a view to wishing him luck, 'If you want to resign, put it in writing' was unlikely to find the task of exerting charm to win votes a very congenial one. Again, throughout his years of power Heath had cultivated isolation: it was neither easy for him nor convincing of him to try to unbend when he had his back to the wall. Perhaps the best judgement on this sudden burst of socializing was given to her biographer, George Gardiner, by an unnamed young backbencher:

I met my Leader for the first time over lunch yesterday. He seemed slightly uncomfortable, and spoke for twenty minutes justifying the way he handled the miners' strike a year ago. He seemed convinced he had been totally right, both then and in October. Any doubts I'd had about whether to support him were certainly dispelled. I came away determined to vote for Margaret.

In fact, as the first ballot drew closer it was becoming increasingly clear that the much-feared Heath campaign team was ineffective, blundering and inaccurate to a degree.

Of all the national press only the *Daily Mail* seemed to have much consistent faith in Margaret Thatcher as the day approached. On Saturday, 1 February, the *Mail* published the results of a survey conducted among Tory backbenchers by their own staff. Ninety-three refused to say where their preference lay, and twenty-five confessed to doubt. Of the remainder three said they would vote for Fraser, forty-seven for Heath, and sixty-four for Thatcher. Heath, the paper concluded, was in grave peril for, if the balance of positive responses proved true for the whole body of MPs, then the slighted challenger would poll 112 votes. It was the closest a newspaper came to her eventual figure.

Still, weight was bearing down on her. On Monday 3 February Sir John Taylor reported to the 1922 Committee that 70 per cent of the Party in the country were for Heath, although four-fifths of those polled would have preferred a wider choice of candidates. This was good news for the Whitelaw men. Then, as expected, Lord Home cast his immense prestige into the balance against Margaret Thatcher; now she had the whole Shadow Cabinet, with the exception of Keith Joseph and Joseph Godber, who had said he would abstain, against her.

On Sunday the Thatcher campaign committee met at Flood Street, but the only result of their deliberations was a decision to check and re-check their canvass returns, especially because as many as twenty-five Members claimed to be still undecided and nearly as many again were considering abstention. The other major problem Neave faced was how to handle the press, now digesting the flood of optimistic statistics and super-confident prediction emerging – with what imagined foundation in fact nobody has ever been able to discover – from the Heath camp. Neave decided to play it hot and then cool. First, he expressed quiet confidence that there would be a second ballot. Then, on Monday night, he and his team went around the House of Commons expressing no more than the hope that she would poll as many as seventy votes: the object of this operation was to try to ensure that any Member who did not want Heath, but preferred a wider choice, would vote for her in order to ensure a second ballot. Since pessimism is the most dangerous mood of all to project in a political struggle this was Neave's most daring move so far: it was also his most successful – as was to be shown the following morning – though it gave rise to a series of problems later. In any event, the papers on Tuesday morning, with the honourable exception of the *Daily Mail*, were certain that Heath would win, and Tuesday's *Evening Standard* carried the headline 'Ted forges ahead'.

Just after she had finished cooking her husband's breakfast on Tuesday (he had a meeting that morning in Swindon) Mrs Thatcher took a call, at eight o'clock, from Shelton. Making the most pessimistic assumptions about her strength and the most optimistic assumptions about Heath's, he and Neave made it a tie at 122 votes: a second ballot was certain.

At nine she arrived at the House of Commons, at about the same time as Philip Goodhart, the Member for Beckenham, who brought with him the black ballot box he had used to conduct a referendum on EEC membership in his constituency. After a morning spent in committee on the Finance Bill she voted, just before departing to a City lunch (again to discuss the Finance Bill). On her return she went to Neave's room to wait.

From noon to 3.30 Du Cann, with Shelton and Kitson acting as tellers for the two main candidates, waited in Committee Room 14. Peter Walker had already told Heath that he could expect between 138 and 144 votes. Ominously, however, sixteen MPs, under the chairmanship of Sir John Rodgers, who had decided earlier to abstain, had already met and, appalled by the prospect of a Heath triumph, decided to swing to the challenger: perhaps another dozen did likewise. When the news was brought to Neave he smiled. Heath voted late and, after he had departed, Kitson bet Shelton £1 that his man would get more than 130 votes. Shelton responded with another £1 that his candidate would poll more than 110. At 3.30 the poll closed and the counting began.

About eighty MPs and the whole of the Westminster press corps waited in the ample corridor outside. A little later Shelton emerged, poker-faced. Kitson's normally ruddy complexion was white. Du Cann announced 130 votes for Margaret Thatcher, 119 for Edward Heath, and sixteen for Hugh Fraser. It was, as Gordon Greig said in the *Daily Mail* the following morning, 'Sudden death in Committee Room 14'. Shelton told Neave, who went to Margaret Thatcher and said, 'It's good news. You're ahead in the poll. There will be a second ballot, but you got 130 votes.' Meanwhile, Kitson attended Heath, waiting in his room with an old friend, Lord Aldington. 'So,' said the Leader, 'we got it all wrong.' He began to draft a statement of resignation; she returned to her work on the Finance Bill.

It was not the end of the battle; but it was the beginning of the end. By the time Heath's resignation was broadcast – on the early evening news – it was thought that there would be a multitude of hats in the ring for the second ballot. In the event two outsiders – Maurice Macmillan and Julian Amery – decided not to stand. Even so, Margaret Thatcher now found that she had to face, besides Whitelaw, James Prior, Geoffrey Howe (Solicitor-General and then Secretary of State for Prices and Consumer Affairs in Heath's government) and John Peyton, Shadow-Leader of the House, former Transport Minister and a politician of legendarily acid wit. When the now greatly enlarged committee of Thatcher supporters met in a subterranean committee room on 5 February, two fears were expressed – that Whitelaw's appeal to the centre might yet still destroy her chances; and that Howe, with his remarkable combined reputation for right-wing views in economic affairs and compassion in social matters, might take enough votes from her to let Whitelaw in. In retrospect, however, it seems that Howe was merely leaving his visiting card for collection on a future occasion: one of his closest supporters expressed to me with utter confidence the prediction that Margaret Thatcher would win on the second ballot.

More clearly than any other organ of opinion the *Daily*

Telegraph on Wednesday caught the mood that would finish Whitelaw. 'Consider her Courage' was the title of the paper's first leading article. In the course of it the possibility that Whitelaw might yet seize the crown was canvassed, and the *Telegraph* – the majority of whose leader-writing staff had left their hearts with Joseph, but were now firmly in the Thatcher camp – added: 'Before the Tory Party allows anything of this sort to happen, they should consider what it is going to look like to ordinary people in the country . . . a whole herd of faint-hearts left it to a courageous and able woman . . . ' The *Telegraph* went further: 'if they ganged up to deny her her just reward . . . it will smell all the same'. This widespread instinct Whitelaw found it impossible to eradicate.

Still, he had resources. When the Thatcher supporters met on 5 February – a cheer greeted the entry of the now decided Norman St John Stevas – they realized that Whitelaw's best course, as a highly popular chairman of the Party, would be to stress the dangers arising if the Parliamentary Party voted in a way opposite to the apparent desires of the Party in the country: from his position, it would be said, he could act as the great unifier. That evening Neave's and Shelton's initial canvass suggested ninety-nine votes for Thatcher and forty-one for Whitelaw, with the rest nowhere. By the following evening, according to the same canvassers, her tally had increased by seven, his by five. It was by no means a foregone conclusion, and it seemed exactly right that she should have looked – according to one observer – 'pleased but apprehensive' at the press conference she gave on the evening of the defeat of Heath.

But the next week was an anti-climax all the same. From the dramas that had frequently marked the first stage of the campaign, the whole affair sank to bathos. Whitelaw was photographed in an apron, doing the washing-up in his kitchen. So increased was Margaret Thatcher's confidence that she declined – because the conditions were unsatisfactory and there were still voters to see – to appear with the other candidates on *Panorama* the day before the second ballot, a decision predictably described as fatal by all politicians and journalists who overrate the importance of television. Already, on Sunday, she had easily outshone Whitelaw at the Young Conservative conference at Eastbourne; they kissed in public afterwards, something that indicated quite clearly that, whatever happened, the animosity and even viciousness of the fight against Heath was quite gone. Though the actual figures were a severe blow to Whitelaw's self-esteem, it was no very great surprise when, at 3.55 on 11 February, Du Cann announced Margaret Thatcher's overwhelming victory, by 146 votes to Whitelaw's 79. 'It's all right,' Neave said to her in his room; 'You're Leader of the Opposition.'

The unimaginable had happened. 'She looks like an angel cake,' Jean Rook had observed in the *Daily Express* the previous November, 'but God help Heath.' At her press conference Margaret Thatcher struck the note of diffident joy that was to mark most of her pronouncements for the next eight months: 'To me it is like a dream that the next name in the list after Harold Macmillan, Sir Alec Douglas-Home and Edward Heath is Margaret Thatcher.' On the other hand, at the end of this first stage of her romantic journey one should not forget a title first given her in the *Daily Mirror* on 5 February by Marjorie Proops – a title later taken up by the Russians when they were made to feel the weight of her criticism. Mrs Proops called Mrs Thatcher 'the Iron Maiden'.

Chapter three
The Party

In at least one respect Sir Harold Wilson and Mrs Barbara Castle conspired to make life a little more comfortable for Mrs Margaret Thatcher. When Barbara Castle joined Harold Wilson's Cabinet the members sat around the same coffin-shaped table as their successors do now, the only difference being that Edward Heath's excellent taste in interior decoration has radically improved the *décor* of the stuffy and uncomfortable Cabinet room. One meeting was enough to demonstrate to Mrs Castle a singular disadvantage of her new eminence: it was impossible to move her legs without laddering her tights. After repeated protests from her Sir Harold – in his own words – 'gave instruction for the legs of the chair to be encased in cretonne covering, *à la* Victoria'. When the Heath government assumed office in June 1970 Mrs Castle's chair went to Mrs Thatcher. It took some time before Heath could have the room done over: when the job was completed the splintery legs of all the Cabinet room chairs had been made smooth; and a whole Cabinet of women could now sit in them in comfort. It was probably not what the Prime Minister had in mind. The anecdote may seem innocuous, but it has point.

A man can change a shirt in two minutes. He can don a dinner jacket in five; and tails and a dress shirt in ten. He can shave – if he uses, like Edward Heath, an electric razor – while reading over the text of a speech, or studying papers. He knows, moreover, that, even if he appears for some great occasion with his

bow tie askew, or his shoes unpolished, nobody will pay very
much attention. Edward Heath is an example of a man who
cares for his clothes without ostentation, and is always neatly
dressed. Harold Wilson is invariably rumpled, and looks uncomfortable in a well-pressed suit. Harold Macmillan has had
his favourite suits repaired again and again over the years; and
Lord Home – apart from borrowing dress clothes from junior
members of the Foreign Office staff – has worn the suits and
jackets of ancestors. The late Anthony Crosland so begrudged
even the ten minutes required to put on a stiff shirt and tails
(which garments he did not, in any event, possess) that, when
he was Foreign Secretary, he refused to dress up, even on the
grandest of occasions. These resources of informality are not
available to a woman; and particularly not to a political leader
who, having all her life preferred neat, elegant and attractive
attire, finds that even a hair astray attracts more comment than
a statement of policy. Early in 1977, indeed, the *Daily Mirror*
– which paper, by frequently putting its editorials on the front
page, states its claim to be a journal of serious comment – made
a major news story out of the fact that photographs demonstrated that Margaret Thatcher's hair varied in length from one
day to another. Surely any competent woman's page contributor could have informed the editor of the *Mirror* that different
ways of combing the hair can make for very different appearances.

On neither of Edward Heath's visits to China did a single
reporter think it worth mentioning what he wore. Anthony
Holden of the *Sunday Times*, in his first dispatch on Margaret
Thatcher's visit, detailed all her changes of clothing in the first
forty-eight hours. The cartoonist Jon of the *Daily Mail* so
regularly drew her wearing the same hat (not a particular
favourite, and worn only once or twice) that, mildly irritated
and, anyway, with a new hairstyle, she has practically given up
wearing hats. More: when a man appears on television he normally needs to do little more than avoid haircream or too
dazzlingly white a shirt to escape the distractions of studio
glare. Since women have more variety and colour in their

clothes – and wear jewellery besides – much greater care and prevision must be exercised before they do television programmes, if they want to avoid the meretricious glitter of a starlet. Now, of course, much of the extra interest which a major female politician excites is, if often trivial, at worst harmless, at best useful; and discussion of her clothes and tastes adds to the gaiety and life of an otherwise drab political scene. But keeping up appearances, however efficient one is, and however practised, imposes considerable strain. From the beginning, she has done it rather well, though comment on how well she has done it often has an edge: the *Guardian*, describing her appearance at a Finance Bill committee just after her triumph, said that 'she is beginning to look, ever so slightly, like the Queen'.

Before and during the battle for the leadership, however, there was a more immediate sense in which the isolation which convention imposed on her sex – and which was increased by her own tastes – affected her. I do not suppose that more than a couple of women MPs are seen regularly in Annie's bar; and both are Labour Members. Margaret Thatcher was never in any way on easy-going terms with the generality of Conservative backbenchers: such time as could be spared from work was spent at home. That was the way in which she had always chosen to run her life, devoting her considerable energies to running two lives, one wholly professional, the other utterly private. As an individual she has never been tempted to stop at one of the Commons bars for a couple of quick ones on the way home; as a woman she would have been unusual if she did so. What all this meant, of course, was that when her hour of opportunity came all her information about the moods, feelings and instincts of those to whom she was about to appeal for votes had to come from others. Now, although Edward Heath, when he was making his bid for the leadership in 1965, was the reverse of clubbable, he had had the inestimable advantage of having been Chief Whip. During his time in that job, wrote his biographer George Hutchinson,* 'he had come to know every single

* *Edward Heath*, Longman, 1970.

Conservative Member. He was able to weigh them all up dispassionately. He knew their hopes, ambitions, feelings of goodwill and ill-will, deficiencies, strengths and weaknesses (over women or drink or money or whatever): Heath knew them, and he knew what they were capable of.' In 1975 Mrs Thatcher had no comparable advantages.

However, there was nothing priggish about her isolation. I recall a late sitting of the House on a particularly wet and windy night late in 1973. The usual huddled queue of dispirited politicians and journalists waited for infrequent taxis under the awning of the Members' entrance. I was accompanied by a Labour MP in an advanced state of intoxication; he had not been a regular drinking man, but a domestic tragedy had sent him over the top. While I was wondering how to get him home – indeed, whether I could get him home – Margaret Thatcher's ministerial Rover stopped to offer a lift. At the time I assumed that she had offered simply because I knew her. A chat with the duty policeman the following day enlightened me: it was her invariable practice to offer to share her car after late sittings; and considering the somewhat emotional state in which many of her passengers have been in the late and early hours, her kindnesses cannot have been invariably easy ones.

But the isolation of a politically ambitious woman goes far back beyond the years of her public success. The town of her birth, Grantham in Lincolnshire, was hardly central to a political education or to political development: until she went to Oxford she had no knowledge of a wider world. Interestingly, though, it was what Grantham made available, rather than what Grantham lacked, that defined her tastes and supplied her satisfaction. Her family were 'never rich, never poor'. Her father, a Rotarian, a Methodist, a lay preacher, a grocer, a teetotaller and an avid reader, was also a prominent local politician, of Independent persuasion. She was devoted to him, and he guided all her early reading. A hard worker at the Huntingtower Road Elementary School and subsequently at Grantham Girls' Grammar, her spare time was spent serving in the family shop, reading and, especially, attending concerts, for the musical life of her home town was a rich one. Over the years she has grown away from that background – her children were baptized in the Church of England – but it marked her deeply, and it did not confine her imagination.

Apart from the tuition her father gave her in politics she remembers most vividly letters received from her sister's pen-friend, an Austrian Jewess: by the time the war came young Margaret Roberts was emotionally familiar with the nature of the threat in Europe; and she had begun to develop a response of her own to totalitarian ideologies. But her sense of her own heritage was perhaps best expressed in a message which she sent to Grantham on becoming Leader: 'I always believe that I was very lucky to be brought up in a small town with a great sense of friendliness and voluntary service.'

She was set apart – or set herself apart – too, in what she chose to do after school. In 1943 it was not easy for a girl to obtain a place at Oxford: it was especially difficult in the science school. Against the strongest urgings of her school teachers, however, she decided to read chemistry. It was already in her mind subsequently to read for the Bar, and on the advice of a family friend she had thought of an eventual specialization in patent law, where both disciplines would be of use. But the life of a chemistry student at Somerville was a hard one: she began work at 7.30, and mornings and afternoons alike were spent in laboratories. Though she played an active part in the affairs of the University Conservative Association, the political clubs were still not attuned to women. With much of her remaining time given to music, and allowing for the fact that the social life of her academic contacts – including her most famous teacher, the Nobel Prizewinner Dorothy Hodgkin – was dominated by left-wing philosophizing, it is difficult to escape the conclusion that her university life, for all that she remembers it vividly as an exciting time, was a trifle lonely.

A feeling that she was almost physically detached from what was going on around her – a detachment created by her sex, her temperament, her ambition, and by the way she concentrated on the task in hand and carried about with her from her

Grantham days the intellectual and moral power to achieve self-sufficiency – stays with the student of her early years in politics. She entered the House of Commons in 1959 and first gained office as a junior minister for Pensions in 1961. There she remained until the defeat of 1964, if not oblivious to, then at least distant from, the scandals and crises that racked the Party during the last days of Macmillan. She went through a succession of Opposition posts until, in 1969, she became Shadow Secretary of State for Education; and she continued her association with that department until the defeat of February 1974.

Now, although during the 1960s she obtained more varied experience than any previous Conservative woman politician and although, unlike either predecessors or contemporaries of her sex, she was judged certain to achieve Cabinet rank in June 1970, it remains striking that so intellectually capable and wide-ranging a politician did not make even more impact during the period from 1965 when Heath became Leader of the Opposition. The decade of his leadership was one of the most traumatic the Conservative Party has gone through; and for more than half of his time it seemed to offer a fair chance of being one of the most promising. Yet Margaret Thatcher's isolation persisted, and for all that she won friends and acquired allies, she came in no way as close to the centre of power and policy development as did men with equivalent or inferior starts, and much less obvious talents, like Peter Walker and James Prior.

Heath began his leadership as little less than a counter-revolutionary. He did not, however, find a description for what he was trying to do until, at his first Party conference after becoming Prime Minister in 1970 he set as his objective the achievement of a 'quiet revolution'. 'We were returned to office,' he said, 'to change the history of this nation – nothing less' and, above all, he promised 'less government, and of a better quality'. Now, of course, nearly every new government has a favourite slogan, a particularly loved piece of rhetoric, a metaphor to describe its ambitions. But the Heath government was unusual in the extraordinary amount of research, argument and preparation that had gone into its five years of preparation for office: it was the proud boast of every Minister that no Cabinet in British history had been so well prepared for its task. Indeed, until the major reversal of policies that occurred in 1972, it was not uncommon for the Prime Minister to ensure that there was a copy of the 1970 manifesto on the table at Cabinet meetings, so that a check could be kept on progress made in fulfilling its undertakings. Even after the about-turns in economic and industrial policy – the decision to introduce a statutory incomes policy, and the provision of industrial subsidies on a hitherto unimagined scale – Heath pursued the implementation of even minor manifesto pledges with obsessive, perhaps compensatory, rigour.

Much of the 1970 programme was, of course, highly technical, but the moral thrust behind it was essentially based on reducing the role of government in the life of the citizen, and on increasing the scope and responsibility of the individual. Again, as Heath said in his speech on the 'quiet revolution', he intended to ensure that 'Government withdraws from all those activities no longer necessary either because of the passage of time or because they are better done outside government, or because they should rightly be carried on, if wanted at all, by individual or by voluntary effort.' He wanted to encourage individuals 'more and more to take their own decisions, to stand on their own feet, to accept responsibility for themselves and their families'. No programme could have been better designed to appeal to Margaret Thatcher.

But the significance of Heath from the outset of his leadership lay rather less in what he did than in what he allowed and encouraged to be done. I recall his speaking, in 1969, at an all-day conference on mental health organized by the Conservative Research Department. Most of those attending were busy people, and some were not even Conservatives. In the afternoon he came in to thank them for their help, and to reassure them that he would read every word said during the day (the whole of the proceedings were taped) and attend most carefully to their recommendations when he was in office. He spoke off the cuff, so no exact record of his remarks survives. According to my minutes, however, he spoke with real passion, particularly on the subject of the search for truth on which the Conservative Party had embarked under his leadership. He mentioned the elaborate system of policy committees he had set up to provide him with a programme for government, and he added, 'No position, no tradition is sacred. We intend to look at everything afresh and decide what is best to be done for the country. No attachment to earlier ideas, or outdated concepts, will deter us.'

The radical note in what he said that day, and in what he said on many other occasions, was unmistakeable. It was as though a fresh breeze was blowing through the Conservative Party. However, when the day was over, a warning note was sounded to me by the distinguished psychiatrist Anthony Clare, who had spoken at the conference. 'Is he really a Conservative?' said Clare in a rather academic way. 'I always thought that Conservatism depended on an attachment to values.' And it is certainly true that the epitaph his critics, and even many of his friends, would write on the Heath government of 1970–4 was that it rapidly lost any sense of what its fundamental philosophical values were. A senior backbencher, quoted by David Butler and Denis Kavanagh in their Nuffield study of the February 1974 election* put the problem very succinctly:

Decisions in politics are very difficult but it helps if you derive them from a philosophy or a set of principles. Many of us feel that we made too many concessions here. It is not so bad if you can compromise your principles and can justify it by success. But we lost the election as well.

Indeed, in an earlier study† Butler showed a shrewd appreciation of where Heath stood in relation to the swirl of ideas and arguments he had encouraged between 1965 and 1970.

Although Mr Heath agreed with the interventionists on the one hand that there was a continuing need for a voluntary incomes policy and,

* *The British General Election of February 1974*, Macmillan, 1974.
† D. E. Butler and M. Pinto-Duschinsky, *The British General Election of 1970*, Macmillan, 1970.

on the other hand, with the free marketeers that individual enterprise was being stifled and industry harmed by 'over-government',
he had comparatively little interest in their controversies. For he
looked to the solution to the problems of the economy in a different
direction which can conveniently (if inadequately) be termed
'technocratic'. Like the advocates of *laissez-faire*, he wished to allow
individual enterprise to flourish; but, unlike them, he did not see
drastic reductions of governmental activities as the best way of doing
this. He saw in structural reforms a way of cutting the area of public
interference without significantly reducing the level of overall
services provided.

Nonetheless, in tone and style and thrust, Heath was radical.
One could not imagine him beginning his Prime Ministership
with the sort of words Harold Macmillan used at the outset of
his: 'I am slightly amused by the fact that during the early part
of my life I was accused of leaning too much to the Left. I have
seen recently accusations that I leaned too far to the Right.
I propose, as I have always, to follow the Middle Way.' It is,
indeed, always surprising to hear Margaret Thatcher, given her
own radicalism, speak with such remarkable warmth and affec-
tion of Harold Macmillan; and recall so readily the political
saws he has communicated to her over the years.

As the Macmillan years came to an end – with a coda which
saw the defeat of Sir Alec Douglas-Home in the 1964 election –
it became clear that his successful stifling of ideological argument
during the 1950s had left a gap, a hunger, in the Tory Party.
After the 1964 defeat Iain Macleod noted in a leading article in
the *Spectator* (of which he was then editor) that the word Tory
was gaining in fashion over the word Conservative. He welcomed
the change for, he said, the former title was invariably associated with periods of innovation and re-examination in the
Party's history. Such a period Heath, in 1965, seemed ready and
destined to preside over – much more so than his amiable,
intelligent but much less inspired rival for the leadership,
Reginald Maudling. The plain fact is that political parties do
not live by pragmatism and office alone; and Macmillan had
exhausted the resources of both.

Writing in the *Sunday Telegraph* on 2 February 1975 Peregrine Worsthorne said that if Margaret Thatcher won the impending contest the Conservative Party would have become genuinely interested in individual freedom, and genuinely committed to its achievement as *the* end of policy, for the first time in its history. Worsthorne is perfectly correct in his suggestion that the Party, over its long and, indeed, unique history has had far more pressing concerns than individual freedom – authority and hierarchy among them – and in the suggestion he has frequently made that Mrs Thatcher, like most politicians, emphasizes a part of the historical picture at the expense of the whole when she claims that her Party is the sole reliable, and the only ever-standing, guardian of individualist values. But he was wrong in predicting, and has been wrong in repeating, that she would be or is an innovator in this regard. For if there was a single theme to the maze of complex and complicated studies undertaken on behalf of, and proposals made to, Edward Heath between 1965 and 1970 it was the libertarian theme. And in background and class and upbringing Heath, like Margaret Thatcher, seemed well prepared to be sympathetic to it and well fitted to encourage others to adopt it.

Nor was he without well-equipped, if still minority, support, for the 1960s saw the beginnings of an intellectual renaissance of libertarianism. In 1957 the Institute of Economic Affairs was founded; in the second half of the 1960s it grew, and acquired admirers like Margaret Thatcher and Keith Joseph; in the 1970s it has burgeoned and, being itself non-political by the rules of the Charity Commissioners, has spawned a political offspring, the Thatcher–Joseph Centre for Policy Studies. The central purpose of the IEA is to encourage micro-economic studies, that is, studies of how markets operate at levels lower than those controlled by monopolies or governments. Its advocacy – and the advocacy of its many distinguished authors – is invariably on the side of individual enterprise, and against the supposition that governments either can or should determine the rules according to which an economic system operates, or even set the objectives a society should seek to achieve.

When an economy has sunk into a morass because the government is grabbing 60% of gnp, there is bound to be a revival of radical demands that there needs to be a restoration of choice, incentives and rewards for activities which benefit society – even if there is, yes, private profit as a result. The academy of such ideas in Britain has long been the Institute of Economic Affairs.

Thus the *Economist* in 1976. And Ronald Butt, in *The Times* on 8 January 1976, gave the IEA even stronger praise:

... the recent change of climate has been remarkable. Ten years ago, the IEA, with its devotion to Adam Smith, free market economics and the guidance of the economy by strict control of the money supply rather than by collectivist intervention, was still regarded as a bit of a joke by most economic writers.

Today, helped by the pressures of real life, it has shifted some of the best known economic writers in its direction and a good deal of the most influential economic thinking comes from economists published by the IEA.

In the year before the 1970 election Edward Heath's economic adviser, Brian Reading, and several of his closest aides were regular guests at the informal Friday lunches held once a month at the IEA's headquarters in Lord North Street. Today the politicians, policy advisers and journalists to be found there eating rather unappetizing chicken and drinking excellent wine will certainly be those closest to Margaret Thatcher.

In the nineteenth century – and perhaps some way into the twentieth – an organization like the IEA would have attracted to itself members of the Liberal Party above all others. For in the nineteenth century it was the Liberals who placed their faith for human progress in the free operation of markets: nearly every major measure passed by Parliament in that century which was designed to relieve human suffering and which involved the intervention of the state in so doing, was a Tory measure. Lord Shaftesbury, the great social reformer, was in almost every respect what we would nowadays call a reactionary – save in the matter of social welfare. But as they have declined in electoral power in this century the Liberals have taken to themselves a degree of that belief in collectivism, and in the control by the state of social activity and provision for social betterment which is the driving impulse of the Labour Party. It was Tories, therefore, who first made their way to Lord North Street to sit at the feet of F. A. Hayek and Milton Friedman.

Hayek, an Austrian professor of philosophy, was not unknown even to older Tories, those who revived the Party after its crushing defeat in 1945. His book *The Road to Serfdom** was, after 1945, much quoted by the bright young men at the Conservative Research Department who, under R. A. Butler, sought to redefine their Party's philosophy after a general election in which the Labour Party had won 180 more seats than theirs had. Among those bright young men were Iain Macleod, who died shortly after the 1970 victory, Reginald Maudling, and Enoch Powell.

A newer influence, both at the Institute of Economic Affairs and among younger Tories, was the American economist Professor Milton Friedman from Chicago, the apostle of monetarism and subsequently, like Hayek, a Nobel Prizewinner. Hayek is a philosopher with a deep and wide interest in economics; Friedman an economist of exceptional technical ability and interests, who has sought nonetheless to see the political and philosophical implications of his purely economic work. To summarize an argument which will occupy more space in a later chapter, it can be said here that the work of both men brought them to a profound suspicion of the growth, in income and power, of the modern apparatus of the democratic state.

The British welfare state and the growth of nationalized industry after the war Hayek saw as the result – at least in part – of the influence on British politics of the left-inclined émigrés from Nazi Europe in the 1930s. For Friedman the most important conclusion of his life's work was that inflation, which destroyed the Weimar Republic in Germany, was essentially a consequence of governments, pressed in modern conditions to assuage more and more demands from the electorate, constantly

---

* First published 1944, reissued by Routledge and Kegan Paul, 1976.

expanding the amount of money in circulation, even by resort to the expedient of printing notes which had no backing.

To Britain in the 1950s, in spite of the signs of inflation and overheating of the economy (which led at one stage to the resignation from Harold Macmillan's Cabinet of the Chancellor of the Exchequer, Peter Thorneycroft, and his two junior ministers, Enoch Powell and Nigel Birch, all of whom were monetarists by conviction and temperament), the ideas of Hayek and Friedman as they were applied in detail to economic management seemed far-fetched, in spite of the wide regard in which the Austrian especially was held. It was not until the second half of the Heath government that the troubles into which it had run, and the inflation which it had generated, compelled a fresh resort to anti-statist ideas; and not until Heath lost the election of February 1974 that those ideas began to gain wider interest and even acceptance, aided by the passionate advocacy of Enoch Powell (a figure on his own after his dismissal from the Shadow Cabinet in 1968 because of his speeches on immigration) and the later interventions of Sir Keith Joseph, who announced his own repudiation of the economic policies followed by the Heath government from 1972 onwards at Preston on 5 September 1974.

It was in such circles as these that Margaret Thatcher found most of her general spiritual and intellectual solace. For every idea, even the most technical, there is an instinctive political response. Enoch Powell once said that, of all professions, that of politics is the one in which personal experience rather than professional training makes a man what he is. Though she had never been poor, all that she had won as a politician and as a woman had been the product of immense dedication and effort; and it was natural that she should favour analyses and policies which, however unfashionable they might appear for most of the postwar period and certainly during the ascendancy of Harold Macmillan, nonetheless depended on the propagation of individual enterprise, rather than on the extension of the powers and responsibilities of even a compassionate state.

But it would be wrong, in looking back on her career, to

exaggerate the extent of her involvement with the ideas of what has come to be known as the New Right. When Heath, after becoming Leader of the Party in 1965, undertook his vast, complicated and radical re-examination of everything Conservatism stood for or was taken to stand for, Keith Joseph, among her present allies, was far more closely connected with the radical wing of the Party. As the man charged with the design of a policy for industry which would encourage capitalistic enterprise – though, after the 1970 victory he found himself charged with responsibility for the Department of Social Services – he was greatly taken by the arguments put forward by the IEA. Younger and less experienced politicians like Geoffrey Howe were likewise interested in the revival of free enterprise ideas. For Margaret Thatcher, however, detachment from the intricate discussion that was going on marked her career.

Partly this was for reasons already suggested: her bent was for the assimilation and presentation of information; her private pattern of life meant the devotion of a great deal of time to her family. Also she was a new girl: she had entered Parliament only in 1959 and gained office, as Parliamentary Secretary to the Minister of Pensions and National Insurance, in October 1961. Though, as it happened, pensions reform was one of the major achievements of the 1970 government (whose measure was later repealed by Labour) neither that subject, nor education, for which she became Shadow spokesman eight years later, were in the forefront of political argument within the Party.

Looking back on the past now she dates her emergence as a politician constantly engaged in wide debate, as opposed to one with general ideas who nonetheless concentrates mostly on specific tasks, to begin with the adoption by the Heath government of a compulsory incomes policy in 1972. This measure was a direct breach of everything Heath had said both before and after the 1970 election, and in particular it went against an undertaking he gave in a speech at Carshalton on 8 July 1967. In the course of this speech, which for a long time afterwards was called by Tories imitating Sir Robert Peel's nineteenth-century pronouncement at Tamworth the 'Carshalton Manifesto', he said:

> If by an incomes policy is meant a general educational programme demonstrating the relationship between incomes, productivity and prices, this is something we can all support. . . . If it means the Government pursuing a policy of relating incomes and prices to productivity in those spheres where it has direct responsibility, that too is practicable and desirable. Over a period of time these may make a marginal but nevertheless valuable impact on the economy as a whole.

> But if by an incomes and prices policy is meant Government control over all incomes and prices, disguised as a voluntary effort but in fact under threat of Order in Council and therefore compulsory, this is not only impracticable but unfair, undesirable, and an unjustifiable infringement on the freedom of the individual.

It is beyond the scope of this book to discuss in detail how the author of that statement became later the author of an incomes policy of unprecedented complexity which involved government and the agents of government in wage determination on a scale never hitherto visualized. It is certain, however, that the *volte-face* of 1972 deeply distressed both Margaret Thatcher and Keith Joseph. Neither, however, as their critics and all of those who subsequently complained about their assault on Heath always stress, felt moved to resign. During the leadership campaign Mrs Thatcher was inclined to say that she had considered resignation and that, on reflection, she should have taken the drastic step of leaving the government. She then admitted the perhaps unworthy motive of fear that a woman who left a Heath government would, as long as he lasted, have no opportunity of getting back. But to her friends outside government altogether it seemed that the managerial collectivism which eventually became the hallmark of Heathian politics was something that she became aware of only slowly over the following two years: it was nonetheless the mainspring of her challenge in the winter of 1974.

For this reason it is useful to summarize the argument about incomes policy here. To the thoroughgoing libertarian – to, for example, the scholars of the Institute of Economic Affairs – all incomes policies involving government coercion are anathema. Even the so-called voluntary policies – like the now defunct Social Contract – are similarly regarded, for they involve the threat of eventual use of the legislative power, and the distinction between the two kinds of policy is regarded as being without very much meaning. On the other hand, to many members of the Conservative Party both the fact that in modern Britain the state is an employer on a hitherto undreamt-of scale, and the fact that trade unions have become more militant than ever before and, at the same time, frequently more careless than ever before of what is seen from Whitehall as the overriding and complicated economic concerns of the nation as a whole, requires government to take some measures to restrain incomes. Since (at Wrexham in 1976 and again on BBC television in April 1977) Margaret Thatcher expressed a view about incomes policy very much akin to that of Heath at Carshalton in 1967, the difference between these two views remains a very important one for the Conservative Party.

On taking office in 1970 the Heath government seemed to hold very strongly to three propositions about the means by which economic recovery could be assured. In the first place they desired to cut both public expenditure and taxation, the first in pursuit of the monetarist theory about the dangers of excessive government spending, the second because they believed that tax reductions would encourage free enterprise. Their second proposition was that incomes policies of any formal or statutory kind were to be eschewed. This did not, of course, mean that the government was not prepared to take a line – and, as it proved, a very tough line – against wage demands by its own employees which it regarded as excessive. Both the refuse workers and the Post Office workers felt the weight of ministerial determination in this regard. The third proposition was that government should refuse to bail out individual firms unable to make their way without subsidization in the market: this determination was to collapse in the face of the resistance of workers in the Upper Clyde shipyards and of the threat posed to Rolls-Royce because of lavish spending on the still experimental and by no means certainly successful carbon fibres project. When the crunch came Ministers were prepared neither to face the total bankruptcy of the country's most famous company, nor the dangerous militancy of Scottish shipping workers.

More particularly, and much more to their credit, they feared the consequences for the unemployment figures of any excessive ruthlessness in the industrial field. It is a curious and interesting feature of the behaviour of British political parties that once in office each tends to be especially unhappy about accusations of insensitivity or betrayal in fields usually regarded as the prerogative of the other. Thus, for example, in the 1960s Harold Wilson showed himself more grandiose and more committed – more, if you like, Tory – in foreign policy and in the matter of the retention of a British military presence east of Suez than a Conservative Prime Minister might have been. So, too, rising unemployment, and the threat of more of the same, frightened Conservative Ministers in a way that, since 1974, much higher figures have failed to frighten Labour Ministers. There were two main reasons for this. First, Heath, for all his apparent abrasiveness, was in many respects very much of the school of Harold Macmillan, whose life, career and behaviour in power was marked for ever by his distress at unemployment in the 1930s: Heath shared that compassionate sense of waste to the full. Secondly, and quite separately from its economic policy, the 1970 government was deeply committed to reform trade union law. Their attempt, through the Industrial Relations Act, to remove many of the – to them – unjustifiable privileges gained by law and custom for the unions through the years, and to make trade union leaders more responsive to the wishes of their members, had excited remarkable union militancy. Ministers were appalled by the prospect of confrontation with the unions both over the Act *and* over unemployment. Since they were not prepared to withdraw the Act – though Heath again and again expressed a willingness to modify it – something else had to give. What gave was the policy of monetary restraint: the government, like Macmillan's government when it ran into less formidable but not dissimilar difficulties, decided to spend its way out of trouble. Since the attempt to do that, quite apart from being dangerous in itself, coincided with a boom in world commodity prices, the considerable extra expense of preparing for entry into the EEC, followed by entry itself, and a continual failure to increase the productivity of British industry, rampant inflation ensued which combined with the revolt of the coal miners to destroy the government.

For the reaction of the Heath government to these events the radicals in the Party had considerable contempt. If Margaret Thatcher was merely worried, others were far more directly critical, and their attempt to think through a response to what was rapidly proving to be a heartbreakingly disappointing and drifting government itself marked a real change in post-war Tory attitudes. Of all post-war governments the 1951 Churchill government had taken the smallest proportion of the national income in taxation and in consequence had most efficiently expanded the range of the individual's economic freedom; for this reason it began to receive considerable respect from the radicals. As regards the attempt to restrain galloping inflation by the adoption of an incomes policy the same radicals merely observed that the power of the unions was greatly exaggerated or, perhaps more correctly, misunderstood. Certainly, they said, unions would and could enforce excessive wage demands if government did not restrain them. But the result of such demands would be either bankruptcy, a sharp drop in demand for goods overpriced as a result of meeting excessive demands, or unemployment. And unemployment did not bother the radicals a whit, for they believed it could be demonstrated that the one real power the unions possessed was that of pricing their own members out of work – the single certain consequence of wage settlements too great for the profitability of a company to bear.

In any event, the radical argument continued, the rising unemployment which had so deeply affected Ministers that they introduced a mini-Budget in July 1971 to allow for higher spending to create jobs, was itself a delayed result of the credit squeeze of the previous Labour Chancellor. Moreover, the inevitably rough justice of an incomes policy would kill incentives for more skilled workers and, by flattening out differentials, induce yet more discontent in the workforce. And attempts such as Heath was eventually to make – with the creation of the Relativities Commission – to restore differentials by government fiat would merely substitute an artificial and unworkable piece of machinery for the natural forces of the market. All these complications and problems, they concluded, were the inevitable consequences of a statutory incomes policy which would both distort the ordinary workings of the economy and gradually demand all the time and energies of Ministers in attempts to keep it working. In this last judgement at least they were certainly right: the exhaustion of those Ministers most closely involved in the final confrontation with the miners over incomes policy was plain to all.

But then the Party was exhausted too. Whether the sense of disappointment, futility and promise blighted that ran throughout Conservative ranks in the spring of 1974 was the result (as Heath's friends claimed) of the fact that he had been confronted by trade union subversion at home and insuperable accidents (like the commodity boom and the energy crisis) abroad, no one could pretend, however much they might defend individual actions of the Cabinet, that the government's record had been a successful one. Nor did Heath's response to events command confidence: there was a widespread belief that if he had nerved himself to a general election a few weeks earlier he might have been successful (though this I doubt).

He began the February campaign with a call to arms: who, he asked, governs Britain? He ended it with an assurance that if the miners would only be patient they could have everything they wanted in a short time. Nobody was clear what he was fighting for. Then, when the October election came, he changed tack again, and appealed for a national government. All in all, and given the inflation rate, there was a great deal of point in the subsequent criticism of *The Times* of the whole incomes policy argument:

The common-sense view is that the Conservative Party ought to be concentrating on budget and monetary policy, where it is certain they would have to act, and not on incomes policy, where it is very doubtful whether they could act. This is the line which is being taken by Mrs Thatcher, by Sir Geoffrey Howe, and by Sir Keith Joseph. It would be absurd to fight the next general election on the slogan: 'Labour's Incomes Policy has failed; try the Tory one.'

But, of course, while the Heath government went on its way towards an unhappy end, Mrs Thatcher had her own problems at the Department of Education and Science. She was neither as innovative nor as radical in Curzon Street as either the many enemies she earned while there (especially in her first year) or her admirers have sometimes claimed. The set of commitments and principles with which she came to office in 1970 were fundamentally neither ungenerous nor doctrinaire. They reflected her own instincts about the balance of priorities and authority that should exist within the schools system. She was committed to a programme of heavy spending on school buildings, of developing nursery education and of slowing the march to universal and mandatory comprehensive secondary education. To this she had added two distinct preferences of her own: she wanted parents to have more opportunities to exert power in schools; and she was deeply concerned about declining standards of literacy. Because of the order in which the cards fell, however, and perhaps more particularly because, though in no sense hostile to the principle of comprehensive education, she was not prepared to impose it for the sake of fashion, she ran into severe criticism. The fact that she was also committed to, and subsequently implemented, the policy of raising the school leaving age which commanded the support of practically the entire educational establishment was not enough to make up.

In particular, it was not enough to make up for what she had to accept as a result of Heath's initial desire to prune public expenditure. Perhaps oddly, in view of the place it subsequently obtained in the mythology of political hate, the pre-election seminar at Selsdon Park reaffirmed the commitment to spending on primary school buildings which had, in real terms, so markedly declined under the previous Labour government. When, therefore, the Cabinet discussed spending cuts she was able to preserve this part of her programme. In return she made the concession to her colleagues of partly withdrawing free school milk at a saving of £8m. It should be emphasized that, if anything, she quite favoured this step: it was not something forced from her. On any reading, however, it was a measure preferable to postponing or abandoning action on buildings. Since she had already, by her issue of Circular 10/70, outraged fashionable opinion by reversing the Labour policy of insisting that all local authority educational reorganization programmes should conform to a comprehensive pattern, it was hardly surprising that a storm broke around her head over the issue of milk, and she gained thereby a hard-faced reputation that even now she has not quite lost. It was a storm out of all proportion to the importance of the issue and, of course, it need hardly be said that the Labour government has since found neither the will nor the means to reverse her policy.

On the whole I got what I wanted [she told George Gardiner]. I got the primary school building programme, and there was no further postponement of the date for raising the school leaving age. Every Department had to make some cuts, but I was determined that I was not going to make mine in education itself. School milk and meals aren't *education* as such. I took the view that most parents are able to pay for milk for their children, and that the job of the Government was to provide such things in education which they couldn't pay for, like new primary schools. . . . The important thing was to protect *education*, and that's what we did. Indeed, we expanded it.

In those remarks it is easy to see the influence on her of the first principle of the libertarian radical – that governments should only do what only governments can do. It was clearly in operation throughout her time in the undoubtedly important but, relative to the overall responsibilities of government, narrow field of education. It has been steadily more widely applied to all her thinking and speaking since she became Leader. And it is a principle adherence to which arises from her very nature and instinct. It is a principle wholly congruent with the judgement of the radical wing of the Party to which she belongs; but it was not from thought or study that she derived it. Moreover, holding to it as she does, it was inevitable that she should become steadily disenchanted with a government increasingly of the belief that it should do more rather than less.

But if her suspicion of expanding government implied – as it did – a love of individualism, there was no commitment to an individualism that was casual or permissive. As in her youth, she saw individualism as carrying with it the connotation of quality. The purpose of an educational system was neither social nor egalitarian in her view: it was to enable individuals to get the best out of themselves. 'Everyone is born with some combination of talents,' she observed. 'So we want a society, and an education system, that enables people to develop whatever talents they have to the full.' Or, as she put it in a speech made after she became Leader, 'our purpose is to make the world safe for Solzhenitsyn'.

At the time there was a widespread desire for increased nursery school facilities, a desire which she shared, though not always for the same reasons as did other advocates. For many the nursery school was not just a way of starting the educational process but a convenient means of enabling the mothers of young children to go out to work. Not for the Secretary of State. 'I was talking about nursery *schools*, not about day nurseries. For educational purposes you need the youngsters for only half a day. Of course that takes some stress off the mother, but doesn't enable her to go out to work full time.' In the event, circumstances curtailed her nursery school programme, but its achievements were nonetheless substantial, and have been cut back only by the reductions in public expenditure imposed on the present Labour government by the International Monetary Fund.

The same principles of activity – again, very often not shared by others deeply involved in the educational world – could be seen in her attitudes to secondary education. It has been a cardinal principle of those favouring a wholly comprehensive system of education that the ending of the existence of grammar and direct grant schools (and perhaps of public schools as well) would raise the comprehensive standard by compelling the attendance at comprehensive schools of children from the best endowed homes, both financially and culturally. It was an argument with which, for all its appeal, she would have no truck. 'The attack on direct grant schools,' she said in 1972, 'has come, not because they are bad, but because they are very good. What a terrible philosophy to hold back a good school while the others catch up.' Likewise, in the instructions she issued to the James Committee investigating teacher training and the Bullock Committee studying literacy, her preoccupation with the strictly pedagogic rather than the social aspects of education was clear. And if she did not always get her way – Bullock, who reported after she had left office, she found singularly disappointing – she finds it satisfying to reflect now that the broad themes on which she constantly laid stress, particularly those of academic standards in schools, are the constant concern of a Labour Prime Minister and a Labour Secretary of State.

The verdict on her time at the DES must remain mixed as long as there is dispute about the proper aims and purposes of an educational system. In some cases, as in her support of the Open University – on the typically personal ground that it offered opportunities to talent that would otherwise remain undeveloped – she was in the mainstream of educational opinion. Her sympathy for the arguments and ideas of the authors of the Black Papers, which were above all concerned to reiterate the value of traditional teaching methods and the necessity for traditional academic standards (and one of the authors of which, Dr Rhodes Boyson, is among her front-bench spokesmen today) was also considerable and unfashionable, though she has not yet gone so far as to adopt their proposals for reforming the whole system by means of issuing vouchers to parents to the value of the state's contribution to a child's education, so that the parents could select, and therefore dominate, the schools. That she was not able to do more could be put down to the fact that, given her extraordinarily tidy and efficient mind and the wretched circumstances in which she found the schools system, starved of both income and capital, she saw her main task as restoring the physical fabric of the system and rearranging its priorities. Any dramatic reforms were to await another Parliament, office in which she was not to enjoy. By 1974 however, she had, in a strictly public relations sense, largely expunged the unfavourable image initially imposed on her, and her standing ovation at the NUT conference, allied to the fact that she now totally dominated her department, suggests that she would have been an exceptionally powerful and dominant Minister thereafter. But greater things awaited her.

She also enjoyed the advantage of marked popularity in the Party, a popularity which she increased by her conduct in Opposition from February 1974 onwards. Though, as I suggested earlier, it is probably the case that a majority of the Party in the country would have preferred Heath to her as Leader in 1975 she was nonetheless a vastly more familiar figure then than she had been in 1970; and one to whose instincts and priorities the better part of the Party responded with sympathy.

And it was a very stricken Party. Conservatives tend to react in neurotically different ways to defeat. The extraordinarily long and unique history of the Party, and the fact that it has so often and for so long held power, has in the past given it a serenity in defeat which is unusual. For some of its members, however, defeat seems calamitous: they are so accustomed to office that to lose it seems an offence against nature and, often, an indication of unusual sin. Yet, considered objectively, the swings in opinion required to produce major shifts in the parliamentary balance of power in Britain are remarkably small. The Tories were shattered beyond belief by the fact that in 1945 Labour gained 393 seats to their own 213. But it required a swing of only 3.13 per cent to reduce the Labour lead to seventeen seats in 1950. The truth is that, under our present system, neither of the major British political parties is ever very far from power.

But what undoubtedly increased the number of those deeply shocked after the defeat of February 1974 and sent the Party into a trauma not wholly relieved even today, was that the

Heath government had failed in so many of the things that Conservatives were supposed to be particularly good at. True, the majority of the Party had supported the entry into the EEC; but it was not only anti-EEC Tories who looked with unease at their Party's loss, through this policy, of their hitherto exclusive appellation 'patriotic', and the attempts of Labour to seize it. Again, if their administration of affairs had often been unexciting and if from time to time – as in 1945 – the Party had shown itself singularly unable to respond to deepseated wishes for dramatic reforms in the nation's affairs, Conservatives were widely regarded, and regarded themselves, as competent stewards of the national purse. Inflation at more than 20 per cent and a situation of apparently ineradicable confrontation with the trade unions, had destroyed their reputation for competence. Even now, the question is raised more often than is at all comfortable for their new Leader of whether Tories could get on with trade unionists and whether, if they could not, it is worth returning them to office. On all these and other such matters there can be argument over whether the Heath government took right or wrong decisions; was lucky or unlucky; was basically competent or basically inept. But the rights and wrongs of individual questions mattered less than the overall impression. And it was the overall impression that both dethroned Heath and made it exceptionally difficult for his successor to rebuild confidence and, as important, self-confidence.

Nor has application to this problem been helped by the way in which very basic changes in the nature of society have affected both Conservatives' conception of themselves and of the beliefs which have governed their existence. Conservatism, unlike socialism, is not a systematic ideology. Naturally, because of its long history, it is deeply influenced by notions and ideas formed in earlier historical periods. Most scholars agree that four propositions have been pre-eminent in the history of the Party – that man is unequal save in the eye of God and that, therefore, egalitarian policies repudiate human nature; that the fundamental nature of man is religious (a belief that Margaret

Thatcher passionately shares); that a state of hierarchy is a natural condition of human society; and that society is itself organic, that is, it cannot and should not be shaped by political or social engineering, but allowed to develop, with the minimum of political interference, by itself.

The second and third of these propositions are peculiarly difficult to assert with confidence and in the expectation of wide assent in the modern world. Even the first and fourth present serious problems. The difficulties were not, of course, anything like so great when the Conservative Party was most naturally the possession of one class, especially when that class had a substantial landed element. In the nineteenth century the third Marquis of Salisbury and in the twentieth Stanley Baldwin (to name but the most prominent) could quite naturally and convincingly speak and act in accordance with, and even openly define, one or all of the four principles. When, at the 1963 conference, Sir Alec Douglas-Home, deeply embedded in and wedded to the landed tradition of the Party, invoked God and religion in a party political speech he was widely thought either to have made himself look ludicrous or to have given deep offence. Some redefinition of the Party's nature in the light of the character of modern society and its aspirations has, therefore, in recent years seemed called for, especially in regard to feelings following Heath's defeat.

Nor is the Party helped in its search for redefinition by its own changing social structure. True, it has never been averse to finding talent and even leaders in what a sociologist might consider to be, for it, the oddest places. Reflecting on the history of his Party Harold Macmillan once drew attention to its vitality by witnessing its taste for novelty, contrasting the occasion when it chose as Leader 'a brilliant and dandified Jew' with the one when it chose 'a clever and attractive woman', and imply- ing that the results of the latter choice might be as remarkable as those of the former. But it often requires a very settled order of affairs to make such strange choices, and while I remain of the opinion that the Conservative is much less hidebound than the Labour Party, and that while it was not astonishing for the

Tories to choose a woman Leader, it would be almost beyond possibility for Labour to do likewise, it seems nonetheless clear that the present social structure of the Party offers much less opportunity for philosophical reflection on its nature, identity and purpose than it has enjoyed in the past.

In the general election of October 1974 the fact that 52 per cent of Conservative candidates standing and 75 per cent (208 in number) of those elected had gone to public schools – as opposed to 18 and 17 per cent respectively of Labour candidates – no doubt gave a certain homogeneity to the Party. Even here, though, and in spite of the fact that no fewer than forty-eight successful Conservative candidates had been to Eton, the broader, and more particularly the landed, base of the old Toryism had begun to vanish. Indeed, when one compares the educational backgrounds of Conservative with those of Liberal candidates it can be seen that the third Party were much more heavily drawn from the ranks of the public schoolboys, 69 per cent of their successful candidates having been privately educated. Of the 277 Conservative MPs 127 were from the professions, 91 involved in business, and only 23 described themselves as farmers. In other words, the middle class as we understand the term today – what the Tudors would have called people in a middling station of life – dominated the ranks of the Parliamentary Party. It was certainly an able intake – both major Parties have expressed satisfaction with the quality of their intake in the last three general elections, but only the Labour Party was really happy about its members returned in 1964 – but it was one which signalled very nearly the completion of the transformation of the pre-war Party, in terms of background, interest and occupation, into something more modern.

The nature of the candidates contesting the leadership elections in 1965 and ten years later signalled that transformation even more thoroughly. Of those who went into the lists in 1963 (there being no elections to the post then there was a wider possible choice of candidates) two were hereditary peers – Home and Hailsham – one (Butler) came from a family that amounted in itself to an academic and political aristocracy, and only

Maudling and Macleod, both outsiders with no real chance of winning, were from the new professional Tory classes. In the elections of 1965 and 1975 only William Whitelaw (assuming one discounts fringe candidates like Hugh Fraser) was of the old Tory stamp. No doubt this was an excellent thing, and the Party could certainly not go on for ever being run by an unrepresentative section of the community. But it was an addition to the serious problems of definition and redefinition that the Party had undergone so profound a social transformation in a decade. Of Edward Heath and Margaret Thatcher it could be said that their humble backgrounds actually constituted an advantage on the occasions when they won the crown, and that was the first time any such observation could be made about the contestants in a Tory leadership battle.

What Margaret Thatcher inherited – or wrested – from Edward Heath was, therefore, a Party that was confused and uncertain about policy, philosophy and power, as well as one that had been making itself over completely. When he was preparing the Ford lectures on the history of the Party, published in 1970,* Lord Blake chose the period 1833 to 1955 for his study because to his mind it marked a distinct era in the history of the Conservatives, from the accession of the first recognizably modern Leader, Peel, to the resignation of the last of the traditional giants.

I end where I do [he explains] because Sir Winston Churchill's resignation marks the end of an era. Perhaps Britain ceased to be a world power in 1945, but she believed herself to be one for another ten years. Whether or not it was cause and effect, the illusion vanished within two years of Churchill's departure. The consequences are still unfolding in every aspect of public life, not least in the Conservative party itself.

Blake was wise to draw our attention in this fashion to the relationship between what has been, relative to previous years, the decline of the Party in electoral terms, its own crisis of

---

* Robert Blake, *The Conservative Party from Peel to Churchill*, Eyre and Spottiswoode, 1970.

identity and the decline of the country. However much its enemies may jeer at the assertion or even be angered by it, the Tories have always identified themselves with the nation in an unselfconscious way that no other party has done. From the lips of their politicians come patriotic sentiments which, whether justified or not, whether reasonable or not, are natural to them. It is the Conservative Party which will always be in the van to protest against cuts in defence spending. It is the Conservative Party which can most easily find a home for ex-officers with political ambitions. And it is the Conservative Party which can most readily produce a Leader deeply concerned about the threat to the national defences – and defence is merely the subject regarding which that national point can most dramatically be made.

From Macmillan to Heath a major attempt was made, through rhetoric and psychology, to substitute a European role for a country that had lost an empire but, except for the few enthusiastic Europeans and in spite of the fact that a substantial majority in the Party was easily persuaded that Britain had an essentially European future, that role has never been very successful. It was not the least of Margaret Thatcher's problems in February 1975 that the trauma of her Party coincided with the latest stage in a long-drawn-out trauma of the country.

Chapter four
The country

In March 1977, some months after her successful tour of the Antipodes, a New Zealand school teacher wrote to Margaret Thatcher. The teacher was not just an autograph collector. She enclosed a blank card in her envelope and, in the politest fashion, asked Mrs Thatcher to write on it the text that most inspired her. The Leader of the Conservative Party chose two stanzas immediately familiar through repetition to anybody who has known her for any stretch of time. They are from Kipling's 'The Reeds of Runnymede'.

> At Runnymede, at Runnymede,
>   Oh hear the reeds at Runnymede:
> 'You mustn't sell, delay, deny,
> A freeman's right or liberty,
> It wakes the stubborn Englishry,
>   We saw them roused at Runnymede . . .
>
> And still when Mob or Monarch lays
> Too rude a hand on English ways,
>   The whisper wakes, the shudder plays,
>   Across the reeds at Runnymede.
> And Thames that knows the mood of kings,
> And crowds and priests and suchlike things,
> Rolls deep and dreadful as he brings
>   Their warning down from Runnymede!

Margaret Thatcher possesses some thirty volumes of Kipling's poems in different editions, and in various states of disrepair:

she has promised to spend her retirement in learning book-binding. When she was a child in Grantham it was one of her jobs to fetch from the library the books her father wanted to read. His choices were wide and, though herself a schoolgirl with an essentially – in terms of her work – technical taste, she read most of what he read, and discussed it with him.

Moreover, and not altogether usually for a local politician of his period, Alderman Roberts was as acutely concerned with the European as with the domestic political scene. On this subject, too, he discoursed to his daughters, and little Margaret, serving her required stint in the shop, would more often than not find herself overhearing political discussions between her father and his customers. Given the high-minded seriousness of the house-hold, the breadth of her father's interests, and the eclectic nature of his tastes, she certainly received at home a broader literary and political education than would be available at her schools – or, indeed, to most girls in most schools of the period. Apart from music and the theatre, indeed, politics and literature were the stuff both of life and conversation.

It would be wrong, however, to come away with the impression that the Roberts' household in Grantham was too heavily serious a place, or that no fun was to be had there. Margaret Thatcher herself, it is true, says that her upbringing was 'rather puritan', though not with any note of regret. There was no garden behind the shop. The lavatory was outside. The kitchen was a lean-to affair. Of the furniture she herself says that 'Nearly all of it was typical Victorian dark-red mahogany furni-ture – the beds, dressing tables, and we each had our own bed-room wash-stand.'

The demands the business made on all four members of the family were considerable, and fully accepted, even by the two girls. It was rare for the whole family to sit down to eat to-gether; and they never holidayed together, Beatrice Roberts taking her two girls once a year for a week to Skegness, to a boarding house where they did their own cooking; her husband taking his separate holiday at the same place – but during Bowls Week. The lightest of the small child's pleasures were the

Skegness fairground and the holiday visits to the music hall. Though sherry and cherry brandy were kept for visitors both parents were teetotal. There were no newspapers taken on Sundays, and little that might be called work was allowed. Indeed, the Sabbath was almost entirely devoted to church affairs, rounded off by a supper-table discussion between Alfred Roberts and some of those from the community who were equally religious. When he first came to know the household Denis Thatcher described it as 'very Nonconformist'.

It was certainly not a home for a frivolous child. But young Margaret was never frivolous. Austere or Spartan or even dour might be the words that would readily spring to the mind of a modern youth seeking to describe such a home and such an environment, but it is clear that even now such suggestions would arouse in her only amazement. She came from an England fundamentally rural still, and she is inclined to show a little anger when metropolitan interviewers and colleagues question the range and nature of the cultural resources available to a young girl growing up in Grantham. Indeed, to anyone who has talked to her about her origins, it seems extraordinary that the press, even that section of the press already disposed against her candidacy, should have so readily swallowed, during the battle for the leadership, the myth that she was a home counties lady. Her every utterance and almost her every instinct reflect her consciousness and evaluation of her true Lincolnshire background. Indeed, during a visit in the spring of 1977 to Grimsby in the course of the by-election campaign there, she exceeded even her own remarkable normal level of campaigning success by identifying herself to audiences as a Lincolnshire girl, and denouncing the highly unpopular Humberside authority (the creation of the government of which she was a member) to which the fishing port had been consigned.

Even if Grantham might, in the television age, be seen as an isolated and restricted place, it sent her to Oxford exceptionally well-rounded, and with her mind exceptionally well formed – certainly well enough formed and disciplined to take on without any feelings of inadequacy the heavily socialist-inclined and superficially much more sophisticated minds of most of her contemporaries and nearly all of her teachers. In a trivial little volume called *My Oxford** Nina Bawden tells an unlikely story of Miss Roberts's undergraduate days to the effect that she announced her preference for the Oxford University Conservative Association over other party political bodies within the university on the grounds that she could more readily shine there than elsewhere. But all the testimony of those who knew her well in youth, to whom may be added those who have since talked to her about her early days, suggests that independence, with a marked leaning to Conservatism, was the natural political stance she brought with her from Grantham and her father's shop to the glittering world of Oxford. Though neither her interests nor her sympathies have changed much over the years, they have remained tolerant and high-minded.

Even now, when her life is exceptionally busy, books remain a favourite relaxation, and a recurring topic of conversation. Of course, personal taste as well as professional necessity means that she does a great deal of technical, historical and political reading, and it sometimes seems that there is a fissure between, say, her enjoyment of poetry and her ability to digest at great speed the latest philosophical, scientific or historical volume. But she is fortunate and unusual in having not only a highly retentive brain but a retentive imagination as well. If, even in conversation, she recalls a quotation she will usually get it more or less right. More curiously – and more interestingly – she is likely to recall the circumstances in which she came across it, and perhaps express an intelligent appreciation of how and why circumstances as well as merit helped create the influence it has on, and the value it has for, her.

It is this particular function of the imagination that has been so useful in preserving for her not only the memories and the learning but also the sights, sounds and impressions of youth. Once, in the course of talking with her about books, I played the little game of asking her if she could recall which book had made

* Robson Books, 1977.

the biggest impression on her at the time of reading, and which she would care to take to a desert island with her. After only a fractional hesitation she recalled her feelings of mixed determination and excitement on leaving Grantham for Oxford in the autumn of 1943. She recalled that Richard Hillary's *The Last Enemy** (the title comes from 1 Corinthians, xv, 26, '. . . the last enemy that shall be destroyed is death') had just been published, and that she had read it almost immediately. This story, written while he was recovering from burns by one of the first British fighter pilots to be shot down during the Second World War (subsequently he was killed in a fatal air battle), was her great calf book; she emphasized not only the importance of the book in her life, but her particular memory of the last chapter.

Born in Australia, Hillary had been brought to live in Britain by his father, an imperial civil servant who passed to him the assumption that after graduation he too would take his place in the ranks of the King's overseas administrators – possibly in the Sudan, a country (as he put it) of blacks ruled by Blues. At Trinity he rowed enthusiastically, wrote preciously, read widely and, in fine, was the very type of the cultured but somewhat rootless pre-war undergraduate, decrying seriousness as the worst sort of pretension. The book tells of his brief odyssey from boyhood to manhood, from carelessness to responsibility, through deadly service in the RAF. In the last chapter he offers a vivid account of an air raid at the end of which he helped dig a badly injured woman from beneath the rubble of her house, a task in which he was somewhat inhibited by the condition of his hands, badly burned in his own crash. As he forced his brandy flask between her lips she said, 'I see they got you too.'

That that woman should so die was an enormity so great that it was terrifying in its implications, in its lifting of the veil on possibilities of thought so far beyond the grasp of the human mind. It was not just the German bombs, or the German Air Force, or even the German mentality, but a feeling of the very essence of anti-life that no words

* Macmillan, 1942; repr. Pan Books, 1969.

could convey. This was what I had been cursing – in part, for I had recognized in that moment what it was that Peter and the others had instantly recognized as evil and to be destroyed utterly. I saw now that it was not crime: it was Evil itself – something of which even then I had not even sensed the existence. And it was in the end, at bottom, myself against which I had raged, myself I had cursed. Great God, that I could have been so arrogant.

One would either have had to know Margaret Thatcher then, or to know her well and have seen her in unguarded moments now, to realize the significance of the impact a story and writing like Hillary's would inevitably have on a highly sensitive and moral nature not untouched by romance. At every climactic moment in her political life, however well she has used her formidable and clinically powerful mind to prepare for it, it is emotion and concern that appear instantly on the surface. The sense of personal involvement, beyond ambition or resolution or courage, which quickens in action and which public service encourages, is initially and very clearly a product of the wholeness of her upbringing, but nurtured and developed in later life by such writing as Hillary's.

The strength of such feelings suggests that after all Grantham and the shop were in no way narrow places.

But the world – wider, at all events, than Grantham in the scope it offered to an ambitious young politician – was itself contracting. After taking her honours degree in chemistry at Oxford she read for the Bar, and stood as Conservative candidate for Dartford in 1950 and 1951. In her first speech to the Party as Leader, at the 1975 conference, she gave a sketchy account of her involvement in Party affairs from the first conference she attended, which was addressed, of course, by Churchill; his memory evoked a note of awe. It was clearly hard for her – to some extent it still is – to grasp, even after her triumph over Heath, that she herself stood where Churchill had stood, albeit with the potential only of leading a much-reduced nation.

When she first appeared as a parliamentary candidate both the afterglow of the war and the titanic reputation of Churchill concealed from Party, country and the world alike how changed were the circumstances of Britain. Nor is there evidence that the vigorous and thrusting young woman from Grantham had any appreciation of what was happening: few Conservatives, indeed, did, save for the intimates of the eternally cunning and far-seeing Harold Macmillan, himself to become Prime Minister in 1957, and with genius to continue to hide from his countrymen how far they had fallen in strength and competitiveness from the heights of 1945. Anyway, other things than politics preoccupied her.

She had become a candidate for Dartford almost by accident, through the suggestion of an old friend, John Grant, who was a director of the Oxford bookshop Blackwell's. He introduced her to the chairman of the Dartford constituency at her first Party conference – that at Llandudno in 1948. She was adopted early in 1949 – at twenty-four the youngest woman candidate in the country. A dinner was arranged on the evening of the adoption to celebrate the event, and a business colleague of the hostess's husband was conscripted to escort Miss Roberts. She was then living and working as a research chemist in Colchester, but her escort, Denis Thatcher, drove her from Dartford as far as London, and asked to see her again.

In order to fulfil her obligations at Dartford she gave up the Colchester job, and took a flat and a new post in London. She was an enthusiastic, hard-working, popular candidate, but not a remarkable one. In the event, however, at the 1950 election when the swing from Labour across the country was no more than 3½ per cent, she reduced the Labour majority by nearly half, from 20 000 to 13 638. Overall, the Attlee government survived by five seats. It was clear that another election could not be long delayed and, until it came in October 1951, Margaret Roberts divided her time between her profession, her constituency and the business of courtship: on the eve of the 1951 campaign she and Denis Thatcher became engaged. He was ten years her senior and liked fast cars – which she did not – and music, which she did. Active in Conservative politics in supportive roles, he had nonetheless always declined to take office, and was content for her to pursue her larger political ambitions and a new interest – the study of law. When, however, Churchill was returned with a majority of seventeen in the 1951 general election, but it emerged that she had managed to do no more than knock another thousand or so off the Labour vote, it was clear that the time had come to leave Dartford. She did so almost immediately, getting married in December 1951. It was to be eight years before she reappeared on the list of Conservative candidates.

During those eight years she did not divorce herself from politics. Indeed, she set aside her own rule that she would not again stand for Parliament while her twins, born seven weeks premature in August 1953, were in their formative years, in order to put in for the (then) safe seat of Orpington in 1954; but she was not unhappy when she did not get the nomination. Predominantly, however, the years were devoted to work and family.

It was in this period that her phenomenal resilience and concentration showed themselves. She had always been a hard and dedicated worker. She had always displayed industry and stamina. She had always seemed on top of her affairs. In 1953 she excelled even her own standards. In May she took her Intermediate Bar examinations. In August she gave birth to the twins. And in December she successfully sat for her Bar finals. She was dissuaded from undertaking a course in chartered accountancy – which she felt would round off her preparation to be a tax lawyer – only by her husband, who vetoed the devotion of another lengthy period of time to preparation for a profession. For two years after her finals she devoted herself to pupillages at the Common Law Bar, at Chancery, and at the Revenue Bar, sharing chambers with, among others, Airey Neave, Anthony Barber (himself a tax lawyer of distinction), and Patrick Jenkin, who was in 1977 to be her Shadow Secretary of State for Social Services.

If not all-absorbing, her non-political life during these years was very nearly so (she herself has said that, with diligence, application and concentration it is possible to live two lives;

but not three). The family's increasingly easy financial circumstances made it possible to employ a nanny. When they moved
from London to Erith, to be nearer her husband's work, she
commuted to her legal practice. Her ability either to rise early
or to stay up late meant not only that her preparation for briefs
was never skimped, but that the children could enjoy a great
deal of her time. If politics did not sink into the background – she
became gradually more active in the Inns of Court Conservative
Association – they were inevitably relegated. She had not for-
saken her ambition to enter Parliament, but an appropriate
time was not easy to mark down ahead.

The 1955 general election had provided Sir Anthony Eden
with a comfortable majority. The year after, he plunged into the
Suez adventure, perhaps – whatever one thinks of the idea of
embarking on it in the first place – in its effect and results the
most humiliating episode in post-war British foreign policy. It
cost Eden his place at the head of affairs, and it evoked in
Margaret Thatcher a strong support for the view that, having
entered on such a project, the British government should have
seen it through. From the confusion, pathos and bitterness of
the hour Eden's successor, Harold Macmillan, was in part
cushioned in his attempts (aided by his Chief Whip, Edward
Heath) to pull the Conservatives round again by the Tory
majority in Parliament. With so masterly a helmsman, it was
clear that the general election, for which Labour desperately
hoped during the crisis itself, would be postponed for some time.
It was likely, thought the Thatchers, that the twins would be
comfortably settled at school before it took place. The Suez war
and its aftermath, involving as it did both a grand national
trauma and an intense national reappraisal, reawakened all
Margaret Thatcher's old political hunger, and all her fierce
patriotism. She began again the search for a Conservative
nomination.

In her renewed search she imposed on herself one limitation;
and she found herself up against one not entirely unexpected
obstacle. She was unwilling to seek any seat for which fulfilment
of her duties would impose on the family either disruption or

the problems attendant on distance. Thus she confined herself to the home counties. Then, when she applied for Beckenham in Kent in 1957 – though she eventually came second to the present Member, Philip Goodhart – she found that selection committees which had been, in her only experience, indulgent to the ambitions of a young and attractive woman, were less well-disposed towards a mother of two who sought entry into Parliament. In fact she was told by one of the committees that, in spite of her talents, it was their universal opinion that she should be at home, looking after her children.

At Maidstone in Kent she had a not dissimilar experience, though here she again came second, this time to John Wells, an old friend and patron from Dartford days. Finally, there was Finchley where the Tory majority in 1955 was 12825. The selection committee decided to ask all 200 or so applicants the same set of questions, and to score them according to their answers. By this process four were selected to appear before a meeting of the divisional council, consisting of between fifty and sixty representatives of Party workers in the division. On the eve of this trial one of the four, C. M. Woodhouse, was selected for Oxford, and gave up his place. Two days after the meeting Denis Thatcher boarded a plane in Johannesburg and picked up an abandoned *Evening Standard*; from it he learned that his wife had been selected. Her political career was at last under way.

The general election at which she entered the House of Commons, that of 1959 – in which she had a personal majority of 16260 and the party an overall lead of 100 seats – marked the highest peak of the thirteen years of Conservative power which succeeded the defeat of the Attlee government. It marked, too, the acme of Harold Macmillan, and from then on nearly every step taken was downward. However, the stirring unease and the forceful patriotism that had crystallized and perhaps brought forward Margaret Thatcher's decision to re-enter the parliamentary lists did not, at this stage of her life, issue in any distinctive analysis of, nor response to, what in retrospect we can see as the seeding period of Britain's decline.

She made, it is true, an almost instant mark on Parliament with her maiden speech – traditionally a quiet, uncontroversial introduction in which the new Member dwells on the virtues of his or her constituency. Hers was a forceful contribution, made without a note, to the second reading debate on her own Private Member's Bill to throw the proceedings of local authorities open to press and public. (It is a pleasing irony that a political leader not marked by any particular love for journalists should have fired her first parliamentary gun in their defence.) Her first, unruffled, twenty-seven minutes on her feet in the Chamber of the House of Commons drew plaudits from Ministers as well as Opposition spokesmen, as did the way she guided her Bill through committee, where she was aided by a junior Home Office minister, Keith Joseph. 'As a maiden speech,' wrote the *Daily Telegraph* 'it has not been, and is unlikely to be, excelled by any of her contemporaries new to the 1959 Parliament. As a thirty-minute exposition, without a note, of a controversial and complex Bill, it was of Front Bench quality.' Henry Brooke, then the Home Secretary, observed that 'she spoke with a fluency which most of us would envy. She achieved the rare feat of making a Parliamentary reputation on a Friday, a reputation which I am sure she will now proceed to enhance on the earlier days of the week.' The Bill passed, and she proceeded to fulfil Brooke's prediction, so much so that in October 1961 Macmillan sent for her to offer her a job at the Ministry of Pensions. She was to spend three years there.

It is arguable whether her failure to get elected in 1951, and her subsequent early success and promotion, were good or bad influences on her later political development. She missed the opportunity of real fellowship with the brilliant Conservative intake of 1950 and 1951 – the group which included Heath, Powell, Maudling and Macleod, and some of whose members, in forming the One Nation group and producing the powerful and influential booklet of the same name, consolidated the work of R. A. Butler and the Research Department in bringing the Party to terms with the greatly changed world of post-war domestic politics. In that renaissance Margaret Thatcher had no part. Again, her early appointment to and long stay in a Ministry which at that period offered little opportunity for political creativity may have stunted her growth, or at least ministered to the more implacably efficient side of her mind, rather than to her romantic and philosophical impulses. On the other hand, when her time came to challenge for the leadership, she was as fresh as paint.

She has had the good fortune to have been too young to have seen or felt the deepest part of the Depression: thus she is much less emotionally hamstrung in her formulation of policies on the economy and unemployment than are those Conservative politicians, like Macmillan and Heath, who were so deeply scarred by those years as to be all too ready to interpret modern recession as though it were a replay of the 1930s, and to imagine that the same economic methods would serve to repair its tragedies. Then, too, in junior office and in Opposition, she was not associated either prominently or emotionally with the apparent success story or the subsequent collapse of the Macmillan years. That she was not untouched by their magic and their assumptions – particularly those of steadily accumulating national wealth, an economy whose most prominent parts were under the mixed management of private capitalism and the state, and a country which would see the steady disappearance of deprivation and inequality through the operations of government – can be seen by the fact that in the deadly battle for the leadership of the Party in 1963 she looked no further for a successor to Macmillan than R. A. Butler, the universal choice of the most (in the conventional rather than the philosophical sense) liberal elements in the Party.

Then there was her personal attachment to, and admiration for, Macmillan himself. To be sure, junior ministers so unexpectedly promoted as she was tend to develop an often exaggerated assessment of the qualities of their patrons. But to Margaret Thatcher Macmillan was as much mentor as patron. Even now, she excitedly recalls his lectures on political tactics, and the various saws with which he entertained willing juniors. When asked to provide an overall judgement on him, 'visionary' is the word she invariably chooses, and it was interesting that even in 1976, when he reappeared in a television broadcast to call for a national government – an idea immensely fashionable in Fleet Street, Whitehall and parts of Westminster at the time, but at odds with Margaret Thatcher's own combative political instincts and likely to damage her chances of undiluted triumph – she would allow very little criticism of him in her own circle.

The extent to which Macmillan was or is genuinely visionary – that is, that he has an ability to foresee at least the general picture of future events and to adapt political policies accordingly – is debatable. The one certainty about him is that he was *the* Tory Leader of the post-war period. He was not the man Churchill was, and the achievements of Churchill both in Opposition and in the 1951 government should not be underrated. But Churchill after the war does not compare to Macmillan for the overall grasp he had of Party and national affairs; for the way in which he adapted to and even influenced circumstances, while often persuading both his followers and the electorate that things were actually the reverse of what they really were; and for the fashion in which he set both the limits and the character of British political debate. His rivals do not compare at all. Eden served briefly, and left amid disaster. Home was granted little time, and in that little time, apart from very nearly winning a general election which he was universally expected to lose, showed no creative disposition, at least in domestic policy. Heath gave promise at the beginning of being the most unusual, and the most radical, of Conservative Leaders at least during this century, but served long enough to reverse or abandon all his major policies, and was ejected from office an embittered and sullen, if not broken, man. For the historian the dominant figure of post-war Conservative politics up to 1975 – and therefore, with Attlee, one of the two dominant figures of national politics after 1945 – was Harold Macmillan.

Macmillan came to office because of a failure in foreign and military policy. That was the occasion of his rise. But the rise itself might have come earlier, and probably would have done had it not been for the extraordinary position of heir apparent which the past and circumstances had given to Anthony Eden. For intellect, skill and performance in office – particularly in domestic office – Macmillan's only rival was Butler, the man fated never to be in quite the right place at quite the right time, and never to have quite the required will or quite the necessary support to achieve the palm. But, for all that Macmillan came to power through foreign policy, and for all that he had had considerable diplomatic experience as Churchill's Minister in North Africa during the war, where he demonstrated exactly that combination of guile and vision which was to make him a remarkable Prime Minister, he was above all a domestic political animal. It was in that guise that he had his greatest influence both on the Conservative Party and on British politics. Although it has seemed that during the leadership crisis and since, Margaret Thatcher has had to struggle with the legacy of Edward Heath, it is the legacy of Macmillan that has in fact presented her with most of her problems.

Macmillan's career as Prime Minister was dominated by two convictions and one real sense of opportunity. His first conviction was that, after Suez, both the history of the British Empire and the possibility of a genuinely independent British foreign or military policy were over. His second was that whatever the quality of international economic competition, and given the existing part-state, part-private control of British industry, there could be a steady increase in prosperity, and a steady expansion of welfare and other services. More: he was convinced that only by holding to such a policy could the Conservative Party hope or deserve to continue to govern Britain. As the period of his rule proceeded, this supposition about domestic policy, more than any of the other things that went wrong for him, was increasingly open to question. It was then that Macmillan blew flames back into the dying fire of a long-held conviction that the future of his country lay in Europe, and he applied, in the event unsuccessfully, to join the Common Market.

This is not the place to analyse the merits or demerits of

Macmillan's European policy, or his contention – in which he was followed by many others – that access to the larger European market would provide Britain with the stimulus to achieve that level of economic growth which, as the fifties turned into the sixties, increasingly eluded government after government. It is extremely important, however, to understand precisely the nature of the dilemma he was in and the character of his response to it if we are to understand the problems now faced by Margaret Thatcher, and her response to them.

The great crisis of Macmillan's government – which he dismissed at the time as 'a little local difficulty' – came in 1957, when his three Treasury Ministers, Peter Thorneycroft (now Lord Thorneycroft, and recalled to active political service as chairman of the Conservative Party by Margaret Thatcher), Nigel Birch (now Lord Rhyl) and Enoch Powell, resigned. Essentially, their objection was to the Prime Minister's refusal to bring government spending more into line with government income.

When Thorneycroft became Chancellor it appeared that the assumptions of steady economic growth and steadily increasing provision on which Macmillan depended were in peril. It was agreed among Ministers at the beginning of 1957 that there should be nothing in the forthcoming Budget that would stimulate inflation. It was, if not generally, at least widely recognized at the time that excessive government spending was a major cause of inflation: that interpretation is now generally accepted (though its pure monetarist form, that excessive spending is the *only* cause of inflation, has yet to gain full acceptance). In February, Thorneycroft made further, though minor, cuts in spending. In the Budget itself Thorneycroft both reduced taxation and planned for a Budget surplus. The significance of this strategy – and even more the significance of its subsequent rejection – for the subsequent history of the Macmillan government, for the prospects of Margaret Thatcher and for the economic future of Britain is so great that some explanation of the theoretical nature of the argument is at this point desirable.

Since Macmillan first introduced a rudimentary policy of

incomes restraint – which he did some time after Thorneycroft's resignation – every British government has at one time or another resorted to the device of incomes restraint when inflation has risen. For most of the 1960s the opposing argument, implicit in all that Thorneycroft did, that controls (whether of incomes or prices) are irrelevant to the problem of tackling inflation, was ignored. In 1977, monetarism – the economic doctrine which states that since inflation is caused by excessive government spending the only way to tackle it is to reduce that spending – is accorded much more respect, but it has been adopted only to an extent that allows continued large Budget deficits, and it has been run in tandem with policies for the control of both prices and incomes.

The Thorneycroft Budget of 1957 was in a classical liberal Conservative tradition, and it may well provide the historical shadow of the first Budget of a Thatcher government. Thorneycroft's conviction was that, in the circumstances of that year, when the balance of payments was in danger and sterling was under pressure, Britain needed *both* reductions in taxation and reductions in social and public expenditure. The latter measures would reduce inflation and stabilize the value of the currency: Conservatives have ever been attached to the idea of a stable currency. On the other hand, Thorneycroft believed, in the traditional spirit of liberal economics, that the wealth of a country increased in proportion to the extent to which, by lenient taxation, its citizens were encouraged to earn more and do better for themselevs. Thus, his cuts on both sides of the board – on spending and on taxation.

Monetarist doctrines have become, in recent years, so much a possession of the Conservative right that it is important to stress that they are not, at least in theory, repugnant to a responsible socialist government, assuming socialism here to stand for greater and greater control over communal provision of goods and services by the state. There is, of course, a romantic fallacy here, which assumes that the removal of power and property from a limited number of hands, and their transfer to the hands of ministers, means the passing of control, or power, or ownership, to the people as a whole – hence the use of the clichés 'nationalization' and 'public ownership'. In fact, and whether one judges it to be desirable or undesirable in its effect, nationalization gives power in the first instance to ministers and ultimately, in the context of today's vastly complicated governmental machine, to bureaucrats. It is in my view also the case – as most Conservatives, and particularly those closely attached to Margaret Thatcher, would accept – that excessive control of national resources and the national productive capacity by government inhibits the creation of wealth, and radically reduces efficiency. Nonetheless, in principle, a socialist government as much as a Conservative should be able, by applying monetarist insights, to keep its spending in some sort of balance with its income; and if this necessarily, in a country whose generation of wealth has been declining, reduces the grandiosity of the ambitions of such a government, it should not prevent it from asserting that centralist and socialist domination of the commonwealth which is the *raison d'être* of left-wing politics. Indeed, it is occasionally possible to see, in the statements of some left-wing theoreticians like Tony Benn and Stuart Holland, a refusal to accept the rhetoric of all recent governments – Labour and Tory alike – to the effect that the generation of wealth is a political imperative, and indications also of a preference on their part for austerity if not exactly a hair-shirt. It is important, however, to understand the real logical difference between the two creeds which dominate British politics, and the sameness of the problems which have confronted all governments – as well as the sameness of their response to it – in order to appreciate Margaret Thatcher's view of, and answer to, those problems.

In the event, in 1957, Macmillan was becoming progressively uneasy about Thorneycroft's approach to economic management. For one thing – and in this, again, the Chancellor was a pioneer – the Budget in his hands was gradually ceasing to be the great set-piece of the economic year. As Chancellors since his day have increasingly done, Thorneycroft was willing, and indeed anxious, to use various mechanisms available to him to make further adjustments to financial and economic policy even between Budgets. Only thus, he considered (as did his junior ministers), could consistency of policy be maintained. We are much more familiar now than were politicians and their critics then with the staggering possibilities of error in Budget forecasts, and in economic prediction generally. That is perhaps because, as the economic ratchet has tightened steadily in the twenty years since Peter Thorneycroft resigned, the errors too have multiplied, and there is scarcely a month in which the Treasury is not obliged to confess that some previous calculation has been in error.

But the purely political picture got worse after the 1957 Budget. The Tories lost a by-election in Lewisham. They performed badly in a Labour seat at Wednesbury. At the end of May they saw their majority in Hornsey decline dramatically. By the end of the summer nothing seemed to be going right: the Budget had not had the effect intended on inflation; and the government was steadily losing ground in the esteem of the voters. The grand question – the same question which was to confront Edward Heath in 1972 and 1973 – was whether Thorneycroft was right in supposing that it was necessary to apply rather more of what we would now call monetarism, and sit matters out until things got better – a possible policy, given that there did not have to be a general election until 1960 – or whether a policy of more relaxed credit, and higher government spending on credit and through borrowing, would provide the impetus the British economy seemed to need.

In considering his options Macmillan was not, however, influenced just by the considerations as I have posed them. When, in September, Thorneycroft increased the Bank Rate by 2 per cent, cut bank lending, and reduced public investment, his instant reaction was to consider the social as well as the political impact of such measures. It was now certain that deflation would bring increased unemployment and at this the Prime Minister jibbed – especially when Thorneycroft proposed to keep the Civil Estimates for 1958–9 at the same level as for the previous year, thus, because of inflation, actually reducing spending in real terms. The Cabinet discussed the matter many times and at great length. At the end of the discussions there remained a gap of some £50m – a much greater sum twenty years ago than it would be considered now – between what the Chancellor wanted and what the Prime Minister would concede. Thorneycroft, Birch and Powell resigned.

The significance of this dispute, and the consequences of Macmillan's policy, have been argued ever since. In the view of the Prime Minister, Powell and Birch had had excessive influence on their chief: '. . . they seemed,' he said, 'to have introduced into the study of financial and economic problems a degree of fanaticism which appeared to me inappropriate. If they did not actually welcome martyrdom, they did nothing to avoid it and seemed rather to seek and enjoy the crown.' Ever since, in his numerous writings and broadcasts, Macmillan has sought to make a contrast between the relatively trivial level of inflation and excessive expenditure which he allowed and the huge inflation and massive spending deficits which governments allow now. By implication at least, he has consistently denied that he might have started anything dangerous in 1957, or that his conduct of economic policy up to his retirement in 1963 might have increased the dangers and the problems. Most critics would now agree, however, that he bears at least some responsibility for setting in train events that had catastrophic inflationary results.

On 4 December 1976 Thorneycroft, who over the years had been much more reticent on the subject than either his master or his two former juniors, and who by now was Margaret Thatcher's chairman of the Conservative Party, wrote an article for the *Spectator* on Denis Healey's latest clutch of economic measures. He included a defence of his conduct in 1957. 'In plain terms', he wrote, 'we refused to finance inflation.' And he added, 'we are now told that to cut spending back by £5000m (about half the deficit on public account) would create desperate injury to the whole social fabric. I remember being told the same about £50m twenty years ago. Would that we had started earlier.' There is no doubt that in this momentous argument, which has bedevilled British politics and the state of the nation for nearly a generation, Margaret Thatcher would side decisively with her chairman, rather than with the man who gave her her first political job.

The argument is momentous because it is far more than mechanistic. To be sure, some at least of the longer-term effects of either economic policy are predictable. In the history of modern industrial countries the record in controlling inflation of those governments who chose to rely on a monetary policy alone – Germany under Schacht in the 1920s and Erhard in the 1940s, France under Poincaré in the 1920s and de Gaulle in the 1950s – is very much better than that of countries, or periods in the history of countries, when there was a combination of over-spending (to achieve growth), incomes policy and, sometimes, a degree of monetary control. On the other hand, with its enormous natural wealth, admiration for and encouragement of individual enterprise, and decentralization of economic decision-making, the United States has been able to sustain its prosperity and position without excessive resort to monetary controls. Of course, it should be remembered too that in the United States the system of trade union law makes strikes, even when they occur, both more predictable, and more susceptible to controlled resolution than is the case in Britain where, over the years, the unpredictability particularly of short stoppages and unofficial strikes has more than once upset consistent economic performance.

But the major question lies beyond the arithmetic of the argument. A policy may be right without being either acceptable or successful. And as the years have gone by since the return to power of Churchill in 1951, the expectations of the British electorate – or at least those expectations as understood by politicians – have been steadily increasing, while the means of fulfilling those expectations have steadily declined. At the same time, the corporate power of the trade unions has increased, and the resistance of their leaders to the adoption of policies which would reduce monopoly and increase competition – for jobs as well as customers – has been increasingly successful.

On the whole, governments have sought to avoid confrontation with the unions. The Heath government was an exception in this regard, but it is important to understand the nature of its confrontations. Through a massive expansion of the money supply, and through the unprecedented subsidies to industry offered in the 1973 Industries Act, that government greatly increased inflation.

Ministers sought to prevent some of the consequences of that inflation by an extraordinarily elaborate and ultimately unpopular control of incomes. It was the combination of inflation and incomes control against which powerful unions, notably the miners, struck. To the monetarists the right circumstances in which to allow confrontation are those in which the government would be exercising a very tight control of money but not, save where it is itself an employer, seeking to control incomes. Then, if excessive wage demands were not to be fuelled by government subsidy, they could issue only in unemployment. The monetarist message, therefore, is that the only real power unions have is to price their own members out of work. The accompanying thesis is that government control of incomes does not control inflation, introduces distortions into the economy and ultimately (as in 1973 and 1977) by reducing differentials between the skilled and the unskilled, creates widespread discontent and the frustration of that productivity on which economic progress ultimately depends.

For all that, it is perfectly clear that no post-war government has ever been prepared for very long to depend on a tight money policy alone, if the consequence of that policy is seen to be higher unemployment. No government, whether Labour or Conservative, has been willing to face sharply increasing unemployment without itself taking measures, and especially spending measures, to bring the figures down. Consequently, especially after the fall of the Heath government, virtually the whole of the Labour Party, and substantial sections of the Conservative Party, have preferred instead to seek some sort of social contract with trade union leaders. Naturally, this is a task much more congenial to a Labour government, for the

Labour Party, apart from its present close relations with the unions, was itself founded in order to give their movement a voice in Parliament. Conservatives in favour of such policies have rationalized their position by arguing that concessions to the unions are a necessary part of the evolution of the body politic, and constitute very little more than the recognition of the fact that another estate of the realm has come of age.

Very few Conservatives, however, would accept the policy which Labour has followed in its period of power since 1974, that is, the passing of a great deal of legislation, including measures to protect jobs in specific areas of work *whatever the market demand for the products of such labour is,* legislation increasing trade union privileges (such as that establishing the closed shop) and expensive steps in nationalization. Indeed, a series of strikes by skilled workers in 1977, as well as the behaviour of the electorate in such by-elections as Workington and Ashfield, suggests that a great many trade unionists, themselves afflicted by inflation, and angry at the disappearance or reduction of differentials, are likewise discontented. The rationalization of the post-1974 Social Contract has been to the effect that, even if it has meant less money in the pockets of many workers, the combination of governmental Acts (including those passed through Parliament at the express request of trade union leaders) has produced a 'social wage', a combination of cash and services which, for the time being at least, should make trade unionists content. The conviction of the Leader of the Conservative Party and her closest allies is that the hollowness of that argument will soon be apparent.

It is no use, however, to deny that very different futures for the country are visualized by those in the centre or on the left of this argument and those on the right or libertarian wing. After Edward Heath had spoken in the economics debate at the Conservative Party conference in 1976, calling for austerity measures and emphasizing that in his view they were the necessary prelude to the building of a prosperous economy in which the social ambitions attendant upon high public spending could at last be achieved, Margaret Thatcher observed, 'He doesn't seem to realize that we are against high public spending on principle.' And, indeed, the strictly political (or perhaps philosophical) difference between the two schools of economic thought is between people who believe that high state spending and very considerable state intervention in the provision of services and the regulation of individuals is inherently un-desirable, and those others who believe that most extensions of state provision are irreversible marks of progress.

This fundamental belief is quite separate from the practical consideration, which is the belief shared by many Tories – and adumbrated in the quotation from Peter Thorneycroft above – that too rapidly or too dramatically to decrease the role of the state in the life of its citizens would produce social disruption of an unmanageable kind. This thesis is voiced again and again by Labour politicians and trade union leaders as part of their argument against the return of a Conservative government. And some thinkers and critics – perhaps most notably Peter Jay, who in 1977 became British Ambassador to Washington – although they would almost wholly agree with the monetarist argument that dramatic reductions in state activity are neces-sary for the survival of freedom let alone the achievement of prosperity, are so convinced that the adoption of any such policy would produce near-revolt that they have been inclined to suggest that the decline of Britain is irreversible. The argu-ment cannot be settled now. But it is certainly the case, as a great deal of her private conversation shows, that Margaret Thatcher, despite her deep emotional and intellectual sympathy with the monetarist or libertarian thesis, realizes that a remark-able and perhaps unprecedented degree of consistent and powerful public support would be necessary to give it a trial in policy.

It is this awareness on her part, rather than the politician's natural desire, especially in Opposition, to stress the evidence of public support for him and his Party, that causes her to lay such heavy emphasis on what appears to have been, throughout the October 1974 Parliament, a genuine sea-change in voting behaviour. 'We are the people's party now,' she cried after the

Ashfield by-election. And she is certainly correct in drawing attention to two unprecedented developments in the by-elections she has fought: first, although in each the percentage poll has been lower than that of a general election, as it normally has been in the past, the number of Conservative voters has gone up; secondly, all the evidence suggests that Labour voters have been switching in substantial numbers to the Tory side rather than, as has been normal in the past, abstaining in discontent with their own Party.

It is probably also the case that whether or not one judges the Macmillan balancing act to have been successful and Peter Thorneycroft's call for sterner measures unnecessary, the extent of government intervention in the economic process has, by the middle of the 1970s, reached an unpopular, and perhaps intolerable, level. In the course of building the post-war welfare state, and in the process effecting a revolution in British politics and society perhaps even greater than the celebrated Gladstonian revolution of 1869, Attlee and his Cabinet still took no more than 25 per cent of the Gross National Product for the state. Even after the various measures undertaken by the Callaghan government in response to the behest of the International Monetary Fund, the percentage of the take is now well above 50 per cent. At times in recent years it has come closer to 60 per cent. It is an old saw of political philosophy that there can be no freedom without economic freedom; and no less distinguished a Labour spokesman than Roy Jenkins, before he left for the presidency of the European Commission, gave it as his view that democracy itself could not long survive so substantial a consumption by the state of national resources. In so far as any Opposition party thrives on the discontent excited by the actions or inactions of government, Margaret Thatcher, all of whose deepest instincts are against such depredations, has benefited politically from the extent of Labour's spending.

But there is a wider and deeper aspect to the problem, one which is to some extent associated with the fact that no government since 1945 – save, to some extent and with particular tact, the 1951 Churchill government – has sought fundamentally to oppose the gradual growth of state power and state responsibility. Until very recently there has been no challenge by politicians with any hope of gaining power at Westminster to what might be called the Macmillan assumption. This is that the politician in power, given that above all else he cannot tolerate marked increases in unemployment and all the social misery and degradation that goes with it, *can* work on the assumption that there is a trade-off between unemployment and inflation. By 1977 this assumption has been discredited. For, while inflation has been moving in cycles, and although every cycle has seen a higher rate of inflation, inflation has not, as it was assumed in the 1950s it would, decreased unemployment. The unemployment rate at the bottom of the 1958 recession was almost exactly the same as that reached at the height of the 1973 inflationary boom. In consequence it is clear that the view expressed by Macmillan in the course of his arguments with Thorneycroft in 1957 – that one could juggle with the inflation rate in order to restrain unemployment, without doing too much ultimate damage to the economic structure – no longer is true, if it ever was. Nor has any government since that of Macmillan looked remotely like achieving the rate of growth which, it was thought, would compensate for the inflation, and ultimately provide the resources to create jobs.

It follows, and this is certainly the view of most of those who support Margaret Thatcher, that there is something structurally wrong with the whole operation of the British economic and political system. At least one piece of evidence that they are right is readily to hand. Not merely is it the case that the present rate – and all recent rates – of inflation in this country is very much higher than in any one of our competitor countries except Italy (the Swiss rate of inflation is nil; that of Western Germany less than 4 per cent). It is also the case that while in recent years wages in Britain have grown at roughly the same rate as in other countries, productivity has grown much more slowly. Since 1960 real output per head in this country has grown at a rate of 2 per cent per head per annum. In Germany the percentage is 4; in France 5; in Japan 10.

None of this – not even the much lower British performance – means that it would be impossible to achieve equilibrium, and perhaps even equality, in Britain; as long as we are prepared to become much poorer. What cannot be sustained on our present productivity performance is the high level, in quality as well as amount, of public provision of goods, services and subsidies. But the degree to which such services have been provided in the past, and the extent to which political parties have vied with each other in undertaking to increase them, has generated enormous and excessive expectations on the part of the electorate. At the same time, the failure of government after government to keep its promises has gradually split the nation into competing groups, each seeking a larger share of the cake for itself. Among the most dominant of such groups are the bigger trade unions, and those unionized workers operating in particularly strategic sectors of the market.

In moments of gloom Margaret Thatcher has doubted the possibility of reversing or destroying any one of the numerous incompatibilities in this economic system. The question which she faces is: how much of the natural potential for national unity, which in the past has produced for Britain an enviable international reputation for political and social stability, has survived the blows inflicted on the body politic and social by the events of the last generation? Perhaps she was not so deeply involved in the germination and development of these fundamental arguments as she might have been had she come into Parliament earlier or not gained office so soon, but she nonetheless has always demonstrated an inherent ability to understand both sides of a balance sheet. She once, for example, created something of a furore when, as a junior minister, she resisted pressure to increase pensions with the riposte that in examining the problem of pensions it was necessary to consider the interests of those who, ultimately, paid them as well as the interests of those who received them. It was not, perhaps, the most tactful of replies at a time when every politician, whether giving or refusing pension increases, was obliged above all to wring his or her hands, and express little more than the deepest or gravest concern. But it was a hard-headed appreciation of the facts.

Her major problem now, as she well realizes, is that each successive inflationary cycle has both further weakened the capacity of the country to fight its way out of its difficulties, and increased the divisiveness which makes resolution even more problematic. She was greatly interested, at the time of the December 1976 sterling crisis, to see a Swiss journalist on television, in company with a number of British financial writers, who expressed his amazement at the stress they laid on the way in which the pound had just been strengthening in the market. To the Swiss the whole story of sterling for twenty years had been one of steady decline, interrupted by brief periods of recovery, while to his British colleagues the history seemed to be one of steadiness interrupted by crisis. There was no doubt that Margaret Thatcher agreed with the Swiss.

'However,' as she once said briskly after a gloomy discussion of these matters with a friend, 'I'm not in this business to be pessimistic.' For a woman of ideas and temperament, the development of her country in her adult years has of necessity consisted of a series of shocks. The world in which she grew up, for all the threats with which it was faced from the continent, was at bottom a world of certainites. Not only was her home life and the life of Grantham composed almost wholly of certainties. So, by and large was the life of her country. As the depression came to an end, and even as the clouds of war appeared, Britain was still a very great power, possessed of an empire lapped by peace, prestige and satisfaction. Now, not only has the empire gone, but the power of the country contracted and the former international vision of its people dimmed, and the purely domestic problems of Britain have mounted.

Enoch Powell once said that, of all the great empires, the British was the only one which was liquidated without marked effect on the domestic body politic. (His argument on that occasion, however, was that the continuation of a lax policy in regard to coloured immigration would produce just that disintegration of the mother country as had finally destroyed the character of Rome.) I once put his contention to Margaret Thatcher, and she fiercely resisted it. The speed at which the empire vanished and the circumstances in which it went were certain, she thought, to leave a deep mark on the people who had created it. An extra turn, she thought, had been given to our preoccupation with our own problems by the vanishing of our glory. After all, it is a truism that success abroad frequently compensates for dissatisfaction at home, especially in the case of a people accustomed for many generations to rule or be involved with a substantial section of the peoples of the earth.

To another contention of Powell's, however, she has been heard to give assent. In a speech to the Royal Society of St George in 1964 he reversed a maxim of her favourite, Kipling. From Kipling's 'Recessional' he quoted the famous line, 'What do they know of England who only England know?' He went on, in a staggering display of knowledge and romantic feeling, to descant on the memorials of old England and its people:

. . . that marvellous land, so sweetly mixed of opposites in climate that all the seasons of the year appear there in their greatest perfection; of the fields amid which they built their halls, their cottages, their churches, and where the same blackthorn showered its petals upon them as upon us; they would tell us, surely, of the rivers, the hills, and of the island coasts of England.

'Perhaps after all,' he added, 'we know most of England "who only England know".' When Margaret Thatcher heard of that passage she sensed and acknowledged its power, and what was for her its truth.

Interestingly, the passages of Kipling from which she draws most strength are less those of the poet of empire than those of the poet of England and of liberty. What, if it has not come to her late, has nonetheless flowered late in her personality, and what she has had most opportunity to express since she became Leader of her Party, has been the consciousness – or the conviction – that beneath all the travail and the failure of recent years the pulse of the values she was brought up with, and which brought her effortlessly into politics, still beats as strongly as ever. Perhaps the detachment from the ordinary social intercourse of politics which her sex imposed on her has preserved for her an uncommon awareness of the separateness of the identity of the politician from the identity of the people. Again, popular and successful though she has always been as a platform speaker in the country, most of her political life has been lived within the confines of Westminster and Whitehall. Yet few politicians share her ability to understand and identify with the almost inchoate ambitions and feelings of those outside the political village in which she lives. There is a genuine populist streak in her, and her initial decision, on becoming Leader, to get out and about in the country owed less to her desire to become known than to her instinct that this was where she would be strongest. She came to the top of a Party in trauma while the country was also in trauma. The extent to which she shares the traumas will have a great influence on her chances of success.

Chapter five
The right

Against the settled advice of her schoolteachers, Margaret Roberts went to Oxford a year early, at seventeen. There was something of the impatience of ambition in her stubborn resistance to mature advice, but something also of an open eagerness to see and get involved in the bigger world. Although she has carried Grantham and its heritage with her ever since she left the town, and although its mark is on her and worn by her with pride, she had drained the place by the time she was seventeen. Indeed, the assiduity and discipline with which she investigates, absorbs and digests every experience that comes her way is perhaps the most noticeable feature of her character. And, of course, the Oxford to which she went in 1943 was by no means an undergraduates' paradise, or the city of gleaming towers which scholastic legend perpetuates. She was a year younger at least than most freshmen; and the place, too, had many students who were a great deal older than the average, especially in 1944 and 1945, because of war service. Now, when she returns there, she still finds it surprising and unfamiliar that students are so youthful: hers was certainly not an Oxford in which even an unusually self-possessed young woman could easily find her feet. Nevertheless, it was here that she first began to read widely and select judiciously in a fashion that made her ripe, more than thirty years later, to set herself at the head of a renewed intellectual tradition in the Conservative Party.

Her chosen field of study also set obstacles in the way of her benefiting in full from the diversity of undergraduate life. Then as now, students of science had a considerably more, punishing schedule of work than their fellows in the arts. Chemistry took up a great deal of time. Every morning and most afternoons were spent in laboratories. From five in the afternoon until seven Margaret Roberts attended lectures. Later on Friday evenings she attended, assiduously, the Scientific Society. Though never a truly outstanding student – she eventually got a good second – she was good enough, and socially attractive enough, to enter to some extent into the society of dons; and visits to the homes of her teachers, particularly to that of Dorothy Hodgkin, took up more time in a scientific atmosphere. As she recalls now, her period of freedom from work normally began only about eight in the evening. Even allowing for the fact that she got up between six and six-thirty, she did not enjoy a particularly generous amount of time for extra-mural interests.

And there were a great many of these, outside both science and the political world in which she was eventually to make her mark. She did not give up her interest in music nor, in particular, her passion for choral music. The Oxford Repertory Company, the Bach Choir, and the Balliol–Somerville choir all took up some of her attention. She regularly attended, in tribute both to her faith and to her past, a student Methodist group. She was markedly unwilling to give up any spiritual or intellectual possession she had already acquired. At school she had learned to read poetry properly, with due attention to metres, and she has never quite lost that gift which, though it is often beyond the range of people who are musically talented, is frequently possessed by those altogether without musical gifts. But there were also aspects of even her strictly professional life that helped to knit together the other facets of her still developing mind and personality.

The scientific Oxford of her day was in no sense dry. Indeed, she recalls that other fields of endeavour were themselves, in the mouths and minds of teachers and pupils alike, imbued with great reverence for the scientific method. The political and philosophical inclinations even of scientists were strong; and usually led them in the direction of socialism, for it was that political creed which seemed most congenial to those who by training and temperament were accustomed to reason logically, with respect for experimental evidence, and with regard to cut and dried solutions. When she talks today about the wave of scientism which swept her Oxford it is as though she is trying to recapture, in a time when there is nothing like the same confidence in the applicability of conclusions reached in the laboratory to human life, a vanished world which was to her both impressive and alien. It has never been her way to sweep aside and out of her path systems of thought or ideas which she finds are seriously rooted, even when her instinct rebels against them. Her philosophy therefore began to take shape in opposition to the prevailing fashion of her time at university; and she had to work at it.

She did not come to Oxford fully formed as a Conservative. Her father's natural political position was somewhere between an even then increasingly old-fashioned Liberalism and the views expressed by the more reformist-minded wing of the Tory Party. But in active politics he was always an Independent, not complaining even when, in later years, a Labour triumph in local elections in Grantham deprived him – unfairly and unkindly, many thought – of his aldermanic seat. The truth was, however, that the fashionable collectivism of her day came up against an instinctive judgement already unusually well-formed. When today she insists – as she does practically every day, and invariably when speeches or articles are being prepared – that it is vital for her side to win the argument as well as the votes, she is prone to refer to having had exactly the same problem at Oxford; and one can see in the face of the adult woman the dislimned countenance of the tough-minded and determined student, feet solidly on the ground and ideas already deeply rooted, resisting the intellectual tide sweeping over her in wartime Oxford.

It was the pressure of the conclusions being drawn from work in science that led her to the spare-time study of logic and

philosophy. But there were more subtle influences abroad which
did bring about some changes of outlook. She read widely in
religion in her spare time, and settled very largely for the works
of C. S. Lewis as her favourite. Thus began a move away from
the Methodism of her childhood. 'I gradually went higher and
higher,' she explains of the process by which she shifted slowly
from a fundamentalist to a sacerdotal outlook. 'I did not read
Lewis just to keep up,' she adds, explaining that a great deal of
her reading in fields far outside her professional or even political
concerns was 'just to keep up'.

One author who was very much on the 'keeping-up' list was
T. S. Eliot, about whom she has to this day notably ambivalent
feelings. Nowadays she is prone to compare him, not to his
advantage, with Solzhenitsyn. Then he was required reading,
and she felt the power of his insights into what she calls the
lower side of the human mind, without being at all attracted by
them. 'He couldn't be ignored,' she says now, almost as though
that is a cause of regret to her. But she found friends also among
more ancient and traditional writers, and especially the two
Brownings and Byron. Her taste in fiction, to which she was
never greatly inclined for its own sake, was less taxing: she was
content with J. B. Priestley and Howard Spring, and enjoyed
A. P. Herbert. She read *Insanity Fair*, Shirer's *Berlin Diary*,
and *Out of the Night*. The influence on her of Hillary's *The Last
Enemy*, which became a *vade mecum*, has already been mentioned. And although she did not read Hayek until, she thinks,
1945 or 1946, she began early to dip deeply into political philosophy, in order to find the resources to bolster and defend her
own instinctive but not untrained view of things.

At the same time, more practical involvements kept her from
what might have been the danger of excessive academicism. She
had an instinctive fear that her life in science would become too
limiting. 'I felt,' she says, 'very much how *impersonal* work in a
laboratory was. I think a lot of scientists in my generation were
looking for ways in which they could apply their knowledge,
not in a laboratory, but out in the field.' There was, of course, a
war on, and from her already crowded life she set aside time to

work, twice a week, in the Oxford forces' canteen, washing up, making sandwiches, and serving food. She also joined the Oxford University Conservative Association. The Union, which then had the disadvantage of denying membership to women, did not in any event attract her: the polished and somewhat meretricious style of its arguments and debates had very little appeal for the rather serious-minded young woman from Grantham, and she rarely took the opportunity even to sit in the gallery as the guest of a member. OUCA was much more practical. Besides the usual round of undergraduate speeches and papers it entertained guests from the great world of Westminster, and its members were active as canvass fodder in local and parliamentary elections. As she demonstrated most obviously in the 1945 general election (when Quintin Hogg was again returned for the City of Oxford) she was more than willing to work. And that willingness brought her up rapidly through OUCA's ranks, until she succeeded Edward Boyle as its president.

To all this she added, in 1944, a part-time teaching job (chemistry, mathematics and general science) at the Grantham Central School for Boys. Money had always been short, and she was perhaps depressed, not only by the advantages conveyed by somewhat ostentatious wealth on many of her contemporaries, but by the similar affluence of the steady number of returned servicemen taking up residence at the university. From the first at Oxford she had depended largely on her father and, to some extent, on her own savings, hoarded when she was a child. She had a fall-back position, for Kesteven Girls' School was perfectly willing to grant her a small scholarship, but only on the understanding that after graduation she would return there to teach. Her eyes were, however, then fixed immediately on a job involving scientific research and, ultimately, when she had had time to qualify for the Bar, on a career in patent law. Discipline and frugality enabled her to resist the temptation to any extent to mortgage her future. Her major luxury after taking the school job was a bicycle.

As happened all over the country, and in very many

universities, the Conservative defeat of 1945, unexpected and even shattering as it was, caused an instant revival of interest in Conservatism, and even of Tory sympathies. By then, Miss Roberts was well prepared for the message of freedom that, at first as a trickle and then as a flood, began to issue from the Conservative Research Department and from senior Conservative speakers. From her reading and from the challenge and counter-challenge of Oxford society, she emerged as something of a mixture of the traditional Conservative and the newly fashionable libertarian; and she has not greatly changed in subsequent years. 'My ideas,' she says, 'took form at Oxford.'

One of the OUCA speakers whose views most impressed her was Peter Thorneycroft. He was not then among the most prominent or most effective of those who, working with R. A. Butler in the Research Department's headquarters in Old Queen Street – and including Maudling, Macleod and Powell, though not, contrary to a persistent legend, Heath – were devising a Tory response both to defeat and to the difficult and probably dangerous circumstances of post-war politics. Then as since, Thorneycroft was a convinced and unabashed libertarian. His speech to OUCA could, indeed, have formed the skeleton for a subsequent pronouncement from the Treasury Bench, for he concentrated all his considerable forensic skill on deploying the case for scrapping the wartime controls introduced by the coalition government, and retained and even added to by Attlee and his colleagues.

To Thorneycroft, in the classical formulation, the wealth and success of Britain lay almost solely in the energy and initiative of her people. The right policy for government was therefore to interfere as little as possible with the impulses of economic man. To him the result of adopting measures based on such a view would be not merely greatly to increase the wealth of the nation, so that many of the ravages of war could be repaired, but also to renew the independence and freedom of the individual, to the greater glory and health of British civilization. He had little patience with the more specifically egalitarian notions of the Labour movement. In particular, he was scornful of what has remained a vital part of the Labour philosophy, colouring and influencing even Conservative budgetary and financial policy in the post-war years – the adoption of a redistributive system of taxation, with the ultimate aim of shifting resources from the upper end of the scale of wealth and income to the lower, and, meanwhile, sharply reducing the disparity of income between those earning a great deal and those earning very little. All that he had to say on these maters to OUCA was meat and drink to his young hostess.

The atmosphere in which this redefinition of Conservatism was taking place has been very well captured by Lord Blake:

The Conservative revival was helped by an intellectual movement in their favour. *Etatisme* which had been all the rage in the 1930s lost its charm in the highly regimented England of the war and post-war years. A very influential book at the time was Professor F. A. Hayek's *Road to Serfdom*, published in 1944. It was essentially anti-Socialist in its implications. The universities saw a notable revival of Conservative sympathies among the undergraduates and to some extent among the dons too. The Conservative Research Department headed by R. A. Butler contained as members during the period . . . people of whom many things have been said, but not that they are stupid. The Labour Party had lost its near monopoly of intellect and ideas.

It would be wrong, however, to suggest to those who have not read it that Hayek's book had something of the nature of a trumpet call to individualistic virtue as its essential tone. There was that element in it, certainly; but it had more of the character of an awful and apocalyptic warning. As early as 1944 the Austrian Hayek was warning Britain that all extension of the activity of the state constituted a danger to freedom and that, more particularly, the growth of the power of the state, whether undertaken in the interests of a supposedly left-wing or right-wing ideology, would inevitably produce in the end a tyranny of the same kind as that to which birth was given in Nazi Germany. To Hayek, as to Miss Roberts – who had a surprisingly intimate acquaintance with the development of German culture and the recent history of German politics, not only through her sister's pen-friend, but because her close interest in German science had led her to read widely in the history of the country which had produced that science – Nazism and Fascism were, above all, aspects of left-wing philosophies, not of those of the right. And it seemed to the historical philosopher an irony of the most tragic kind that the ideas of British thinkers had been substantially influenced by many émigrés settled in this country as refugees from Hitler's Germany, the ultimate implications of whose beliefs were not notably dissimilar from those of Hitler himself. Tyranny, to Hayek, was and is, like freedom, indivisible.

In 1976 his London publishers, Routledge and Kegan Paul, brought out a new edition of Hayek's seminal work. Not long after it appeared I asked Margaret Thatcher to choose for me the passage that she considered most encapsulated the message of the book, and most affected her. She selected this paragraph from the introduction:

The author has spent about half his adult life in his native Austria, in close touch with German intellectual life, and the other half in the United States and England. In the dozen years in which this country has now become his home he has become increasingly convinced that at least some of the forces which have destroyed freedom in Germany are also at work here, and that the character and source of this danger are, if possible, even less understood here than they were in Germany. The supreme tragedy is still not seen that in Germany it was largely people of goodwill, men who were admired and held up as models in this country, who prepared the way, if they did not actually create, the forces which now stand for everything they detest. Yet our chance of averting a similar fate depends on our facing the danger and on our being prepared to revise even our most cherished hopes and ambitions if they should prove to be the source of the danger. There are few signs yet that we have the intellectual courage to admit to ourselves that we may have been wrong. Few are ready to recognise that the rise of Fascism and Nazism was not a reaction against the Socialist trends of the preceding period, but a necessary outcome of those tendencies. This is a truth which most people were unwilling to see even when the similarities of many of the repellent features of the internal regimes in communist Russia and national-socialist Germany were widely recognised. As a result many who think themselves infinitely superior to the aberrations of Nazism and sincerely hate all its manifestations, work at the same time for ideals whose realisation would lead straight to the abhorred tyranny.

There is no doubt that the skeleton of such a conviction formed in Margaret Thatcher's mind by the end of the war; and that she is much more deeply convinced today, in the midst of the memorials of a generation's steady decline in wealth, resources and self-confidence, and the monuments of an ever-more encroaching state.

Of course, a great many Conservatives, as well as the members and supporters of the Labour and Liberal Parties, decry the Hayekian doom-saying as ludicrously exaggerated, and his identification of socialism with National Socialism as absurd beyond belief. I will argue a little later that there is, in fact, a great deal to his contention. What is worth observation at the moment, however superficial a point it may be to make, is the extent to which Hayek's reputation has risen again in the 1970s (he spent some years in virtual seclusion and silence), and how he has commanded a far greater audience than he ever enjoyed immediately after the war. This is relevant not merely to Margaret Thatcher's position and to the policies she has adopted, but to what might be called her rhetoric of warning. Her passionate and vehement denunciation of socialism in what often seems to others to be merely its moderate forms has been criticized, not infrequently by people on her own side. The insistence of her utterances, and their frequent repetition, have often been considered to have a shrill note unfamiliar and unbecoming to the British political ear. In the past, though Conservative spokesmen have often denounced the evils of socialism in measured terms (it used to be the fashion to refer to the other major Party when it was in Opposition or in quiet times as 'Labour', but to switch to 'socialist' when it was in power or at times of general elections), theirs has been a pretty ritual incantation.

Her warnings and denunciations, on the other hand, come from the depths of her instinct, and are fortified by convictions given weight from her reading. Whether the rhetoric is palatable to fashion, or even to men and women of genuinely moderate feelings, who deplore the escalation of violence in argument between politicians, there is no doubt that it is both considered and sincere; and that she considers herself to be offering to her country a warning and a vision of the future no less momentous than Churchill's after 1933. Though it did not immediately lead to any outright political action, her agony of mind during the second half of 1973 – when Heath was desperately striving for a system of economic management in which decisions would be taken collectively by Ministers, union leaders and businessmen – was palpable; for this was the growing shape of the syndicalism that Hayek had warned against. She is so combative a politician, so definitely a Party partisan, that it would be wrong to suggest that she was other than a fully working member of the team in February, 1974. But it may well be that somewhere in the recesses of her heart and mind there was a feeling of relief when Heath went down to defeat. To a journalist who visited her immediately after his resignation she expressed a genuine sympathy for his personal plight, but seemed remarkably undistressed herself. And those who know her best seem even now convinced that she would have resigned had his proposed deal with the Liberal Party come off; or even if his dreams, later in the year, for some kind of coalition between the Tories and men and women of all parties and none (as he put it himself) looked like coming off.

The depth of her feeling, the strength of her rhetoric and the unforced passion of her conviction that the present British crisis is probably the deepest the nation has ever had to face – certainly in peace time – is, of course, a more recent development in her thinking: the events of the late sixties and early seventies awakened an instinct and an understanding that had lain dormant since the close of her time at Oxford.

As she emerged from Oxford and took up scientific work in Colchester and political work in Dartford, Butler and his young men had set to work in Old Queen Street; but it would be wrong to suggest that the insights of Hayek, much read though he and similar authors were, entered as deeply into their thinking as they had done into hers. Perhaps only Enoch Powell, recently demobbed with the rank of brigadier, had as much radical appreciation of the libertarian message as she had; and he was fifteen years older, much more experienced, and had many other political problems on his mind.

It is clear that it was not the intention of the Research Department after 1945 to make preparations in any way radically to alter what the Attlee government was doing. Labour after the war was essentially committed to taking control of the 'commanding heights' of the economy for the state and, secondly, to take large-scale steps – like the establishment of the National Health Service – for improving the welfare of the citizenry, while also altering the equilibrium of the economy in favour of the less well-off. The Conservative reaction was threefold. First, there was a long tradition of Tory support for welfare measures. During the nineteenth century the Party had invariably been the exponent of governmental intervention to succour the weak. Moreover, those who led for the Conservatives in opposition to Attlee had often been deeply involved in wartime governmental committees preparing for the reform of welfare once the great conflict was over. It ill behove them to criticize on more than details, administration and method the measures that Labour advocated.

Secondly, it seemed to the Conservatives after the 1945 election that the people had willed a much more radical shift in economic and social policy than it thought the Tories could, or would, provide. The Conservatives were shattered by their defeat, and by the Labour majority of 146 in the House of Commons. To be sure, a cooler appraisal of what had actually happened in the election might have reduced their concern. After all, it required no more than a swing of 3 per cent to take the Opposition within striking distance of victory in 1950. Nevertheless, the hunt was on after 1945, not for a radical critique of the Labour revolution, but for aspects of the programme that Conservatives could adopt, giving it their own special colouring of concern for freedom and enterprise rather than equality and centralism. Indeed, it seems clear that Churchill looked on benevolently at Butler's efforts, rather than interesting himself in their detail. Nevertheless, the great war leader had himself helped Lloyd George to lay the foundations of the modern welfare state before the Second World War, and he was ever alive and sympathetic to schemes for social improvement. Butler could count on that powerful goodwill, especially as his task was to educate the Party to an appreciation of modern concerns and modern fashions as much as to persuade the country that the Tories, while they would reduce taxation and relieve the country of the irksome burden of socialist controls, could also be relied upon to preserve intact the basic system of nationalized care and concern established by the Labour Party. The implied promises were more than adequately fulfilled by the 1951 government.

But, thirdly and in some respects most importantly, the measure of consensus which revisionist Conservatives were as (perhaps more) keen to establish after the war as they were to propound a radical Toryism was also to apply to a very great extent in economic management. Their acceptance of what the Attlee government had done in economics was not, however, mindless. The Tories intended to leave in state hands such industries as mining and the railways where it could be argued that private enterprise was unable to cope sufficiently well: they would denationalize only such industries as steel, where private capital and management were expected to be able to come up to scratch.

Thus was born the concept of the mixed economy, the broad character of which was accepted readily by both Parties. It was not until after their defeat in 1970, indeed, that the Labour Party abandoned the concept. Today, such leading Labour figures as Tony Benn believe as a matter of Socialist principle that successful as well as unsuccessful industries should be taken over by the state, though such as James Callaghan and Sir Harold Wilson prefer the government's taking shares in major concerns to outright nationalization. Even this, however, marks a major departure from the policies advocated in the 1950s by the late Anthony Crosland, the senior theoretician of the Labour movement, who specifically disavowed any further major extension of economic activity by the state.

Especially after the failure of the Heath government, which had first broken with the consensus by announcing its determination not to sustain ailing enterprises with public money, the Conservatives found it difficult to erect an opposition of principle to the activities of a Labour government. Their failure to do so goes back to their decision, after 1945, to accept the main body of whatever economic legislation they found in force on their return to office. The difference between 1945 and 1974, however, was that in the latter year, inside and outside Parliament, there was a convinced and powerful body of opinion keen and willing to advocate a strategy alternative to that pursued by Labour and the Heath government alike. How this came to be the case is itself a fascinating chapter in the long history of Conservative politics.

The Tory defeat of 1964 was not unexpected. What perhaps was unexpected was that it was so narrow. The narrowness of the margin made it fairly certain that the Parliament would last nothing like its full term, and nearly everything Harold Wilson did – and he was, at the time, at the height of his powers as a political manager with the added advantage that most of the press, in one of its typically uncritical moods, was bewitched by him – was geared to the assumption that the country would again resort to the polls at an early date.

'I never went back to collect anything after the election,' Margaret Thatcher says. 'A department is always interested in the incoming Minister, not the outgoing one. Once you're out, you're out. And I didn't want to embarrass anyone by saying goodbye.' For the moment, however, she was left with the job of shadowing her previous Pensions Ministry, while her Party and its leaders looked around and took stock.

As in 1974 the first problem the Party faced was that of the leadership. To his small and devoted band of admirers Alec Douglas-Home had done spectacularly well. Taking over a shaken and in many respects discredited government and Party he had, in the year that he was allowed, come as close as defeat would allow to snatching a victory from Wilson. Like their hero, these Tories had an unforced contempt for Wilson as nothing more than a clever manoeuvrer, and they believed that in a fairly short space of time his vices would be seen to stand in strong contrast to Home's virtues of simplicity, straightforwardness and patriotism. To others, however – and they were in the majority – it was still considered a mistake to have chosen as Leader of the Party a fourteenth Earl who had had to give up his ancient title and descend to the House of Commons to assume his new duties. They felt both the implied slur on their own House – that the Tories had been unable to find a Leader from the ranks of the Commons – and the widely believed accusation that the aristocratic Home was an anachronism.

It is important, too, to remember that the essence of the Wilson image at that time was not that of the great party manager and wily exponent of the art of instant politics which he later enjoyed, but that of a thrusting, classless technocrat. It was perhaps the last moment in party politics – in spite of the fashion in which Heath's reputation later developed – in which victory went to a man because he appeared to be about to bring the fresh brush of expertness to the dusty corridors of British politics. As the Parliament began its business Wilson's qualities as a debater, a showman and a headline stealer became day by day more evident. Home simply could not handle him in the House of Commons, and discontent with the Leader of the Opposition mounted. In response to some of the pressure, and to a great deal of the criticism of the way in which he had become Leader in 1963, Home devised a new scheme for electing the leader, the first draft, as it were, of the system adopted in 1974. To the dismay of his loyal supporters he made it clear that he did not want to keep the leadership badly enough to fight for it, and on 22 July 1965 he announced his resignation. The grace of his conduct then and subsequently was made the excuse for sharp criticism of Heath's behaviour after October 1974. Home's resignation depressed Margaret Thatcher who, without being close to him, was one of his strongest admirers. After a good deal of wavering, she voted, in the leadership ballot of 27 July, for his successor, Edward Heath.

In the first three years of his leadership Heath rewarded her with a variety of responsibilities which greatly increased both her experience and her expertise. In October 1965 she was appointed to a junior Opposition post on Housing and Land. March the following year saw her as number two Treasury spokesman. In October 1967 she entered the Shadow Cabinet to speak from the front bench on Power; and exactly a year later she became Shadow Minister for Education, a job which, in shadow and substance, she held for five and a half years.

Hers was not exactly an uncommon experience in the early phase of Heath's leadership. For, before he finally settled on the policies and the team with which he was to fight the 1970 general election – he lost that of 1966, but it had to be fought in impossible circumstances and nobody expected him to win it when all the cards were in Wilson's hands – he experimented with a great many ideas, and with a number of people. In the course of these experiments he gave full rein to the burgeoning radical wing of the Party, and gave to them a position and a base within the Party which they were never to lose, and which left them with considerable power and influence in 1974, even after the apparent discrediting of their ideas from 1972 onwards.

Immediately after he had lost the 1964 election Home, trenchantly advised by Heath, put in hand an overall review of policy. The Party had held power for thirteen years. Subsequently, when he was Leader of the Opposition, Heath was to say on a party political broadcast that that long tenure had left them exhausted, and bereft of fresh ideas, with impetus and direction gone. Home gave him a free hand (he was then Shadow Chancellor) and he set up an extensive and complicated series of policy committees to re-examine everything from taxation and public expenditure policy to local government, the arts and voluntary social services. His instructions were clear, and they were repeated at frequent intervals when he became Leader: no subject save that of the commitment to enter the EEC was sacred. (In fact this was not, as events

showed, quite true, but it is certainly still the case that no
political party in modern times has so thoroughly opened its
mind to new ideas.)

There were, nonetheless, a few indications of where the
Leader's prejudices lay, and these were to some extent influential in the way policy developed. He had become known for a
remark to the effect that there was something wrong with anybody in business who was not earning £10000 a year by the
time he was thirty. (It is a curious fact, all the same, that
Heath's own business experience was sharply limited, to a
traineeship at Brown, Shipley: he had all the fascination with
commercial success of many a politician who has never gone
deeply into commerce.) And it was beyond doubt that he would
smile above all on those who gave him policies with which to
encourage the thruster, the entrepreneur and the tough-minded
businessman.

It is a fact of life that such a programme as he set up is most
likely to encourage also the political thrusters, the more radical-
minded among the followers. Throughout the period from 1965
to 1970 two main objects of policy gradually took shape. Major
efforts were to be made substantially to cut personal and company taxation, the objective here being to recreate business
incentives on a massive scale and thus through private effort
to regenerate British wealth and growth. It followed that
public expenditure had to be cut back, and the state's slice
of the national income reduced. In the second place, there
gradually developed the determination to reshape the machinery of government itself and even the fundamental way of
doing things in various areas in order to promote efficiency.
Thus it came about that the 1970 government found itself
committed not merely to reduce taxation, but to make over the
system of taxation itself. It came about too that Ministers in
that year found themselves with the task of restructuring
housing and rental policy, and making their first brave attempt
at a new industrial policy.

It was a heady time for all those with ideas. Yet as time went
by it became clear that the brief was less open than it had

initially appeared to be. Save in relatively small matters, for example, Heath was unwilling to tamper with the machinery of the welfare state: two radical schemes for the reform of the National Health Service were turned down, and it became obvious that he would tolerate no major shift of power in education from state provision to parental control. Extra commitments, indeed, were entered into by the Opposition, notably in the field of pensions, and a scheme – later enacted and then repealed by Labour – was adopted to shift the pensions burden from the state to private pension funds. This was perhaps the only major reform in the social field undertaken by a Conservative government since the war and it was a strikingly imaginative one, which was never given a chance to work. As regards the Health Service the Tories ended up with no more than the commitment to reform its administration, which they later did, under Keith Joseph, with marked lack of success.

Over all this activity Heath brooded to great effect. The times were exciting for those with ideas not only because he encouraged them in public, but because of his openness to novelty. Apart from his network of policy committees he came, on average once a month, to the Research Department in Old Queen Street and sat in the big boardroom there with the thirty or forty bright young men and women who worked not only on the day-to-day formulation and presentation of policy but also on longer-term projects. No subject was sacred, and no one was required to stand on ceremony with the Leader. Anybody who had ideas, schemes, plans, or even dreams, as long as he or she had considered carefully their logic and the facts that supported them, was encouraged to speak his piece. Beside Heath would sit one of his Parliamentary Private Secretaries, carefully noting the suggestions that interested him. It was especially exciting for young people, many of whom were not long out of university, especially as they knew that the Director of the Research Department, Brendon Sewill (probably the best Director the Department had seen in its history, and with an extraordinary gift for motivating those who worked with him) would make sure that position papers and ideas dreamed up within the

Department would go directly to the Leader and would be carefully scrutinized by him.

To the public and the press at this time Heath presented an image that he was later to regain, in his time of trial, as a dour, unresponsive man, possessed of few public gifts and wholly bereft of either charm or openness of mind. To those who came in contact with him, despite his lack of the political gifts fashionable at the time his refusal to indulge in political gimmickry was refreshing. He had a powerful Private Office, and two of their number, his economics adviser, Brian Reading, and his principal speech-writer, the late Michael Wolff, had offices in Old Queen Street, He was obsessive about good briefing, could read any amount of paper and master the most complicated arguments in a very brief compass. Any project which interested him – one was women's rights, a radical and humane policy which he forced through with the aid of a handful of Party officials in the teeth of much Party opposition – was checked on continuously; and again, in a Party not hitherto noted for the systematic nature of its policy-making, his continual encouragement and interest sustained many an innovator, and many a new idea, against all opposition. If he lacked charm or persuasiveness, he nonetheless gave the powerful impression of a man who could sustain anything he was convinced of by sheer force of will. Many who worked with him during those years formed an attachment to him which survived everything that went wrong later, and every change of mind which the attractions and pressures of office forced upon him.

From 1965 onwards, stimulated and presided over by Heath, a head of steam built up behind a new development in Toryism. Until October 1969, when she became Shadow Secretary of State for Education, Margaret Thatcher was switched regularly from job to job, and it was widely assumed that a gifted woman who had had no more than some experience of junior office was being deliberately put through a testing apprenticeship, at the end of which she would be given a leasehold on some high appointment. Nor was hers a unique experience, save in the variety of the tasks she undertook. For the pattern of Heath's appointments, both during his period as Leader of the Opposition, and when he became Prime Minister in 1970, was an interesting one, which indicated his desire to replace an older generation of frontbenchers with a new one.

It was widely believed that Macmillan had been ill-advised in refusing to bring new blood on a large scale into his government after the victory of 1959. It was not until Thursday, 12 July 1962, the famous 'Night of the Long Knives', that he made really drastic alterations to his Cabinet, which included the transfer of Reginald Maudling – by 1965 the most experienced of the post-war generation in high office – to the Treasury. His delays had meant that many of the politicians who were to dominate the Conservative Party and its thinking in the sixties and into the seventies had had very little departmental experience. Heath himself, when he became Leader, had had only nine months in the Department of Labour (a diplomatically taxing but then an administratively unburdensome job) and a year in the office specially created for him of Secretary of State for the Regions and President of the Board of Trade. Between these two appointments – the first by Macmillan and the second by Home – he had served as Britain's negotiator with the EEC countries. This onerous task he discharged with intelligence and zeal, and to high praise, but again it was not the kind of experience which had hitherto been thought to fit a man for the leadership. Enoch Powell, who has bedevilled Heath since his dismissal from the Shadow Cabinet in 1968 and whose fate has somehow seemed inextricably linked with that of his former Leader, had served in a Cabinet for only nine months, as Minister for Health. For Heath both in 1965 and again in 1970 there was the difficult task of appointing a front bench wisely balanced between experience and vigorous youth, at a time when some of the most experienced of his colleagues seemed to be over the hill, and his most able juniors woefully inexperienced.

He solved it by three means. First, during his time as Leader of the Opposition, he gradually replaced – by dismissal or through retirement – some of the more senior men of the Macmillan era. Butler retired to the Mastership of Trinity. Selwyn Lloyd,

Duncan Sandys and others were dropped. Henry Brooke and Peter Thorneycroft lost their parliamentary seats. Edward Boyle and Enoch Powell, among those thought of as gifted men of a new epoch, respectively retired from politics and was dismissed in fury. When he became Prime Minister Heath presented a new-look government: among the ranks of his Cabinet were two men, Peter Walker and the Prime Minister's Parliamentary Private Secretary, James Prior, who had never before held office of any kind. The curious thing is that though Heath between 1955 and 1970 gained a deserved reputation for innovation, experiment and bringing on new men, after his victory he gained an equally deserved reputation for reluctance to change, and an unwillingness to make any alterations at all in his team. It was not until November 1974 that he made widespread changes again; and then it was too late.

Secondly, after 1965, though he was disciplinarian in his insistence that his colleagues should stick rigidly to their briefs and not ramble generally over the field of political philosophy in the manner of their predecessors (he once sharply reprimanded the Shadow Home Secretary and distinguished lawyer Quintin Hogg, for speaking on the planned Industrial Relations Bill), he continually rotated junior front-bench spokesmen, and brought backbenchers on to the front bench for particular assignments, to test their mettle. Then, through the maze of revisionist policy committees he set up, he tested the intellectual calibre of everybody who was anxious to contribute to the business of policy preparation. It was by this means that Keith Joseph as Shadow Industry Minister, with a powerful and zealous young team around him, first established a senior position in the counsels of the Party. It was perhaps a sufficient indication that Heath's heart was never in the radical proposals that they produced that, on his victory in 1970, he broke up the team, and despatched Joseph to the Department of Health and Social Security, a denial in itself of his repeatedly declared philosophy that his concern in Opposition had been above all to train men and women for specific jobs, and to draft watertight policies of a radical nature.

During the period of Opposition Margaret Thatcher served first (under Home) in her old job on Pensions; then as a junior on Housing and Land; then as a Treasury junior to Iain Macleod; then in the Shadow Cabinet as Shadow Minister of Power; and, finally, as Shadow Education Minister. Not only was this regarded by friends, colleagues and rivals as a period of training, it was, and still is, so regarded by herself. 'I was glad to be moved about so much,' she said, 'because it gave me such a wide training.' Of Iain Macleod, who appears to have contributed most notably to her development, she told George Gardiner, 'He was superb at managing parliamentary business, but most of all one admired his capacity for oratory, and his great knack of hitting on the really telling phrase.' All this variety, she believes, contributed greatly to her later effectiveness for 'If you are to make a contribution to a Cabinet, you obviously need to know a good deal more than what goes on in your own department.'

As has already been stated, the very first days of the new and unexpected government of 1970 saw Margaret Thatcher in difficulties. One of the first things announced by Heath on the blazing June day on which he assumed office was that the new administration would make no major decision rashly, or in haste. This was in keeping with his conception and presentation of it as well-prepared – uniquely so – for office. Indeed, when the Conservative Party conference met at Blackpool the following October, it proved still impossible for either senior Ministers or the Prime Minister himself to announce the measures that above all were awaited by Party and country alike – those pertaining to the economic management and future of the country. The first steps to be taken were not put before Parliament until the economic debate, and mini-Budget, of 4 November 1970.

But there was another and sharper side to the image of the new government, as conceived and presented by Heath himself. It offered a decisiveness, a willingness to break with fashion as well as consensus, which contrasted with but did not contradict the Prime Minister's own picture of a sedulously deliberate and careful band of counter-revolutionaries. Such a term is appropriate and fair because, despite taking the whole summer to decide what economic measures were to be taken, he announced at Blackpool that his ultimate purpose was to bring about a 'quiet revolution', 'to change the course of history of this nation – nothing less'. The sharper edge of the Heath counter-revolution was seen as early as 30 June 1970, a bare fortnight after the general election, when the new Secretary of State for Education and Science repealed the Labour ministerial circular requiring all local authorities to submit to the DES schemes for the re-organization of their schools on the basis of a comprehensive system. By that date only fourteen of 163 authorities had failed to follow the instruction. But the issue remained one potent in practice as well as in emotion: perhaps the logical end of what Margaret Thatcher did on 30 June 1970 can be seen in the an-nouncement of official Conservative policy in 1977 to the effect that local authorities would be at liberty to submit to a Con-servative Education Secretary of State schemes of reorganiza-tion which reversed, as well as those which simply declined to implement, the comprehensive system. She has never forgotten, nor regretted, her decision in June.

Nonetheless it was an action which marked her down as a target for many critics and enemies. It is, perhaps, impossible in the late 1970s to recapture the full force of the passion of the moment, a passion so great that it was to lead later in the year to her husband suggesting that the pressure on her was so great, and her distress in its face so marked, that she should resign altogether from politics. After all, if the issue for or against the principle of comprehensive education is as yet far from decided, enough evidence of disorder and incapacity has been presented against comprehensivization in the intervening years to cause many (especially parents) to doubt its value. A distinguished ex-headmaster of a comprehensive school – Dr Rhodes Boyson – is one of Mrs Thatcher's front-bench spokesmen on education. Much evidence has been found to support the contentions of the once notorious, now famous, Black Papers on education – to which Boyson was a regular contributor – that comprehensives inhibit the academic achievements of their pupils. Even the

BBC and the *Observer* have presented images of chaos, particularly in larger comprehensives. Even so, it should be noted that neither the Conservative government of 1970, nor the Conservative Opposition of 1977, have declared themselves against comprehensives given the right conditions: the first comprehensive system in the country was instituted by a Conservative local authority.

Be that as it may, the repeal of a five-year-old circular in 1970 made Margaret Thatcher a marked woman among radical teachers in state schools, and among most educational correspondents. To the proverbial man from Mars the issue might appear somewhat academic. One the one hand there were those who believed that in the state system all children should go to the same school, and have their varying talents and needs catered for in different kinds of classes – but in and within a single system with a single body of teachers; on the other there were those who wanted to preserve the traditional division between 'academic' state schools (grammar schools) and those more orientated to practical work (secondary modern schools).

Of course, a great deal more lay behind the controversy than the simple question of reorganization. Not to be controversial and not to engage in too lengthy an analysis of modern schools of educational thinking, it is still possible to make one or two points relevant to the controversy which surrounded Margaret Thatcher from June 1970 almost until the present day.

Those who were and are in favour of the reorganization of state-financed schools according to the comprehensive principle had and have more than a strictly academic ideal in mind. So far as the quality (at its simplest, capacity in the three Rs) was concerned they believed that it could be at least as well nurtured in a comprehensive as in a grammar school. But they had one or two other things in mind as well. They believed, first, that children who were socially deprived – who came from disturbed or uneducated or inadequate homes – should receive exceptional attention from the educational authorities. To them, therefore, education had a social as well as an academic function. They also believed that the bringing together under one school roof of deprived and advantaged children would benefit the former without loss to the latter – whatever the parents of the latter might think. And they believed that the education services, at local and national level, should be devoted as much, or nearly as much, to making up in terms of social and even physical provision – as in the soon-to-be controversial question of school milk – for what children missed at home as they should be devoted to academic provision. For such people – that is, for the majority of the Labour Party and the majority within the National Union of Teachers – teaching had a social work content of large and expanding proportions. So far as organization was concerned it was assumed that the state would and should be the final arbiter so far as organization of schools was concerned.

It was and is the conviction of many Conservative thinkers who have addressed themselves to these matters that the *élan* of comprehensivization ensured the vast exaggeration of social at the expense of academic ends in school education – and to no great benefit to children. Moreover, the whole thrust of Conservative views has been to believe that power in matters of education should lie as close to parents as possible. Local authorities are closer to parents than is the often distant Department of Education: they, rather than the Secretary of State, should decide what is right for their area. Above all, two views lay behind the Secretary of State's thinking in June 1970 – that much of what passed for educational thinking then represented social attitudes and theories rather than educational aims strictly considered; and that power in education should be moved back from the DES and the teaching profession towards the parents, even if neither they nor the local authorities they elected gained complete control over the system. Certainly, the state should not be allowed to ordain the nature of systems.

Controversial though that initial decision was it was to become more furiously argued after the results of the Cabinet's summer-time deliberations became known. As already related, the decisions made at the pre-election Selsdon Park seminar enabled Margaret Thatcher to preserve from the spending cuts which were to be the foundation of the new government's economic programme all that she regarded as the most substantial parts of educational policy – notably the renovation of the primary schools and the raising (in 1973) of the school leaving age. What, as the work of the summer went on, it became clear she could not preserve (indeed, she hardly wished to, save as part of the tactics of negotiation) were certain of the ancillary social services schools had begun to be accustomed to provide. When the Chancellor, her old legal colleague Anthony Barber, who had attained his office as a result of Iain Macleod's untimely death shortly after the election, rose on 4 November it was to announce that the existing charges for school meals were to be raised in two stages from one shilling and ninepence to two shillings and tenpence. The upper figure was no notional budgetary ploy. It was the actual cost of meals, and the principle was thus established – with certain exceptions for the badly-off – that parents should be responsible for the full cost of meals provided at school. Further, school milk would no longer be provided free – save when medical considerations supervened – for children between the ages of seven and twelve. The total savings to the Exchequer were expected ultimately to reach about £50m. The total cost to Margaret Thatcher's political reputation in the popular press and among those involved in educational work who stressed the social function of schools has never been recovered.

It is hard to recapture without bemusement the spirit of the months that followed. Margaret Thatcher was in an exceptionally difficult situation because, unlike other Ministers who had to make cuts in their departmental spending, she could not take action by statutory Order, but had to introduce legislation which prolonged controversy, lengthened her time in the firing line, and exacerbated differences. The full fury of fashion – represented by the still-used slogan 'Thatcher – Milk Snatcher' – was turned on her, and it took nearly the whole of the life of the Heath government before, by assiduous work and the implementation of her major promises, she won general respect for her stewardship.

Even then not all that she did was uncontroversial. The inquiry she set up under the chairmanship of Lord James into standards at teacher training colleges, amply vindicated though it was, aroused the suspicion of the teaching profession. Her appointment of the Bullock committee to examine standards in literacy was rightly suspected of implying a disapproval of most that was being done under the banner of progressive education and a conviction that standards were declining. She was more than once in conflict with teachers over pay. Perhaps only the success of her primary school rehabilitation and building programme, her concern with nursery education and her raising of the school leaving age convinced the cooler-headed among her critics that she was a serious and concerned Minister.

But of all the things she did and said perhaps what most prolonged controversy and most engendered hostility and even hatred was her absolute conviction that everything she had done, if not wholly or completely right, was nonetheless fully, logically and morally done in the sensible service of the only tenable idea about the nature of education. One of her worst moments was being forced to leave the designation ceremony at the Liverpool Polytechnic before its conclusion because of hostile demonstrations. One of her best was the announcement in the same month (June 1971) of the allocation of the required funds for primary education. She and her friends remain convinced that the campaign against her was irrational where it was not deliberately and destructively revolutionary, an index perhaps of the kind of hostility she has so often generated. On purely pragmatic grounds it is worth observing that those who have the strongest logical case against her for her DES record are her right-wing monetarist allies: against £58m or so that she had cut, she spent an extra £186m on primary schools alone. And she has never wavered in her conviction that 'the important thing was to protect *education*, and that's what we did. Indeed, we expanded it.'

But during the summer months of deliberation something unrecognized was happening, something that would ultimately have great impact on the fate of the Heath government and

more than anything else ensure for him the subsequent criticism
and hostility of the radicals in his own Party.

Although it was certainly the case – and certainly understood
by most politicians and critics – that the new government was
unwilling to subsidize inefficient industry, and that it would
early embark on a series of cuts in public expenditure, the
general appreciation of such undertakings both in the Cabinet
and the Treasury was that cuts in spending were above all
designed to make room for the cuts in taxation which would be
needed to restore incentives to individuals and the economy.
Nobody in the higher reaches of the government, few enough
in the Conservative Party, and only a limited number of critics
outside, were opposed in principle to high public spending and
deficit budgeting. Indeed, it is worth observing that, although
Leader, Margaret Thatcher has placed the reduction of public
spending at the forefront of her economic policy and gathered
to her cause virtually all of those who accept the views of
Hayek and Friedman, Edward Heath himself, at the Brighton
conference of 1976, regarded reductions in spending as necessary only because of the exigencies of an inflationary situation
and not as part of a long-term and settled policy. If, when so
much opinion has changed between 1970 and 1976, he still holds
to that view, it is hardly surprising that he was not opposed
to it in 1970.

Yet, even while he and his colleagues prepared for a June
election, something was happening the importance of which
they altogether failed to appreciate during the deliberations
they undertook after their victory. Between April and June the
Bank of England allowed the supply of money available to increase by £700m, the largest quarterly increase ever. It is difficult to say to what their inattention can be attributed. Certainly, the new government was somewhat dislocated by the death
of Iain Macleod on 20 July, and his replacement by the inexperienced and unprepared Anthony Barber. But it is by no
means certain that Macleod himself would have noticed what
was going on, let alone been aware of its danger, in spite of the
fact that most Conservatives recognized, at least privately, that

the monetary restrictions of the last two Labour Budgets (by Roy Jenkins) were wise. Then, too, Heath came rapidly to an informal agreement with Barber (who was far from ambitious to be Macleod's successor) according to which the Chancellor would concentrate his efforts on the much-prized reform of the taxation system, while the Prime Minister would himself take care of broader economic strategy.

Whatever the reasons, the monetary expansion that had begun just before Heath took office undermined the usefulness and hopefulness of all that was done in the mini-Budget of November 1970. Moreover, at no stage in its life did the Heath government more than flirt with monetary contraction: throughout their time in office the stock of money rose by 60 per cent, and while the rise in the first quarter of their period of office was only 8.5 per cent, by the last quarter of 1972 it was 28 per cent. One does not have to be a strict monetarist to suggest that such policies dangerously fuelled inflation, nor a strict free market opponent of compulsory incomes policies to believe that the controls introduced personally by Heath in Lancaster House in November 1972 could not conceivably hope to stem the inflation thus created.*

Indeed, it is staggering, even with hindsight, to look back on the monetary record of the Heath government. Its principal problem, however, appears to have lain less in any settled philosophy depending on monetary expansion than in a failure of perception. Barely a handful of even the most critical Conservative backbenchers grasped the significance of what was going on; and scarcely a single commentator did so. Indeed, the *Economist* newspaper – which, with its international circulation and, then, an editor (Alastair Burnet) who was both an admirer and a friend of Edward Heath – did comic damage to its reputation by its continual support of the expansion of money, a policy

---

* There is a wealth of literature on all aspects of the argument about the Heath government's economic policies and record, but perhaps the most convenient introduction is Ralph Harris and Brendon Sewill's *British Economic Policy 1970–4: two views* (Institute of Economic Affairs, 1975). Sewill, Director of the Conservative Research Department until 1970, was Barber's adviser at the Treasury thereafter. Harris is Director of the I E A.

to which a belief in controls of income and prices was added when Heath's economic adviser, Brian Reading, joined the staff in 1971. Reading was ahead of his old employer in advocating the introduction of the incomes policy so rigorously eschewed in Opposition.

Now, without going into too detailed (and, for this book, in any event unsuitable) an economic digression, it is worth observing – given that there is invariably a lag of at least nine months between the introduction of a particular policy on money and demand and its effect on retail prices – that the last quarter of 1971 and the first three quarters of 1972 saw a steadily declining level of price increases: for the four quarters the percentages were 9.2, 8.0, 6.2, and 6.5. The monetarists judge this to be the effect of the monetary contraction of 1969. On the other hand, the steadily increasing monetary expansion of 1972 had its effect too, and the four quarters of 1974 saw price increases of 12.9, 15.9, 17.0, and 18.2 per cent. Two elements in the political equation had, so Ministers said, affected their course. The first, already referred to, was unemployment. The second was their dash for growth: they believed that both the economy and industry needed the stimulus of public money to achieve growth.

This was an argument with which Margeret Thatcher had for a long time been familiar; and one on which she took the opposite side from that taken by Edward Heath and his Chancellor from 1970. In her 1968 address to the Conservative Political Centre (an invitation to address the CPC's meeting at the annual conference is highly prized by leading Tory politicians) she said:

There is another aspect of the way in which Incomes policy is now operated to which I must draw attention. We now put so much emphasis on the control of incomes that we have too little regard for the essential role of government, which is the control of money supply and management of demand. Greater attention to this role and less to the outward detailed control would have achieved more for the economy. It would mean, of course, that government had to exercise itself some of the disciplines on expenditure it is so anxious to impose on others. It would mean that expenditure in the vast public sector would not have to be greater than the amount which could be financed out of taxation plus genuine saving. For a number of years some expenditure has been financed by what amounts to printing the money.

This, of course, is nothing like as rigorous as some of the things she has said in more recent years; and nothing like as rigorous as some of the things said by close associates of hers such as Keith Joseph and John Biffen. Her reference to demand management by government would, moreover, excite the criticism of senior monetarists. But, given that the debate had not – outside the Institute of Economic Affairs – reached any great sophistication in 1968, her words can be taken as a fair account of what she would now take as a sound view. Certainly, her speech shows that she was well aware of the guts of the argument.

It seems clear that such opposition as there was within the Heath Cabinet to its monetary policy and later to its attempts to control incomes, was expressed by her. But it was as late as 1972 that her friends became aware of any real concern on her part; and only after she became a candidate for the leadership was she heard expressing the view – frequently trumpeted since early 1975 by Enoch Powell – that she should have resigned in the face of the November 1972 incomes policy. Certainly, whatever worries or reservations she expressed in private or in Cabinet, she was no standard bearer in those years either for the economic cause which has won so much attention since, or for the wing of the Party that, espousing it, did more than anybody else to put her in charge. One must, however, face the brutal fact that had she not stayed in the Cabinet it is unlikely that she could have made a successful bid for the leadership from the back benches. Not that the leadership was something she had in her mind late in 1972: I merely state what seems to me undeniable.

There are many, more or less complicated, reasons* for

*Probably the most succinct and comprehensive account of them is to be found in F. A. Hayek's Nobel Prize lecture for 1974, published with other essays by the IEA as *Full Employment at Any Price?*

opposing attempts by government to control incomes and prices, the most important of which centre around the proposition that repeated attempts to do so both distort the market process and weaken a nation's economic structure. So far as the record of the Heath government is concerned, however, its attempt thus to legislate in 1972 and thus to control in early 1974 – the middle stage of its incomes policy was reasonably well accepted and reasonably popular – could not, as his critics on the right foresaw, conceivably achieve the stated aim of ending inflation because the controls were imposed on the top of a monetary policy which, on even the most non-monetarist of calculations, increased inflation. The belated expenditure cuts of the autumn of 1973 were quite insufficient to offset this balance, largely because the rate of expansion of the supply of money under Heath and Barber was so unprecedented and so dizzy. But the real promise that underlies the imposition of incomes policies in Britain – and, to be fair to Heath, one should add that in the ancillary instrument of the Relativities Commission he sought to persuade employees to accept a rough idea of social justice as well – is that they will bring an end to inflation. When they do not do that their initial appeal fades, for workers see little point in accepting controls if the end of those controls shows no sign of being achieved. At the time of writing (early 1977) the same thing is happening to Stage Three of a Labour incomes policy as happened to Heath, even though that government is pursuing a more responsible monetary policy – not *very* responsible, but more responsible – than did Heath.

When the Cabinet discussed the imposition of incomes controls in 1972 Margaret Thatcher was deeply involved in the preparation of a White Paper on education which was intended to govern both policy and the disposition of resources over the following ten years. It is very clear that she had added to the demands of an unusually busy department the impulse of her own almost fanatical conscientiousness. But, while it may be said in her defence that she was absorbed in the DES and had no part in the inner economic debates of the Heath government, a gap remains in any assessment of her. This is the gap between her judgement and the instinct, long ago established in her upbringing, education and experience which led her to the conservative position on economic policy which she now adopts and her quiescence during the period from 1971 to 1974. Certainly, she had not begun, in those years, to think strategically, as, being Leader, she now must. Certainly, the isolation her sex alone imposed on her within the Party was a factor. So also was the limited nature of her ambition and her vision.

One other thing is important. Although the doctrines and the rules of financial and economic conservatism are in no sense a possession of the Conservative Party – socialist politicians here and abroad have from time to time both practised and followed them – they do, today, have a readier appeal to a particular kind of Tory mind than to any other.

But more changed between 1970 and 1975 than the extent and nature of Margaret Thatcher's ambition and vision. Circumstances changed. And if many Tories took the view that Heath had gone down to electoral defeat because he too gallantly or too honestly confronted the new spectre of trade union power, a sizeable number had serious doubts about the rightness and the effectiveness of the policies he had pursued. Successive governments, after all, had failed to control inflation through the instrument of policies on incomes and prices.

From the very outset of the life of the Heath government the most popular single politician in the country, from 1970 to 1974 still a Conservative, Enoch Powell, had proclaimed the inevitability of its destruction, because of the policies it followed. Many, perhaps most, Conservatives believed that in his long campaign of opposition to and denigration of his Party leadership Powell was moved above all by malice and envy. Most people believed that his unrivalled command of popular opinion was the product, almost solely, of his opposition to coloured immigration to Britain. Anthony Barber denounced him at one Party conference (in 1973) as a frustrated fanatic. On that occasion the leadership had been expecting an inflammatory speech of a kind to which they had become accustomed since

Powell's dismissal from the Shadow Cabinet in 1968. In fact he spoke moderately and constructively, somewhat to the disappointment of his most fanatical supporters. But, acting on the direct instructions of Heath, passed along the table to him after Powell had sat down, Barber nonetheless went ahead with his prepared attack. It was an indication of the irritation – hatred would sometimes not be too strong a word – that many of his former colleagues felt for the Member for Wolverhampton South West. Later on the same day, however, outside the conference itself, Powell brought a quite unsophisticated audience to its feet with a detailed and scathing intellectual critique of the government's economic policy.

It is certainly possible that his ability to do that was the product, not only of his extraordinary rhetorical power, but of the reputation he had already gained as the hammer of immigration. But the fact remained that he could do it, even on so abstract a subject as monetary policy. Whatever may be due to the growing impact of events and failures on public as well as specialized opinion, whatever may be owed to the disciples who had laboured so long in the vineyard of monetarism, there can hardly be any doubt that the very special place Powell had won for himself in the public arena made the whole range of alternative economic policies which the right wing of the Conservative Party advocated throughout the years of Heath's residence in Downing Street better known, better understood and, perhaps, more palatable. In the first – and still the best – of the books on Powell,* T. E. Utley suggested that he would be around for many years to trouble the Tory Party. This has proved true; and he raises a great many issues which concern his former Party. But perhaps it has been his prescience on economic policy that has, in the long run, most aroused his own ire with such as Margaret Thatcher and Keith Joseph, who have – so it seems to him – entered on an inheritance he had prepared for himself.

But whatever sequence of events and causes finally brought

* *Enoch Powell*, Kimber, 1969.

about the defeat of Heath; whatever men and women nudged circumstances this way or that; whatever the heritage Heath left to his successors in both Parties, he went down to defeat in February 1974. And this brings us back to the beginning of the story.

Chapter six
The Leader

Among the more absurd features of our political system is one of the least remarked, but by no means the least important – the ever-increasing bulk of the party manifestoes. The mystique which a grotesque perversion of democratic theory has imparted to these documents, together with the multifarious details of the commitments they nowadays contain, conduces to bad government and the discredit of the parliamentary system as a whole.

With these words – and prompted by the fact that in the general election of October 1974 the Liberal manifesto had run to ten pages, that of Labour to seventeen, and that of the Conservatives to twenty-six and a half – Professor F. E. Finer (writing in *New Society*, 13 November 1975) began an onslaught on the whole modern system of issuing manifestoes. *New Society* is not, in its entirety, a regular part of Margaret Thatcher's reading. In truth, she probably does read more journalism at its semi-academic level than do most senior politicians. By far the greater part is, however, selected for her, and arrives in her box (the red ministerial despatch box she had at the Department of Education and Science) by courtesy of her Parliamentary Private Secretaries, her Private Office, the Conservative Research Department and individual politicians. The organization behind any senior politician rapidly learns several things about the principles of such selection. There are certain outside individuals whose views the Leader is known to hold in particular regard: anything written or recommended by them is naturally included. There are certain themes known to interest the Leader; certain attitudes which he (or, in this case, she) is known to want to cultivate; certain lines of thought which the staff know he or she is already pursuing. Finer's article was immediately clipped and put in the box, above all on the basis of the last principle. She has quoted it constantly since, and so frequently recommended it to friends, colleagues and interlocutors that a copy is always readily available from her Private Office staff.

Finer's four columns of text encapsulate a good deal of philosophical thinking about the nature of democracy, as well as a certain amount of hard practical advice for modern politicians. A more elegant, lengthy and analytical approach to the same subject, reaching the same conclusion, was a paper on the nature of democracy proffered to the Leader by the American philosopher Shirley Robin Letwin in the summer of 1976; and many of Shirley Letwin's papers have been studied with close attention not only by Margaret Thatcher but by Keith Joseph and others of her allies as well.

The nature of the relationship between a politician – whose essential job is to act – and thinkers is, indeed, usefully illustrated by the progress of the argument on just this one point. Not only did the suspicion of manifestoes constitute a decisive break – in terms of political style perhaps the most decisive break – with the attitudes of Edward Heath, whose last manifesto was his longest; but the question of whether or not to go into detail on matters of future policy has been the one which has been most used by the press to plague the Thatcher leadership. It was only with the greatest reluctance that she gave her consent to the preparation of the (extremely well written and almost as well received) mid-term policy document *The Right Approach*, which appeared in 1973; and that was, in any event, a philosophical document rather than one which offered detailed proposals. It is important to understand, however, that her attitude to the lengthy description of policies proceeds first from an instinct, second, as we will see, from an intellectual conviction, and only third from a sense of tactics.

Because of this, it is important to understand Finer's reasoning. He calculated that the modern manifesto contained something between sixty and eighty specific proposals. The process
of presenting proposals in such numbers he described as being
'without meaning'. It destroys, in his view, the doctrine of the
political mandate, for it is virtually inconceivable that a political party, once elected, can claim majority support, even among
those who voted for it, for every one of its policies; and the
view that it can is even more ludicrous when one considers that
no party or government since 1935 has won more than 50 per
cent of the overall vote. Moreover, the *claiming* of a mandate
for such a lengthy shopping list is a useful technique by which
politicians in office evade criticism of what they plan on grounds
of reason, logic, morality or commonsense. (The example Finer
chose is that of Barbara Castle resisting attacks on her plan for
phasing out pay beds in the National Health Service.) Most
importantly, in Finer's view, the lengthy and detailed manifestoes 'debauch public policy', simply because of the obligation
felt by a political party, and encouraged by the pressures within
it, to carry out to the letter undertakings which experience may
show to be unwise or undesirable.

The same point is made on a higher level in Shirley Letwin's
lengthy dissertation on the nature of democracy, where she
argues that the very meaning of the authority of the electorate
in a modern liberal democracy depends on the voter being
offered only a programme in which a government undertakes
to do a very limited number of things. If it does not impose that
discipline on itself, asserts Shirley Letwin (who believes that the
exercise of the vote is the only conceivable exercise of authority
by the people if the nature of liberal democracy is to remain
intact) then the choice between a party and its rivals will be a
meaningless one. Apart from its logic, this case might be expected to appeal to Margaret Thatcher's instinct, because of its
implication that less government means better government.
Indeed, there was always a potential contradiction in the attitude adopted by Heath of at one and the same time propounding
the desirability of the withdrawal of government from many

areas of individual and national life and producing massive programmes for government.

The dilemma, which has run on throughout her leadership, has, however, consistently suggested to some politicians and commentators, most of them probably people uncritical of the modern assumptions about the inevitability if not desirability of constantly expanding roles for government, some ambiguity or evasiveness in her character. The raising of the dilemma, and the hostility which her solution of it aroused in some quarters at least occurred within days of her great triumph over Heath. It arose first as a questioning of her attitude, and second as a method of analysing and criticizing the matter that arises most immediately, most urgently and most tantalizingly for all concerned when a new Leader appears. That is the matter of appointments.

The Leader of the Conservative Party in Opposition has a striking advantage over his opposite number in the Labour Party. A large portion of the Labour Shadow Cabinet is elected by the Party's Members of Parliament. Their vote may impose on the Leader senior colleagues he would wish consigned to some infinitely faraway place. Even though, if he becomes Prime Minister, he may, with the Queen's Commission in his hand, dispense with their services, it can be unwise to do so: it may be much more prudent – a forced prudence – to keep on the ones he does not want, but who were elected, for a time at least. The Conservative Leader has no such disadvantages: he or she may also be influenced by prudence; but the fact that all jobs come from the Leader's bottomless fund of patronage is a significant accretion of power – just as is the similar fact that no policy can be forced on the Leader by a vote and, indeed, that nothing really is policy until the Leader has pronounced it to be so. In return for this empire, the Conservative Party is ruthless in demanding that its Leaders be successful.

The two questions asked about Margaret Thatcher on the morrow of her victory were whether she would hold to the attitudes of mind and policy which she had revealed during the campaign, and whether and to what extent she would reward with office those who had stimulated and managed her campaign. Such mystery as there was about the second question arose from two considerations. Most of her closest supporters were both unknown and inexperienced. This was necessarily so, since the whole Shadow Cabinet except Joseph had ranged themselves against her. Then, too, since it was universally assumed that all who supported her were right-wingers, the answer to the second question would cast light on the first.

On the whole, the reaction of press and public to her election was generous and delighted. For all that most commentators, and many individual citizens, had a good deal of concern for Heath in his humiliation, there was much natural pleasure in the arrival of a new and, in terms of sex and personality at least, attractive political phenomenon. She had had, of course, little support from the press during her campaign. Now, however, only the *Economist* and *the Observer* were initially snide and hostile. This happy state of affairs was not to continue: many reporters, and not a few parliamentarians, continued to believe or began to express the notion that some ghastly and nightmarish mistake had been made, and that time would see a reversal to the natural state of affairs. For months, indeed, the *Daily Express* appeared to believe that events would bring about the return of Heath as Leader of the Party. *The Times* likewise persisted in the strange logic that had characterized its attitude between the first and second ballots, when it had argued that Tory MPs should choose Whitelaw on the grounds that he would get on better with Heath than would the woman who had encompassed her Leader's destruction – as though, in spite of the massive repudiation of the former Prime Minister by his followers, he should still be allowed some position of exceptional authority – something in the nature of a power of veto – over the Party's affairs.

But, of course, everybody was in a state of shock. When, after Mrs Thatcher's range of second-tier appointments had been completed on 25 February, the new chairman of the Party, Lord Thorneycroft, dismissed its Director General, Michael Wolff – who had risen to that position after years spent as

Heath's closest personal adviser and favourite speech-writer – *The Times* denounced what it called 'the act of a downright fool'. One frontbencher, James Prior, refused to vote in a division on the Finance Bill in protest. This little storm indicated something of the nature of the problems she was to face for nearly a year: problems of disobedience and disloyalty arising out of a continued fervent loyalty to Heath, a deep conviction that she was a dangerous usurper, and an almost unthinking reaction against everything she did or appeared to be doing. In the matter of Wolff's dismissal it took outsiders and relative outsiders to reassert proportion in the matter of what was merely the replacement of a Party official in Central Office which is, after all, in the Party's constitution, the Leader's private property. Writing in the *New Statesman*, Alan Watkins, who is certainly no Thatcher supporter, said of Wolff that 'those who live by patronage shall surely perish by patronage . . .' and Anthony Lambton, who had resigned from the Heath government over a personal scandal, added in the *Evening Standard* that since one of Heath's most serious faults was universally agreed to be an inability to communicate, the fact that Wolff had been his senior speech-writer was in itself 'sufficient reason for his dismissal'. Still, it was not until Margaret Thatcher's hugely successful tour of the United States the following summer and her equally successful debut as Leader at the Party conference in October, together with what was generally agreed to be Heath's churlish behaviour there, that the sniping ceased.

But in the few days following William Whitelaw's appearance in tears before reporters, the reaction of what was now in truth Margaret Thatcher's Party to *her* victory had to be put in four ways, one of them very definite. First, of course, she was not yet confirmed as Leader of the Conservative Party: only nine days after the second ballot did peers and commoners alike confer on her her new title. And it should be said that these delaying formalities had a useful purpose: until she was really there, so to speak, she had a freedom of action that might later be denied her. Certainly, until the meeting in St Ermin's hotel that put her finally on top, she could display a seemly modesty in the face of her elevation, and a decent hesitancy about telling colleagues senior in experience to herself what jobs they were now to do – or whether they had jobs at all. Nor could anybody reasonably expect anything like a policy statement from her. She had time to take breath.

Yet, as she immediately made plain to her friends, what she did in those few days might have marred her leadership for some time to come. Caution was necessary, as well as allowed. The incredible enthusiasm of the press, abroad as well as at home, fascinated, excited, carried away even, by a new phenomenon, with little regard to what the phenomenon might portend, meant very little either to her or to those politicians in the Conservative Party who felt instantly that their task was to prevent *her* being carried away by her victory. Above all they felt that their task was to smooth the sharp edges off Margaret Thatcher, to bring her into the broad centre of Tory politics and ensure that no real change should take place. Perhaps only those – and not all of those – who had been her supporters from 21 November gave themselves up to that delighted euphoria which arrives with the feeling that the hour has come. After her first glass of champagne, however, it was clear that she was moved by none of this: such excitement as was evident in her was that of worry and concern. Within the few days that she brooded over what she should do, two members of the Shadow Cabinet, impatient with their sojourn in the anteroom, announced that they did not wish to serve her. They were Peter Walker and Geoffrey Rippon. Their announcements constituted the second, and most definite, element in the Party's reaction to her election.

We should not, of course, make too much of this. It could be that both men guessed that they would not be asked to serve. Their announcements had none of that immediate quickness of spirit, immediate decision about the future, that characterized the refusal of Iain Macleod and Enoch Powell to serve under Alec Douglas-Home in 1963 once *their* hero, Butler, was refused his chance. It could be, too, that both men felt that Margaret Thatcher was about to lead the Party off in an utterly new direction, one they felt to be wrong, and that they decided to take a hard line of principle against her. Whatever their feelings, it is not unreasonable to mention that, at the time of writing, Rippon has returned to the fold, if not to power, as leader of the Conservative group in the European Assembly; and Walker has more than once declared both his support and his willingness to serve in either a Shadow Cabinet or a Cabinet under her.

Even before these two had announced their decisions, however, there was one poignant task Mrs Thatcher had to discharge. She had to visit Edward Heath.

Heath was the first Leader of the Party to be dethroned against his will since Austen Chamberlain. In 1922 the body of the Party, led for the occasion by Stanley Baldwin, decided that they did not wish to prolong the life of the coalition led by Lloyd George, in which their Leader, Chamberlain, took second place. Chamberlain was not of their mind: he went into the wilderness with Lloyd George. But he returned in 1924 as Foreign Secretary in a government headed by Baldwin. Baldwin himself retired, loaded with honours. His successor, Neville Chamberlain (Austen's half-brother), though he was forced out of office as Prime Minister in 1940 by those dissatisfied with his conduct of war, remained as Leader of the Party until a diagnosis of cancer of the throat compelled his retirement, which was followed rapidly by death. Churchill retired, full of years, and grumbling, but in favour of a successor chosen by himself. That successor, Eden, presided over the Suez campaign so disastrously that he would probably have been forced to give up anyway; a collapse in his health, however, made further humiliation unnecessary. Macmillan, who followed him, had his will sapped by successive failures after years of triumph: when his prostate gland caused trouble, he, like Churchill, was able to determine the succession of a favourite, Home. Home himself, having lost – but so nearly won – an election, chose not to prolong his leadership against criticism, and resigned it after pledging – and subsequently giving – total and unselfish loyalty to his successor, Heath. Of all of them only Heath was, at the time he was defeated, full of health, ambition, conviction, and a deep sense of having been wronged. Since February 1975 many Conservatives have compared his seeming disgruntlement and his opposition to, even dislike of, Margaret Thatcher unfavourably with the conduct of Home. The implication going with that judgement is that Home's behaviour was of a piece with that of previous Conservative leaders. On the contrary, it is clear that it was unique, as is Home himself. Of all previous Tory leaders in this century who had a choice of conduct only Arthur Balfour, who was forced out of the office after a bitter struggle in the early years of this century, behaved with the loyalty and restraint that marked Home's conduct; and Balfour did not begin to show the same traits of character until years had elapsed after his replacement by Andrew Bonar Law: even then, it was during the middle of a world war. In the case of every one of the others circumstances and health conspired to make their exits graceful.

Such panoramic historical analyses, however, are brought to their root in the common clay of modern politics by the circumstances of Margaret Thatcher's visit to Heath at his house in Wilton Street – rented to him on generous terms by the Duke of Westminster, after his defeat in February 1974 had left him without a home in London. She had said, as had every contender for the leadership, that a post in the Shadow Cabinet would be offered to Heath. The circumstances of his career and of his defeat had been so extraordinary that nobody could have expected him to wait upon the new Leader; nor did he offer to do so. On the other hand, though she had visited Conservative Central Office within hours of the second vote in the House of Commons, she had not yet sought, nor had her delighted, bewildered, vestigial staff discovered, what perks were hers. The Leader's official car had not yet been relinquished and so she was driven to Wilton Street in the battered white Mini belonging to Joan Hall, the former Tory MP who had served her during the campaign in a voluntary capacity. (She it was who had once on a most public occasion given Heath a gift of carpet slippers with the suggestion that a little more domesticity in his life would make him more appealing to the public.) The Leader's official car was parked in Wilton Street when Miss Hall and Mrs Thatcher arrived there.

What happened at that meeting remains a matter of some dispute, a dispute perhaps symbolical of the divisions persisting in the Party, divisions of principle as well as personality. In his book on Mrs Thatcher* Ernle Money gave an unlikely account of a discussion conducted on her part with briskness, on Heath's with a childish acerbity. Months after the event Heath told his friend, George Ffitch of the *Daily Express,* that he had never been offered a job at all. Had this been the case Mrs Thatcher would clearly not have fulfilled the spirit of the promise of reconciliation inherent in her election platform. In preparing his story, however, Ffitch omitted to ask for her version of the occasion; he went strongly on his own exclusive material.

The first journalist who addressed himself to the subject at length, and as a reporter rather than as a partisan, was George Hutchinson (Heath's official biographer) in a story on the front page of *The Times.* Hutchinson recorded the statements of both sides, and emphasized the extraordinary discrepancy between them. It took a day or two more for political journalists to recall that, immediately after the meeting, members of Heath's private office had told them that an offer had been made and refused, because Heath now wanted to spend some time in reflection on the back benches. It did no good to relations within the Party, however, for him to seek subsequently to alter the record. So far as I understand the matter, their conversation at Wilton Street was brief and cool. Margaret Thatcher made her offer in the most general of terms, and Heath refused without either discourtesy or warmth: the meeting was not unlike their earlier one, on 21 November of the previous year, when she told him she was planning to stand against him for the leadership. It seems clear, too, that both parties were relieved to have their conversation over, and relieved, too, that they were not going to have to work closely together in the immediate future.

* *Margaret Thatcher: First Lady of the House,* Frewin, 1975.

Timothy Kitson, Heath's Parliamentary Private Secretary, detained Mrs Thatcher in the hall for casual conversation for some minutes, so that the waiting press would not feel that the meeting between past and present had been too abrupt; and she went back to the waiting Mini. The worst moment – perhaps the only really bad moment – of her accession was over.

After that she moved rather quickly. When her first Shadow Cabinet was announced a few days later, six names from the Heath team were missing. In addition to Rippon and Walker, Robert Carr (her notional boss in the Opposition Treasury team, and something of a hero to middle-of-the-road Conservatives), Paul Channon, Nicholas Scott and Peter Thomas were all dropped. Only in the period between February and October 1974 had any of the last three attained senior positions, though Thomas had been for a time chairman of the Conservative Party after the 1970 general election. Such disturbance as was felt at her choices was less on account of any feeling that the new broom had rubbed too furiously against senior members of the Heath entourage than because the dismissed Shadow Ministers were taken to represent a trend of enlightened and progressive Toryism which she seemed to be repudiating. It is never easy, of course, to define what enlightened and progressive Toryism is; at that point in 1975 it seemed to be a conviction that most of the things done by the Heath government, in spite of their consequences, were right. Later, when the Tory Reform Group Nicholas Scott seemed for a time to present itself as a sort of opposition within the Opposition, all the more so in that its chairman, James Gordon, had been dismissed his post at Central Office shortly after the leadership election, the new Leader asked one of its members, 'What is it, exactly, that you want to reform?' and got no answer. It is hard to resist the conclusion that, at least in the days immediately following the election, the opposition to and criticism of her leadership was – with the exception of Channon – the opposition not of the principled, but of the 'outs'.

'You will not,' she said to a friend just before her first Shadow Cabinet was announced, 'see what I really want to do until the reshuffle before a general election. But you will have some genuine indication when I change the first lot around in just about a year.' It was almost exactly a year before she made serious changes.

As much interest was directed towards those 'in' as towards those 'out'. In obeisance to what had become a tradition – albeit a short-lived one, dating from Heath's leadership victory over Maudling in 1965 – she asked Whitelaw to assume the duties of deputy leader and, as she remarked at the time, she was fortunate to have available a man who enjoyed both the advantages of a more comfortable method of presentation than herself and a complete lack of rancour over her victory, Heath's defeat, or even his own eclipse. But next to him, and giving special mark of her favour by a public statement to the effect that he was to rank number three in the Shadow Cabinet hierarchy, came Keith Joseph. His brief was to superintend both overall research and the formulation of policy but, to the chagrin of some of his admirers, he was not given the coveted post of Shadow Chancellor, which went to Sir Geoffrey Howe. Neave came for the first time into the Shadow Cabinet as both Head of the Leader's Private Office and senior spokesman on Ulster. Timothy Raison at Environment, Sally Oppenheim at Consumer Affairs and George Younger at Defence were all regarded as encouraging appointments, showing her concern to give opportunities to new men and women.

There was no root-and-branch extermination of the Heathmen: with Margaret Thatcher's retention at the Home Office of Ian Gilmour (subsequently transferred to Defence), who had been the author of the most virulent of the public speeches attacking her candidacy, she indicated a desire to close the breaches that had arisen in the Party. Her only great regret was the refusal of the Member for Oswestry, John Biffen, one of the outstanding right-wing critics of Heath, to join her, apparently on the ground that he – opposed to Britain's membership of the EEC – preferred to await the outcome of the forthcoming referendum on that subject. Her relationship with Biffen continued to be dogged by uncertainty and disappointment. At the end of the year he did join the Shadow Cabinet, as spokesman on Energy. Later, Mrs Thatcher transferred him to Industry, and it was widely believed that a spell in that post was in the nature of preparing him, by acquainting him with all the manifold complexities of industrial subsidization, to be her Iron Chancellor in government. Every mark of favour and respect was lavished on him, but his health gave out under the strain, and he was forced to resign. Before the sighs of relief from those who feared the application of his radicalism to feather-bedded and unsuccessful industry had had time to be heard, however, she announced that Joseph would take the portfolio in addition to the one he already held: the much regretted incapacity of Biffen was, clearly, not going to be allowed to make any difference to her intentions for government. If anything, Joseph is more determined a monetarist than Biffen, and more convinced of the need drastically to reduce government spending on industry.

We will return to the matter of her subsequent appointments to the Opposition front bench, for her two reshuffles since she became Leader clearly indicate not merely her growing control over the Party, but the survival under pressure from events and criticism of the radical Tory instincts and belief with which she took office.

It was entirely natural that in the weeks and months that followed her election public attention should be focused, intensely, on what she was like, and on whom she liked and disliked. In reality, though, she faced more serious difficulties than that of picking a Shadow Cabinet. After all, it would be widely expected that her first consultative committee (as the Shadow Cabinet is more correctly called) would reflect that she was new to the job; that she was anxious to promote reconciliation between factions; that she wanted to try out new faces and combinations; and that she would need time to find her feet: her 'real' Shadow Cabinet would not be expected to make its appearance for some time. Of more immediate concern were matters of general tactics, and matters concerning both the Party organization and the huge gaps in her own knowledge and experience. Her tactical judgement and reaction to it was the third significant aspect of her early days.

For some time her private organization remained what it had been when she was elected – vestigial; and there was no disposition to hurry appointments to it. Before all else came her belief that, with the date for a general election uncertain, it was impossible for any Opposition Leader – even one whose novelty and unexpected success had attracted so much worldwide enthusiasm and interest – to keep up with the Prime Minister (then Harold Wilson) in the race for election victory. One had to define ahead, she said, what the natural peaks and troughs of events would be, and to alternate between periods when she would be exceptionally accessible to would-be interviewers and profile-writers and the ordinary run of radio and TV current affairs programmes. Within a few days she had given all the interviews she was willing to give for the moment, and made a trip to Scotland, where the size of the crowds that turned out to greet her exceeded by far both the expectations of her own staff and the precautions taken by the police. It was already time, she felt, to go quiet for a bit.

Her other rule, within the context of her theory of peaks and troughs, was that the peaks should be tied as far as possible to Party events – most notably the annual October Party conference – and in serving that end she was prepared immediately to take on a gruelling tour of the United States, timed for the following September and ending just before the faithful assembled at Blackpool. Some of her advisers were dubious about this decision, partly because she was so inexperienced in foreign affairs, partly because a trip to America so early in her leadership, and before she had really got on top of things at home, might easily be disastrous. For all her innate caution, however, she knows when to plunge. Planning for the United States went ahead, and it proved to be probably the best decision she could have made.

The rule about alternating between periods of exposure and periods of privacy was varied in only one respect. She knew very little about either the Party organization in London or its branches in the country. She had few friends or allies in the National Union of Conservative and Unionist Associations – the voluntary body that runs Conservative affairs in the constituencies. Information from Central Office showed that over her career she had spoken less than almost any other senior parliamentary figure on strictly Party platforms. The instruction went out, therefore, that in addition to keeping all her engagements already contracted for before the second ballot, she would be as receptive as possible to requests for her appearance at individual constituency and area functions. It was imperative to become known as quickly as possible, to show the flag to the Party's workers, and to show the Leader as well. Somewhat to the amazement of all but a few, pressing the flesh – to use the American term for this kind of political circus activity – proved to be something at which she was extraordinarily adept, and which she seemed greatly to enjoy. Even relatively hostile journalists – like James Fenton of the *New Statesman* – were both impressed and delighted by her performances on the stumps.

Between her election and the beginning of the following December, she made no fewer than twenty-four visits to different parts of the United Kingdom, besides trips to Turkey, Luxembourg, France, Germany, Romania, and the United States and Canada. Four of her trips were to Scotland. Her colleagues now began to understand what her friends had known for some time, that she had the deepest suspicion of the eight-year-old Conservative commitment to devolution for Scotland and Wales, as enshrined in a promise known as the declaration of Perth, made by Heath in a speech to the Scottish Party conference. When, under severe pressure from both the Liberal and the Nationalist Parties, the government eventually introduced a Bill to provide Scotland and Wales with their own elected assemblies, the Conservative Party faced serious difficulties. A number of Margaret Thatcher's spokesmen on Scottish affairs, and particularly the Shadow Secretary of State, Alick Buchanan-Smith, felt that they could not go along with her deep opposition to the Bill. They could not be persuaded that her determination to combine with Labour opponents of devolution *tout*

entière to throw it out did not necessarily represent an abandonment of the Heath promise.

To her gratification she found that Whitelaw, after years of
loyal support of Heath on the issue, was now of her own mind
and considered that devolution in the form proposed presaged
the break-up of the United Kingdom. He also felt that Heath's
account, since he had lost the leadership, of the origins and
nature of the devolution policy, was less an accurate historical
picture than the expression of his continued discontent with the
the new order in the Party. In particular, he resented Heath's
insistence that the policy could still be justified in 1976 because
it had emerged from detailed consultation and confabulation
within the Party in previous years for, Whitelaw insisted, that
simply had not been the case. In the event, Buchanan-Smith
and his friends resigned. An ardent anti-devolutionist, Teddy
Taylor, the Member for Glasgow Cathcart, was made Shadow
Secretary of State, though Heath's former Chief Whip, Francis
Pym, was made responsible for opposition to the Bill. His performance was a masterpiece of parliamentary tactics and the
Bill was duly thrown out.

In February 1975 this was all a year and more in the future.
The number of Mrs Thatcher's visits to Scotland during a particularly crowded and testing period for her suggests, however,
both the high priority she gave to that country's affairs and her
feeling that the Scots had been for a long time misgoverned by
London and neglected by faint-hearted Tories who had witnessed
the steady erosion of their Scottish position over the years since
the general election of 1955, when they had last held a majority
of the seats there. By the middle of 1977 she had paid more
visits to Scotland than any previous Conservative Leader who
had not lived there, and her optimism about the Party's prospects in the north, if it had not completely carried conviction
with her colleagues, had gained some weight from events – from
the improved performance of Tory candidates in local authority
elections, the revival of morale in the Scottish Party, and a vote
against established policy on devolution at the 1977 Scottish
conference. She has still not completely abandoned the under-

taking to give the Scots an assembly of their own, but her repeated emphasis on the extent to which Scotland, like the rest of the kingdom, would benefit from her kind of government, and the whole thrust of her words and attitudes, has completely altered the outlook of the Party. Friends and allies who at the very outset of her leadership urged her to the dramatic step of repudiating the declaration of Perth, seem for the most part highly content with the way in which she reached her 1977 position.

In the spring of 1975, however, much of her success must have seemed still distant. The four points of consideration of her leadership – its initial hesitancy, the refusal of some to serve or express loyalty, the puzzled distance between her and the Party organization, and the question of how she would set about both establishing her authority and hammering out rejuvenated policies – all caused headaches for herself and those around her. There were moments in those early months when she appeared frail and tired beyond belief, and when her staff seemed to have time for nothing but the ceaseless round of engagements, paperwork, and the exhausting business of getting the show on the road administratively. The initial flush of delight and pleasure faded from many parliamentary cheeks. Questions and doubts were raised about her attitudes and her potential. Rumours of plots and coups were rife, and the press in general allowed her very little time to adjust to her new circumstances. If hearts did not fail, not a few fluttered.

Of all her difficulties it was her inexperience in foreign affairs that gave rise to most concern, and not everybody was happy with the first step she took in that area of policy. Reginald Maudling, the former Chancellor, had resigned from the post of Home Secretary in the Heath government because of rumour, suspicion and criticism arising from his earlier association with a now bankrupt and imprisoned architect, John Poulson. As both Heath and Maudling understood the matter, there was neither prospect nor possibility that he would be prosecuted, nor likelihood that anything more than a carelessness in business matters which colleagues did not find inconceivable in one of so amiable and casual a temperament had occurred. Maudling found it improper, however, to remain in his job as long as police investigations were continuing, since he was, as Home Secretary, the ultimate chief of the police force. Despite Heath's every effort, he could not be dissuaded from his purpose.

By February 1975, though it would be wrong to say that the affair was settled (a report of a House of Commons committee on political aspects of the affair was still to come, and has since appeared, castigating Maudling for negligence and lack of frankness) it seemed clear that his protestations of innocence could be believed. After a good deal of consultation, and following in particular the advice of the party's *doyen* of foreign policy, Alec Douglas-Home, Margaret Thatcher invited Maudling to return to the Shadow Cabinet as Shadow Foreign Secretary. He was delighted and she, though she had many critics, was pleased with those who pronounced it to be an imaginative appointment. Whatever his failings were thought to be Maudling was generally and deservedly a popular and rather admired man. In matters of economic and social policy he was, moreover, decidedly on the left of the Party, and it was correctly reckoned that he would fight strongly against the rigorous monetarism of Keith Joseph, and for such still widely popular techniques of economic management as an incomes policy. Alas, the relationship did not work out as well as either party hoped, and Mrs Thatcher ultimately decided to drop him from her team, thus almost certainly bringing to an end a long and generally speaking successful ministerial career.

There was one quarter, however, in which Maudling's appointment caused particular concern – as, indeed, did Margaret Thatcher's own attitude. Britain was already preparing for a referendum on continued membership of the European Economic Community. Though governments of both Parties had, in their time, applied to join the EEC, it had been left to the Tories under Heath – from the very outset of his career in public life a devoted and unshakeable proponent of a European policy – actually to sign the Treaty of Brussels. In Opposition, it became clear that a very large number of Labour politicians – certainly a majority of the Party in the country – were against membership. To placate them Wilson and his Shadow Foreign Secretary, James Callaghan, undertook, if elected, to make provision for a referendum following a period of renegotiation of Heath's terms. More: immediately before a Bill authorizing the holding of a referendum was presented to Parliament, Wilson made constitutional history by announcing that he intended to abandon the principle of collective Cabinet responsibility, according to which each member of the Cabinet is bound to support each and every one of its decisions, and to allow Ministers to campaign as they wished. A number immediately joined the National Referendum Campaign, as did the majority of senior trade union leaders, and a number of respectable, if not at all comparably senior, Tories. In the course of the campaign itself the chairman of the 1922 Committee, Edward Du Cann, was to lend his weight to this side. Pro-Marketeers doubted the strength of Maudling's commitment to the EEC.

The argument about the Common Market centred around two issues and, although this is not the place to go into a detailed analysis of the rights and wrongs of what was and is probably the most important single political issue in Britain this century, it is useful to summarize them.

The first, and to most anti-Marketeers the most important, aspect of the affair was the risk to British sovereignty in becoming a member of a putatively federal organization. Anti-Marketeers were delighted to discover that they were unpersuaded by their opponents' assertion that membership would procure or help to procure the economic breakthrough for which the country had so long waited; but the economic argument was not, to them, the most central one. The pro-Market organizations, to the contrary, concentrated above all on the so-called economic benefits of membership and concealed from the public – dishonestly in the view of the NRC and incidentally myself – the desire of their majority to move towards the creation of a federal Western Europe. Then – although the Treaty of Rome which established the Market made no provision for a common defence policy, and sketched only in the vaguest way the

desirability of a common foreign policy for member countries –
there was a rather muddled suggestion on the part of the supporters of membership that a Western European unity of this
kind was necessary to protect freedom from the Communist
threat in the East. To the other side, however, at least to
Conservatives and more moderate Labour members of the NRC,
the political instability of Italy and the potential instability of
France, together with the steady rise to influence of the Communist Parties in both countries, could well mean that Britain
was being dragged into something that might prove both un-
stable and dangerous, and was risking her sovereignty while
doing so. Yet practically every newspaper and by far the greater
part of the business community regarded any threat to continued membership with something of the horror with which
they might contemplate Armageddon. From the very outset all
the big guns were ranged on the side of continued and loyal
membership.

Europe was Edward Heath's great issue. He had done more
than any other man to swing the majority of the Conservative
Party behind the cause. He had conducted the Macmillan
negotiations on entry with the European powers, and failed. As
Prime Minister he finally succeeded, and when his government
collapsed it was to this part of his record, and among major
issues to this alone, that he could look with satisfaction. For this
achievement he was regarded in Europe itself and among the
domestic supporters of membership as a major statesman. The
vast resources of money and organization (and for flattery) of
the European organizations were at his disposal immediately
after his fall: they provided balm for his wounded soul, and
probably also fed the illusion, certainly shared by his still considerable number of adherents and his still (for a private
Member) considerable political staff, that his replacement had
been some kind of ghastly mistake.

On the face of it a critic could be forgiven for assuming that
things might well be different in the Thatcher camp. Maudling
himself, when he had been Commonwealth Secretary, had been
profoundly suspicious of the EEC, and had negotiated the

creation of the rival European Free Trade Association. Protestations that he was now a loyal European cut very little ice. Heath had brought the full weight of Party discipline to bear on the small but courageous number of backbenchers in his Party who had opposed his will on the issue. Almost certainly, all of them had voted for Margaret Thatcher. Some were numbered among her admirers and in one or two cases she returned the admiration, and even friendship. Her nationalism was sharp and precise and well known: though she had never criticized the EEC she had never been forthright in its praise either, and her rhetoric was very dissimilar from that of those who seemed able to combine praise of the nation and its prospects with praise of the organization. Her friends and supporters outside Parliament were strongly disposed against the Market: some took an active part in the NRC campaign. Finally, it was known that she was distressed by the coolness that had arisen between Heath's government and that of the United States – and particularly by the personal coolness between Heath and Secretary of State Kissinger – and saw her forthcoming trip to America as the beginning of an attempt to repair any breach which had arisen. And, while being anti-American was no condition of being pro-European it was certainly the case that the more enthusiastic a man was for the EEC the more dismissive he was likely to be of the Anglo-American alliance, and *vice versa*. All in all, she was certain to find herself more at home with the Tory members of the National Referendum Campaign than with their opponents, among whose ranks were to be found those most critical of her leadership.

Consideration of the affair – and of her determination to end the pressure hitherto put on anti-Market Tories to conform, while keeping the Party in line on support of the Treaty of Brussels in the referendum campaign – prompted what seemed like an excellent solution. In the event it created more suspicion than satisfaction. Heath was unquestionably the first politician on the European side. Margaret Thatcher knew little enough about the issue, and had no desire to take further limelight away from him. If he would not join her Shadow Cabinet (and there is every indication that she was more than happy that he would not) could he not assume the leadership of the Conservative campaign to stay in Europe? This time she was unwilling to consult him personally, but the proposal seemed both sensible and gracious, and soundings were undertaken among those still close to him. The answer was abrupt and ungracious: though he would speak on Conservative platforms, his principal effort and nearly all his time would be at the disposal of the main pro-European umbrella organization. For the duration he was to be a European first, and a Tory very much second. Perhaps it seemed to him, as to some others, that her move was only a trick, designed to grab for herself the credit if the referendum went the right way, and to shrug the blame off on to him if it went wrong.

As most members of the National Referendum Campaign committee expected, the referendum produced an easy victory for continued British membership. Though Mrs Thatcher had spoken for the pro-European side, affirmed her commitment in more than one interview, and presided over an important pro-EEC press conference, the victory did nothing for her politically. Amid the flood of relief in the press and in the City could strongly be sensed a great undercurrent of gratitude to, and support for, Heath. At this stage of affairs, moreover, there was scarcely anybody in any section of the Party or on any newspaper staff who was not deeply aware that the transfer of power had not gone smoothly and that in some quarters the fact that it had taken place was barely if at all accepted.

After sending her a quite generously phrased telegram immediately on her accesssion Heath declined on platform after platform and in interview after interview to give her open or heartfelt support. He did not attack her – as Powell had attacked him and later her – but he did not help either. The referendum campaign and several grand overseas trips did much to restore any damage that had been done to his self-confidence. He continually reiterated his intention 'to speak out on the major issues of the day', and he pointedly denied that it could in any way be required of him to make explicit declarations of loyalty to his successor. With the referendum over and much of the press settling back into the ordinary grooves of domestic politics there began a considerable flow of comment to the effect that the future prospects of the Party depended on a reconciliation between the new Leader and her predecessor. The sympathies of the journalists penning the comments were amply displayed by their assertions as to who should make the first move. For her own part Margaret Thatcher maintained a marked politeness towards Heath, and her staff were instructed to give what assistance they could in the fairly frequent event of his staff seeking assistance from the Private Office, the Research Department, or Central Office.

The American visit was now looming. It began in the middle of September, and lasted a fortnight. Mrs Thatcher made five major speeches, in New York twice, in Washington, in Chicago and in Toronto. She was received with every mark of respect and even deference by President Ford, by the Prime Minister of Canada, Pierre Trudeau, and by the Secretary General of the United Nations. At a dinner given for her in Washington by the then British Ambassador, Sir Peter Ramsbotham, and attended by some of the most senior figures in American political life, including James Schlesinger and Henry Kissinger, a brief impromptu speech earned her a standing ovation. Nervous to a degree when she left London, she was throughout full of aplomb and grace. The trip earned widespread coverage – initially perhaps partly for her novelty value, thereafter for other reasons – both in America and at home. Almost everybody she met liked her and was impressed by her, which was not something that had been universally expected. Her walkabouts were as successful in North America as they had proved to be in Britain, and all in all she had won for herself by the time of her return the most successful imaginable prelude to her first conference as Party Leader.

Nor was it simply a public relations success. Both what she said and her conduct generally had been taken to represent an important break with the traditional attitude of British Opposition politicians travelling abroad. The vehemence of her attacks

on the conduct of British affairs by the Labour government was
held to be in breach of the (albeit imprecise and ill-defined)
convention that one should not attack one's country overseas.
The Foreign Secretary, James Callaghan was indeed so incensed
by what she did and said that he issued instructions to the staff
of the Washington Embassy to repudiate her message. This, of
course, put the Embassy in an extraordinarily difficult position.
According to the (again somewhat hazy) rules covering such
circumstances they were obliged to offer her such assistance as
they could. They knew, too, that she might well one day be
Prime Minister, and slights might well be remembered. It happened, however, that a significant number of the staff were in
personal sympathy with the Labour government and were a
trifle alarmed, especially by her speech to the Institute of Socio-
Economic Studies in New York on 15 September and her speech
in Chicago a week later. She, on the other hand, was angered by
clear evidence from British newspapers – and most importantly
from the *Financial Times* – that officials were briefing British
journalists against her. When an attempt was made gently to
reproach her for what might be taken to be attacks on her
country she replied, 'I'm not knocking Britain. I'm knocking
Socialism.' Nonetheless, relations with the British Embassy
were the least satisfactory part of the trip.

Much later, when the replacement of Ramsbotham by the
Prime Minister's son-in-law, Peter Jay, caused a great deal of
controversy in Britain, and when the new Shadow Foreign
Secretary, John Davies, felt impelled to come to Ramsbotham's
defence after rumours that Callaghan's Press Secretary had
denounced him to a lobby conference, Margaret Thatcher remained silent. It was clear that neither the incumbent nor his
replacement enjoyed much of her esteem.

To the Americans, of course, a great deal of what she said was
unexceptionable – though perhaps unexpected coming from a
British politician. From the ourset – in New York on 15 September – she launched an attack on the 'progressive consensus', as
she called the general agreement about economic and social ends
between British politicians of all parties since the war. The

'progressive consensus' she defined as 'the doctrine that the state should be active on many fronts in promoting equality; in the provision of social welfare and in the redistribution of wealth and incomes'. She denied that equality in wealth and incomes was desirable or that it was practical. She denied that the British people wanted such equality. And she insisted that attempts to achieve equality and extend the welfare state had weakened rather than helped the national economic performance. Whatever Conservative politicians in the past may have felt on these matters, few in the mainstream would have uttered their conclusion aloud, especially in the ringing and confident language that she chose:

Let our children grow tall – and some grow taller than others, if they have it in them to do so. We must build a society in which each citizen can develop his full potential, both for his own benefit and for the community as a whole; in which originality, skill, energy and thrift are rewarded; in which we encourage, rather than restrict the variety and richness of human nature.

'We,' she told the Pilgrims, 'are an eleventh hour nation. But the eleventh hour has struck.'

The immediate sense that she was sloughing off a generation of consensus was confirmed everywhere she went, and in increasingly emphatic language. Bearing in mind the tradition of not criticizing the country abroad, the Foreign Office was particularly disturbed by something she said to the National Press Club in Washington:

In my country, at present, we have serious problems; it would be foolish to ignore them. We have, to a more intense degree than many other countries, a combination of rising prices, falling output and unemployment. And we have a sense of losing our way. The problem is not a technical one. It is one of the life and death of the national spirit. We are in the midst of a struggle for human dignity.

It is not my job, nor the job of any politician, to offer people salvation. It is part of my political faith that people must save themselves. Many of our troubles are due to the fact that our people turn to politicians for everything.

Then, too, she said of the process of *détente* with the USSR, at that time in the full tide of early approbation, 'No, we did not lose the Cold War. But we are losing the Thaw in a subtle and disturbing way. We are losing confidence in ourselves and in our case. We are losing the Thaw politically.' Thus the Americans as well as the British were castigated; and they loved it.

Throughout the visit, then, she harped on three themes – that it was a dangerous illusion to assume that desirable economic and social ends could be achieved by the action of the state and that it was, indeed, necessary to put the growth of interventionism into reverse; that the growing financial and philosophical encroachments of the state sapped national will and vigour to a dangerous degree, and she intended to return power to the people; and that the West as a whole was in danger of losing its way in history. There was nothing apprentice-like about her, nothing diffident or uncertain, nothing indecisive or hesitant. Colleagues back home put aside such doubts as they might on reflection have had about the hardness of her message, and rejoiced in such an excellent preliminary to Blackpool.

It cannot be said that it is exceptionally difficult for a Tory Leader to be a hit at the annual Party conference. True, there may be embarrassments, difficulties and even serious problems. But the body of the Party is invariably not only loyal to its Leader, but anxious to demonstrate that loyalty. The method of organization chosen, too, gives every opportunity to emphasize loyalty. Indeed it was not until the days of Heath that Leaders attended the whole of the conference. Even now, everything in the few days the affair lasts builds up to the entrance of the Leader on the final morning, to address the mass rally. Even a Leader – like Heath – who does not find it easy to touch hearts, can hardly fail. The audience is strung up: they want to cheer. Supremely skilful stage-management invariably prolongs events before the arrival of the Leader long enough to whet anticipation, but not long enough to allow boredom to set in.

Still, as one of those closest to Margaret Thatcher said about her position in February, she 'had to convince more people of her qualities than had any predecessor'. The breathing space between America and Blackpool was full of business. Thorney-croft had been ill all summer, and the reorganization of the Party machine had gone with nothing like the speed Mrs Thatcher had expected and believed she needed. Apart from her tours in the spring and summer months time had to be spent assuaging the doubts felt about her in Fleet Street (especially at *The Times*) and in the City, where she took to lunching more often than any predecessor. An apparently tame place, the City of London is in fact the beating heart of a web of international high finance and usually highly suspicious of anything that smacks of radical capitalism in Conservative circles. The cautious instincts that fit well with the modern intertwining of private and public finance predominate there.

There were two further problems. The two general elections of 1974 had left the Party's coffers depleted. Although the Conservative Party frequently receives, and to some extent depends on, considerable business donations, the greater part of its income comes from small contributions, and it has no completely reliable source of large income such as the trade union movement offers Labour. Unfortunately, so anxious was business to achieve a success in the referendum that a great deal of the available cash went to the European Movement. Then, after the lurch to the left of the Labour Party in Opposition after 1970, and the collapse of the Heath government, many businessmen began to feel that the radicalism the new Leader appeared to be offering had little chance of practical success. Entranced by a brilliant and rapid campaign through their boardrooms by the Liberal Leader Jeremy Thorpe, a number – including former generous contributors to the Tories – decided to try to use their money to support the cause of a reform of the electoral system and the introduction of proportional representation. This, it was believed, would enable the Liberals to achieve an electoral breakthrough. It would enhance the prospects of moderates everywhere and prevent the emergence of a doctrinaire left-wing government.

Margaret Thatcher set her face against PR from the very

beginning. She opposes it as fiercely for a Scottish Assembly or for direct elections to a European Parliament as she does for elections to the Parliament at Westminster. Every move towards it she regards as the setting of a dangerous precedent. She is convinced that PR would not prevent the triumph of left-wing radicalism; and that if it achieved anything it would be the dominance of a coalition-type government, committed above all to the middle-of-the-road policies she is in business to reverse. She had – and still has – some sticky moments in City lunch rooms.

In any event, Blackpool was upon her. Impressed as the Party was by her tour of America, it was still nervous, a little lost perhaps, in her company. And a weird series of events, which *could* have been the result of a series of misunderstandings, conspired to throw a long shadow before her performance on the last day.

Heath arrived a day later than she did. It is yet another peculiarity – and a rather pleasing one – of Conservative conferences that any past politician of seniority, whether he has been successful or not, and whatever the circumstances of his decline or fall, is greeted with rapture. As Heath entered the hall – the great, garish, amphitheatrical hall of the Winter Gardens – the audience rose as one man. So did the platform, including the new Leader. Heath acknowledged the cheers, and then hesitated before walking around to come to his seat without going past her. The press was on to the affair immediately, and the usual over-excited conference coverage began. Mrs Thatcher's press officer, Derek Howe, and Heath's, Stephen Sherbourne, angrily disputed over responsibility for the failure to organize a joint photograph. That evening, in the Louis Quinze room of the Imperial Hotel, full of politicians and the camaraderie of conferences, Heath walked past her table to his own without making acknowledgement.

Worse was to come. Later in the evening Heath went for drinks to the room of John Moore, a backbencher holding high office in the Party. Among the company were three journalists, Peter Jenkins of the *Guardian*, Christopher Hitchens of the *New Statesman*, and the female representative of Scandinavian Radio and TV. By no stretch of the imagination could any of them be regarded as a Tory sympathizer. The following day reports appeared to the effect that Heath had denounced both his successor and Keith Joseph as traitors and fanatics. In bars throughout the rest of the day various reports of the tone and emphasis of his words were canvassed. It was suggested in his defence that he had dined very well, that he was still in a state of some trauma after his defeat, and that he had spoken in deep gloom and sorrow rather than in petulant anger. He then issued a statement denying the stories; it unfortunately contained an unusually self-justifying note, and referred at length to his continued support within the Party, particularly as evinced by his standing ovation the previous day. He did not, said one senior journalist, seem to understand why he had been applauded – 'not because they wanted him to be Leader, but because they didn't want him'. And he had certainly been indiscreet.

But he had also ensured Margaret Thatcher's triumph at the final rally, by which time he had left Blackpool. The incident was fundamentally a trivial one, and probably more the product of simple hurt feelings than anything else: his conduct had been too inept to smack of intrigue. But the Party was determined to make it up to her and she, all in blue, rose to the occasion with a stinging, light-hearted denunciation of the government and all its works. She began, though, with a recollection of the first conference she had attended, when Churchill was Leader. As she went on to praise Eden and Macmillan, it became clear that she was going to work her way through a litany of predecessors. The tension in the hall when she reached Home was palpable. But her praise of Heath was full and generous – even, thought some of her supporters, lavish. But she had already dismissed all suggestions that she could justifiably be cold to him. She had arrived and, as she said over drinks afterwards, 'Now I *am* Leader.'

There are events and moments in politics that, at the time they occur, may appear trivial but which, on consideration, can be seen as symbolic. There had never been a time, from

February to September, when any of her friends or allies doubted
that they had made the right choice, or that she would ultimately
be successful. But there did seem moments when, if she did not
doubt herself, she seemed not quite to realize what she had already done, or how much she deserved or could demand. The
most striking was an occasion when, after a hasty challenge to
the Prime Minister, she found she had to open a censure debate
in the House of Commons. She was unwilling to do so, and complained that she much preferred to speak later in the order, for
she liked to have something to attack. 'But, Margaret,' said
Airey Neave, 'When you're Prime Minister you'll have to open
debates quite often.' Her start of surprise and her silence convinced several of those present that she had not yet thought
that far ahead.

She was a different woman in March 1976. The Tories, supported by the left-wing Tribune Group, defeated the government on its proposals for public expenditure. Harold Wilson
immediately called for a vote of confidence from the House. (In
similar circumstances a year later James Callaghan declined to
seek the House's confidence and compelled Mrs Thatcher to
table the censure motion that precipitated the Liberal–Labour
pact.) She was unfeignedly furious that Wilson had not gone to
the country, and immediately began to prepare a speech of
denunciation both for the morning debate at Westminster and
for her appearance at a Cambridge rally later in the day. Much
advice, particularly on the historical precedents, was taken;
but she was impatient of academic views that the circumstances
of Balfour, Baldwin and Chamberlain, who had been under
severe pressure from their Party when the first two called general
elections and the third resigned, were quite different from those
of 1976. She was so exercised that one of her advisers cautioned
her against making too much of the matter. 'After all, you may
find yourself in this kind of fix one day.' She looked at him. 'If
I did,' she retorted, 'I would resign.' It says much for her
character that nobody in the room doubted her for a moment.
It says much for the authority she had already won for herself
that nobody doubted that she would be right to resign. Her

command of affairs and her confidence had grown mightily in her first year. But what *difference* had her election made? Having a drink with her later that evening I asked her what she thought she had changed since becoming Leader. 'I have changed everything,' she said simply.

Chapter seven
The change

In the course of her speech at Blackpool in 1975 Margaret Thatcher had a great deal of fun at the expense of the Soviet Union. It was, though, serious fun. She meant every word of her passionate denunciation of socialism in its most extreme form; but she made it, also, the target of her acid wit. She had not, at this stage, gained her subsequent status of bogeywoman in the eyes of the Russian press – that was not to come until the following January – but she had, in a pithy speech consisting principally of one-sentence paragraphs, questioned the whole process of *détente*, cast doubt on the forthcoming Helsinki conference and its usefulness, and reiterated her conviction about the essentially aggressive nature of Soviet policy – all in a speech to the Chelsea Conservative Association the previous July. The speech was noted, but it aroused no particular furore. It was, however, widely believed to have influenced Harold Wilson to make a speech that was much tougher than expected at the conference in Helsinki a few days later. Such influence is not unlikely: Wilson has always been a politician very sensitive to issues, and particularly interested in the new lines his rivals are trying to stake out. It would not be beyond him to try to steal Margaret Thatcher's thunder.

The most immediately useful thing about the Chelsea speech, however, was that after it Mrs Thatcher entertained Robert Conquest, the celebrated political writer and scholar of Soviet affairs, to drinks in Flood Street, and he was subsequently of considerable help in filling out her ideas on East–West relations. Certainly, the Chelsea speech was the beginning of important things for her, and nothing gives her more pleasure than the fact that since she became Leader she has made a world-wide impression in the field of which she was most ignorant at the outset. Yet, aside from the logic of her views on Communism and the ambitions of Soviet Russia, it is striking to reflect that, as on all important matters, the roots of her thinking lie some way back, and lie above all in her instincts. Of all her contemporaries and rivals, and for all her love of intellectual debate and assertions about its importance, she is the most instinctive.

There are two aspects of the argument about *détente* – or, perhaps more correctly, of the argument against *détente* as it has been practised above all by Henry Kissinger. One is strictly military, the other is a much more complicated political affair. The military proposition is that, contrary to the expectations aroused both by the Soviet–American talks on the limitation of strategic arms and the much more broadly based Helsinki Accords, the Russians have gone on expanding their armed forces at such a rate that they now enjoy, or very shortly will enjoy, a strategic superiority over the West. The political proposition is that since the Soviet government undertook at Helsinki to improve the provision of civil rights within their borders – among other things, to make Western newspapers more freely available, to allow Soviet Jews to emigrate to Israel, and to facilitate the reunion of families whose members live on both sides of the Iron Curtain – and since they have not done that, they are likewise untrustworthy on matters more closely associated with life and death. Critics of the critics of *détente*, including Enoch Powell, regard this proposition as both superficial and naive. Security, they say, and the balance of power have nothing whatever to do with the internal and historically determined characteristics of a regime. Nor could anybody but a fool, the argument continues, consider it conceivable that the Russians would change the internal nature of their administration simply to suit a whim of the West. This doctrine, particularly as it asserts the desirability of disinterest

in the internal nature of foreign countries, is a classical view of
the British Foreign Office.

But the matter is a good deal more complicated than that.
The principle of foreign policy according to which Margaret
Thatcher formed her initial judgement about East–West relations owes more to the practice of Churchill in the 1930s than
to the traditionally rigid views of the Foreign Office. Churchill
always saw an indissoluble connection between the domestic
practices of the Nazi government and the aggressive nature of
its foreign policy. The Soviet Union and Germany are not, of
course, adjudged nowadays to be the same; but the relationship
between domestic and foreign policy is frequently asserted to be
similar. To take but one example: the extraordinary development of the Soviet Civil Defence programme, assessed by a US
Senate Committee to be of such proportions that it can only be
taken as a design for preserving life on a considerable scale after
a nuclear war, would be conceivable only in a state where the
population was dragooned. But, of course, behind all these
judgements there is held, on Mrs Thatcher's part, a conviction
of a much older and more fundamental type: it is never advis-
able to allow a potential enemy to become much more powerful
than yourself.

This is not to say that she personally sees what has come to
be called the human rights issue simply as an aspect of a cold-
minded military policy. Her concern with civil rights lies as far
back as her teenage understanding of what was going on in Nazi
Germany. It attained a Russian dimension, and she first began
to read up on that dimension, when she picked up a volume by
Solzhenitsyn – *The First Circle* – at the airport on a journey as
Secretary of State for Education. She read it throughout the
journey, neglecting for this unique occasion her official papers
to do so, and finished it that night. From then on she read
steadily in modern Russian literature, and when she became
Leader the works of Solzhenitsyn in particular became part of
her regular reading.

The first occasion of a public intervention by her on foreign
policy in general, and on Soviet Russia in particular, is worth

recording. In April of 1975 Harold Wilson returned from the negotiation of a trade package in Russia. He had been spending some time sizing up his new rival at the twice-weekly gladiatorial combat called Prime Minister's Question Time – on Tuesday and Thursday at 3.15 – and it was clear that her inexperience was to be the card he would regularly bring into play. Wilson was a renowned master of the Question Time procedure. He rarely answered questions directly, but was particularly expert at discomfiting and embarrassing opponents. The paucity of information given, and the frivolity of both questions and answers at these Tuesday and Thursday sessions has caused them to be criticized by the more serious-minded students of parliamentary politics. But Harold Macmillan, at least, rates their importance very highly. According to him the gratification offered by triumph to one's own parliamentary supporters – which spreads out like gas into the constituency Parties – makes the small effort required to be good at the job into something like a highly successful investment.

When Margaret Thatcher made her first appearance as Leader, Wilson had been oleaginously polite to her, and even rather skittish. But unlike many of his colleagues he did not underrate her. (He once observed that Heath had been the only Tory he had underrated, and that his foolishness in this regard had cost him the 1970 general election.) So he watched her performance carefully. On this occasion she was for all practical purposes unbriefed, since her Research Department advisers, whose job it is to predict what the Prime Minister may say and advise her accordingly, had thought that this was not the sort of question on which she would want to come in, at least as yet. Nonetheless, she rose and challenged Wilson's enthusiastic account of the deal. As usual, he did not take the question directly, but indulged in a little homily about the importance of experience and the dangers of inexperience in foreign policy. 'What the Prime Minister means,' she observed, 'is that he has been around a long time. And he looks it.'

However, the incident inspired her to much more activity. The policy of *détente* had been so accepted for so long, and its principles had become so ingrained, that the Conservative Research Department and even some of Mrs Thatcher's senior parliamentary colleagues were reluctant to consider how desirable it might be for a Britain no longer powerful, with daily shrinking international responsibilities, above all struggling to find her feet in the Common Market, to break with an international consensus. There were, however, many outside the formal Party organization who shared her views, including some in the United States, among them James Schlesinger. Gradually, Margaret Thatcher's mind turned to the preparation not merely of a speech, but of a series of speeches, on the subject. It is one of her most impressive characteristics that once she is convinced a subject is important she is not prepared to drop it simply because, on its first outing, it fails in political attraction. And the Chelsea speech, though it attracted a certain amount of attention, was no bombshell.

Détente [she said] sounds a fine word. And, to the extent that there has really been a relaxation in international tension, it is a fine thing. But the fact remains that throughout this decade of *détente*, the armed forces of the Soviet Union have increased, are increasing, and show no signs of diminishing.

She went on to quote a speech by Leonid Brezhnev three years earlier in which he had said that *détente* 'in no way implies the possibility of relaxing the ideological struggle'. She observed that both Suslov and Ponomarev had more recently re-emphasized the same point. And she added,

They are in principle arrayed against everything for which we stand.
  So when the Soviet leaders jail a writer, or a priest, or a doctor or a worker, for the crime of speaking freely, it is not only for humanitarian reasons that we should be concerned. For these acts reveal a country that is afraid of truth or liberty; it dare not allow its people to enjoy the freedoms we take for granted, and a nation that denies those freedoms to its own people will have few scruples in denying them to others.

After the conference a considerable part of her correspondence dealt favourably with the Chelsea speech. Conquest went to the United States, but there were many other scholars who had increasingly begun to share Margaret Thatcher's apprehensions about the progress of relations between the NATO alliance and the Warsaw Pact. Gradually, her reading came to be occupied more and more by matters of foreign policy and – as more than one of her colleagues found surprising – by military concerns. Because of the way she organizes her affairs she occasionally gives a slapdash impression or leaves herself open to embarrassment. I have already mentioned the system by which any busy political leader receives journalistic and academic political material to read. In addition, however, attempts to buttonhole the Leader at social gatherings are likely to produce an invitation to write to her – or for her – on the interlocutor's interest or obsession. It is frequently difficult, therefore, to trace exactly the genesis of a thought, and not infrequently difficult even to find a relevant paper. (It will be even more difficult for historians accurately to dissect her career, for she never hoards paper; so far as I can see this reflects an excessive modesty which forbids her to imagine that there will ever be a real academic and scholarly interest in her career.) Embarrassment is caused when the easily flattered assume they have established so confidential a relationship during a simple conversation that they can afterwards indiscreetly suggest to friends that they are working with Mrs Thatcher. Nonetheless, nearly everything important or valuable gets to her.

Conquest wrote to a mutual friend from Washington in May 1976, some time after Margaret Thatcher's second and most successful speech on *détente*. He made two points which were both of considerable interest to her and of considerable relevance to the debate, and it seems right to include them here. A scholar of profundity and wide reputation himself, author of a definitive book on the Stalinist terror, and of a remarkable short biography of Lenin, what he had to say about academic opinion was of particular moment.

It is a true and very striking fact [he wrote] that virtually all serious students of the USSR are in accord with the view that its

leaders remain in a state of total enmity towards the West, which
they only fail to translate into action when they are prevented from
doing so. But serious students of the USSR of any repute are a tiny
handful; and most of them, however telling their occasional intervention on the press, are academics without a powerful involvement
in foreign policy matters as such.

He suggested that her approach (which he compared to that of
Daniel Patrick Moynihan, now Democratic Senator from New
York) 'is in accord with the profoundest understanding of the
particular foreign political entities with which our policies must
deal', and he added:

The weakness of the 'Conservative' position – or, more generally, the
patriotic position traditionally common to all three parties – is that
rather few of those in political life who subscribe to it have done a
great deal of thinking and writing concentrated on foreign policy.
The Left, on the other hand, swarms with producers of 'analysis' and
opinion on these matters, wrong-headed and essentially shallow –
but influential out of proportion, and full of the power to distract
from realities.

The letter was shown to Margaret Thatcher, and she underlined
several passages. Clearly, there was a good deal in it that was
encouraging, but a good deal that was depressing as well.
However, the problem it defined was the kind of problem she
liked: it fitted well with her fundamental conviction that in
every sphere of policy the argument had to be won. She was dismissive of the happy assertion of Lord Fraser of Kilmorack
(formerly Sir Michael Fraser, senior deputy chairman of the
Party) that between 1966 and 1974 the Tories had produced as
many as 1000 concrete policy proposals. 'What use is that,' she
said, 'when we didn't win the argument?'

　The second speech on defence, delivered at Kensington Town
Hall on 19 January 1976, was prepared and researched almost
wholly in her private office, with only small assistance from
outside. She was happy to return to the subject whatever the
likely impact, but it obviously made sense for her, particularly
as she intended to force a traditionally unfashionable subject

right into the centre of the political arena, to make it as hard and dramatic as possible. 'The Russians,' she said, 'are bent on world dominance, and they are rapidly acquiring the means to become the most powerful imperial nation the world has seen.' And she went on, in the hardest hitting language she had so far used on any subject:

The men in the Soviet politburo do not have to worry about the ebb and flow of public opinion. They put guns before butter, while we put just about everything before guns. They know that they are a super power in only one sense – the military sense. They are a failure in human and economic terms.

But she saved her most savage castigation for her own country and its government:

We in Britain cannot opt out of the world.

If we cannot understand why the Russians are rapidly becoming the greatest naval and military power the world has ever seen, if we cannot draw the lesson of what they tried to do in Portugal and are now trying to do in Angola, then we are destined – in their words – to end up on 'the scrap heap of history'.

The response exceeded her wildest expectations. The speech was given the fullest coverage by the press and – though a number of correspondents disagreed with both her analysis and her conclusions – most writers gave utterance to a sort of surprised respect at the detailed statistical arguments and the global strategic view which provided the backbone of the speech. Above all, the Russian press launched a protracted and vehement campaign against her, dubbing her the 'Iron Lady' and festooning even their offices with cartoons of her. In itself this both supported her propositions and gave her, overnight, a substantial world-wide reputation. Roy Mason, the British Defence Secretary, whose record and the record of whose government she had savaged, at first reacted dismissively and contemptuously. He was promptly embarrassed by the seriousness of the Russian response. Then, as the months passed, a German Defence White Paper appeared, offering the gloomiest views about the potential of the steadily increasing Eastern forces in

Europe. More and more American voices took up the theme. Even Kissinger, coming to the end of his time in office, began apparently to withdraw from some of his more optimistic positions on *détente*. Mason was ultimately condemned to eat his words; and Margaret Thatcher had achieved one of the most gratifying triumphs known to a politician: she had become a trail blazer.

One passage in the Kensington speech, however, gave rise to some concern. By this time, although the extent of any economic retrenchment might be debated, all senior Conservative politicians had come to the conclusion that considerable cuts in public expenditure would be needed. In attacking cuts in defence spending she promised:

We will reverse those processes when we are returned to government. In the meantime, the Conservative Party has the task of shaking the British public out of the effects of a prolonged course of sedation. The sedatives have been applied by people, in and out of government, who have been telling us that there is no external threat to Britain, that all is sweetness and light in Moscow, and that a squadron of fighter planes or a company of marine commandos is less important than a new subsidy for a loss-making plant.

For the moment she could bask in triumph. Nonetheless, she was not content. The first speech had been made on the eve of the Helsinki conference. The second came halfway through the following year. She was determined to return to the charge precisely on the anniversary of its conclusion. So, a few weeks before that date, her staff were informed of her intention, and preparatory work began. First, she must digest the enormous amount of reading she had tackled and annotated over the previous year, ranging from highly specialist American articles (sometimes barely intelligible) right across to translations of Russian material. The next was to trawl again over a year's publications to make sure nothing had been missed. Finally, the brains of the experts had to be picked, and two days before the event she gave a dinner party at which the subject was much discussed. However, in view of somewhat misleading press reports that appeared at the time, it is necessary to say and to stress that every word of the final draft was written by herself.

For there were storm clouds around. While her Shadow Defence Secretary, Ian Gilmour – popularly supposed to disagree with her on nearly everything – fully supported both her stand and its exploitation, the Shadow Foreign Secretary, Reginald Maudling, did not. He was, not unreasonably, irritated because he had merely been told the speech was to be made, and not consulted on it. He submitted a draft of his own, cast animadversions on her advisers (including myself) and urged her strongly against making a speech of the kind she had already made. He did not question that the speech would gain her some short-term popularity but it would, he insisted, do damage in the long run, because it would anger the Russians. Any commitment to increased spending on defence, he believed, ought to have the consent of the Shadow Cabinet. He feared, too, that a denunciation of Western unpreparedness would annoy the Americans who, after all, had been carrying the main burden. In short, he advocated a line completely different from the one Mrs Thatcher had been taking.

At this stage somebody talked to the press. A rumour spread that as a result of Maudling's objections she had backed down and that the speech would not be made. This story appeared at the very moment when discussions were going on about where she would make the speech: she was about to settle on Dorking where the local Tories could not only provide a large hall, but could guarantee to fill it. Finally, after the speech had been made, Adam Raphael reported in the *Observer* on 1 August, using 'sources close to Mr Maudling', that the final version had Maudling's full support, though it in fact differed in almost every respect from his own recommendations. In particular, as the headline in the *Sunday Express* informed readers, it pledged 'We will re-arm'. Discussing rumours that Margaret Thatcher had been persuaded to tone the speech down, Ian Waller in the *Sunday Telegraph* wondered how, if that was the case, the original draft could possibly have been tougher. It was easy to agree with him when one read:

The signatures were hardly dry before the Soviet Union flagrantly interfered in Portugal. Even more serious was the extension of Soviet activity into Angola, including the provision of weapons and advisers.

In spite of Helsinki the Soviet Union remains a closed and repressive society. It means that the Kremlin can, and does, suppress not only unwelcome ideas, but unwelcome facts too. Their 'freedom of information' consists of their absolute right to tell their subjects what they should believe and what they should hear.

The response was by now predictable. Mrs Thatcher received extensive and, in the main, friendly press coverage at home and abroad. Roy Mason and Tass (the Soviet News Agency) launched their expected attacks, Mason going so far as to accuse her of wanting war with Russia. But the third speech set the coping stone on her command of a particular and vital area of foreign and defence policy and issued immediately in an invitation to China – itself a great success – where her views of the Soviet threat were shared. In a later Shadow Cabinet reshuffle Maudling was dropped.

A serious, intelligent and hard-working politician gains enormously, in technique and understanding and aplomb, not merely from the simple business of engaging on his – or her – round of duty, but from taking up and developing and repeating a theme. To the politicians and statesmen of the countries Margaret Thatcher visited after the beginning of 1976 she was to be known more as an exponent of a particular view of foreign policy than as an unusual and challenging but essentially British politician. There was a focus to her conversations in China, Germany, Australia and New Zealand which would not have existed before those speeches were made, and which scarcely existed on her first visit to the United States, even though the first of the foreign policy speeches *had* already been made.

There is, too, the important matter of technique. There are perhaps half a dozen politicians in Britain who speak extremely well and enjoy a good platform manner. But if, as happens, their speeches go unreported, if they are not visited by TV cameras or radio microphones, they wither from lack of attention and challenge. There is little pressure to develop, no opportunity to watch oneself later and assess how a thing could have been done better. Margaret Thatcher, an assiduous learner in every field she touches, has improved immeasurably both as a speaker and as a broadcaster since she became Leader. For the first year, of course, she had the extra pressure of realizing that her critics readily recalled the aphorism of Dr Johnson to the effect that a man seeing a woman preacher in action would not be surprised that the thing was not done well but surprised, rather, that it was done at all; and her fierce competitiveness reacted readily to her awareness of such a challenge. Then, as time went by, she was as often as not expected to be controversial, to make good copy, and this too helped in her training, particularly as it is her fixed conviction that a minute's attention by television news is worth nearly a whole major current affairs interview. In consequence of that conviction, she has consistently sought to reach the news through speeches from the platform, rather than conceding to the desires of current affairs interviewers.

Yet, there is a curious aspect – at least in her own mind – of her reputation as a performer. Before she became Leader of the Party her reputation stemmed above all from the House of Commons. She had begun to make it virtually on her first day there; and she had increased it over the years. Yet she has been heard to say gloomily that, since February 1975, she has made only one first-rate speech in the Chamber – in the economics debate immediately after she had enjoyed yet another success at the Brighton Party conference in 1976. She is, perhaps, being somewhat hard on herself, but she has undoubtedly had more than one bad let-down in the House of Commons. In public, on the other hand, where she naturally speaks far more frequently, her failures have been few and far between, even when she has appeared without a text. It is probably the case that, whereas she feels an unexpectedly heavy weight of responsibility in Parliament, her delighted discovery of how well she goes down with audiences of voters has spurred her to greater heights and given her greater ease in action.

She has never, though, grown to like television. The redoubtable Clive James, television critic of the *Observer*, who thinks her a poor platform performer – though, so far as I am aware, he has only once seen her speak in public, and that on one of her bad days – considers her to be 'dynamite' on television. She is never comfortable in a studio. She finds the usual table and chair highly restrictive, and is happier and more effective when performing from an armchair. She claims never to know where to put her hands, and to be constantly inhibited from making the gestures which she habitually uses to emphasize a point or interrupt a progression of thought. 'The camera loves her,' says James, but she certainly does not love the camera. If, therefore, she is effective – and the bulk of congratulatory correspondence after each appearance confirms that she is – it is because, whatever her discomfort, she refuses to be inhibited either by surroundings or by interviewers. She never, for example, allows an interviewer to interrupt her, however reasonable the interruption may appear to be, and for that reason is less than popular with the profession. She dislikes party political broadcasts, not least because she is rarely pleased by the formats and methods of presentation dreamed up by Central Office and, in so far as she can be comfortable at all on television, she is happiest when speaking straight to the camera.

Though I have never heard her say this it may be that one of her reasons for disliking the broadcasting media is her inability to feel that she is making any contact with listeners or viewers. Interviewers she seems to regard as a screen, blocking her off from people, rather than as professionals there to elicit what will interest their customers. The drama and the potential empathy of a public meeting she likes, and she finds something of the same satisfaction in her now massive correspondence, often running to 800 letters a day – more after a major speech or broadcast and with, for a political leader, relatively few cranks contributing. She exercises a closer supervision over the correspondence – and over the replies, which are rarely purely formal – than do most politicians, and receives almost every day a representative sample of what comes in.

Of course, the principal topic of concern of her correspondents is the state of the economy, and the solutions to economic problems which she favours. Perhaps more than three quarters of her correspondence and more than 90 per cent of her speeches deal with economic matters; and these are just proportions, for whatever the wisdom or otherwise of her attitudes on defence and foreign policy, education and immigration, if she is not successful in economic policy she will, quite simply, not be successful.

As economics is the overriding priority for every politician today, so it is the overriding concern of most of their constituents. One of Margaret Thatcher's office rules is that she should personally see all letters from children, and she is particularly pleased when a child's attitudes correspond to her own. There was, for example, the child from Northumberland who had organized her schoolmates to create an industry – the manufacture of bubble baths – through which to help pay for a school minibus. The average age of the board of the company, the child gravely informed Mrs Thatcher in a long letter on the economics of the subject and in particular the success of overseas sales, was twelve. They were thinking of applying for the Queen's Award to Industry, and had written to the Prime Minister to tell him so, enclosing some samples of their work. Perhaps because these had been returned from Downing Street, these level-headed youngsters omitted to send samples to the Leader of the Opposition, but they nonetheless sought her help in procuring orders. She replied, ordered twenty-five bottles of bubble bath mixture, and congratulated the children on their enterprise. She concluded: 'If any of your school are coming to London in the next few weeks, perhaps you could bring them to me and we could talk about your trading venture. I feel very excited about it.' That last sentence was no mere politician's automatic response. She *was* excited, and touched particularly by the energy and initiative of children.

In general, though, the very straightforwardness of her delight in her work and her profession pleases and uplifts those around her. For example, in March 1976, when Harold Wilson resigned, the news came to her first as a bald statement. Since she had been alone among her colleagues in believing that there might be a general election early rather than late, and since nobody at this stage thought that Wilson might conceivably retire, her immediate expectation was that there was to be a general election. Half an hour went by before the bubble was pricked with the delivery of Wilson's lengthy statement on his retirement to the Cabinet. Her enthusiasm went, but revived again when Peter Thorneycroft called for a gambler's discussion of the succession. 'Callaghan,' she said, 'and none of them would be harder to beat.' Thorneycroft responded with the accurate prediction that there would be a run on the pound of dangerous proportions by the end of the year.

'It is never very gratifying,' she said when that run came, 'to be proven right when one's predictions were of gloom.' Certainly, her economic predictions have been consistently of gloom and so far she has been consistently right. What has been particularly difficult for her, however, has been to walk the narrow line between taking regular advantage of government failures on the one hand and spelling out what she would do differently on the other, especially as many of her solutions are as yet both unfamiliar and potentially unpopular. Nowhere has this been more difficult than in the field of incomes policy.

Incomes policies have been four times adopted by British governments and have four times failed even to provide a minimal improvement in our economic condition, instead in the end precipitating yet another economic dislocation. Despite this, the idea of a fair incomes policy retains a considerable hold on the public mind, rather, one imagines as did the idea of a just price in the Middle Ages. So strong is this feeling that the politician who wishes altogether to eschew incomes policy, and rely on monetary policy and competition, invariably encounters some difficulties making his message understood. This is particularly so for a Conservative Leader, since many of his supporters will want him to promise strong action against the unions, while many of his potential supporters will fear a destructive confrontation with them. Then, too, so thoroughgoing was Heath's conversion to incomes policy in 1972 that a great many Conservative politicians believe that such a policy is a necessary and unavoidable task of government. To challenge that idea is to invite dangerous dissent, and considerable perturbation.

Thus Margaret Thatcher's responses to questions at a meeting in Wrexham caused a considerable furore. Yet her position, both on incomes policy and on competition could readily have been deduced from what she had been saying with regularity even before she became Leader.

I don't want any head-on clash [she said] because I believe it is perfectly possible to work with the unions. Look, I have been round factories today where they have no labour troubles at all, because both management and people working in them have realised that their future is bound up in the same thing. Whether you are share-holders, managers, workers at any level, your future is bound up in the prosperity of the enterprise. And I think that is the attitude we want to encourage.

Not a clash or a conflict, but to say – Look, your prosperity and your children's prosperity is bound up with giving your fellow workers who are consumers, who consume your product, a fair deal.

Because of her response to the next question the significance and the implication of that answer was missed. In it she had sketched in an extraordinarily clear way her concept of an in-dustrial system in which there is very little role for the state except a hortatory one. Her views on tight money policy have been spelt out again and again, and events have begun to make them persuasive. But politicians as well as journalists and ordinary citizens have almost no concept of a situa-tion in which the state might have no crucial role to play in any dispute over productivity or wage levels. While Margaret Thatcher clearly does not rule out such intervention altogether, she has frequently expressed the belief that the more often government intervenes the more often it is likely to fail, and the more readily it will be bankrupted of real influence and moral credit. All government can really do with effect, she is fond of saying, is control the supply of money, and the borders of practicality within which both sides of industry have to work.

At Wrexham, however, a persistent questioner went on to ask her about incomes policy. On hearing of her reply, Peter Walker insisted that she could not conceivably have given it, and in the House of Commons Labour Ministers again and again jeered her when she repeated it. That was in the palmy days of 1976, when it seemed that their collaboration with the most powerful of the trade union leaders ensured a long and reasonably happy life for the variety of incomes policy they had adopted. The questioner asked:

With all due respect, we have to stand up to the Unions. How are we going to do it? Now, I suggest that this is the way to do it. We will have a referendum and say – right – to the miners – right –, you can have the coal mines. You bring us the coal. You can have £200 a week if you can sell it.

And Margaret Thatcher replied:

We have not come to a clash or a confrontation yet. Let us not say anything that would bring that about.

I believe that we can work in the future with the Unions as we worked with them for thirteen years in government. And remember in the end, the clash only came over a statutory incomes policy, not over anything else but a statutory incomes policy. And I do not intend to have a statutory incomes policy again.

Slowly, informed opinion has been coming round to her view on the matter. *The Times*, very largely under the influence of its then economics editor, Peter Jay, came to a strong preference for monetary methods to tackle inflation, and gave the Conservatives the sound advice that, since the country had been convinced that the Labour Party really had a special relationship with the unions, it would be absurd for the Tories to go to the electorate with the message that now they had seen the failure of a Labour incomes policy they should try the Conservative variety. But her battle – against ingrained prejudice, fear and ludicrously inflated optimism – has been uphill all the way. However, as the shadows gather around both the Labour government and its policies of wage restraint, few of her colleagues or her critics have not now (though often reluctantly) come round to the view that she was right all along. For, it should be remembered that from Joseph's speech at Preston between the two 1974 elections, nobody could doubt that he and his best political friend were heavily committed against a return to attempted controls on wage bargaining.

Yet, for somebody with very definite views on economic matters, views well known before the leadership election if those on other matters were not, she was surprisingly slow to make her weight felt in the economic debate. It was not until 4 May 1976 at the Junior Carlton Club that she made a speech, with which she herself was satisfied, on the subject of future economic policy and the methods she would adopt to attempt to return Britain to prosperity. As in the case of perhaps one in ten of her speeches she gave it a title – *The Path to Profitability*.

She began with the familiar assertion that whereas the Conservative case was almost invariably better than that put forward by Labour, it was rarely as well presented: her near-obsession with the importance of winning the argument was never more clearly evident. Another theme rapidly to become familiar was the statement of the blanket conviction – by no means pleasing to all Conservatives – that Britain and the British have 'for thirty years . . . been subjected to a steady remorseless stream of Socialist propaganda, some of it open and unashamed, but quite a lot of it under the mask of independent opinion'. And she hammered the point home:

Our aim is not just to remove our uniquely incompetent Government from office – it is to destroy the Socialist fallacies – indeed the whole fallacy of Socialism – that the Labour Party exists to spread. Otherwise it will be all too easy for the faithful to say, as they always do when confronted with the facts of Labour failure: 'The doctrines of Socialism are still as true as ever; it is just that they have been badly carried out.'

How to perform this Augean task?

We must become aware of the way in which in our daily lives our own thinking may have become affected, become tainted, without our ever realising it, by the ceaseless flood of Socialist and pseudo-Socialist propaganda to which we have all been exposed for so long.

Mrs Thatcher chose for analysis two examples: the assumption by the left of a moral superiority for socialism, the result of which 'is to leave even some Conservatives with a vague feeling that the idealists are to be found on the Socialist side'; and the attempt 'to make us ashamed of profit and the profit motive'. To believe the first proposition, she said, one had to believe that it was better to have an official taking decisions for one than to take them oneself, since the whole sinew and muscle of a socialist system was its bureaucracy. And she quoted the ever-available Solzhenitsyn:

The decline of contemporary thought has been hastened by the misty phantom of Socialism. Socialism has created the illusion of quenching people's thirst for justice: Socialism has lulled their conscience into thinking that the steamroller which is about to flatten them is a blessing in disguise.

The profit motive she defended with energy and power. Even some businessmen, she observed scathingly, had started to use the term 'surplus' to describe profit, as though profit was almost irrelevant to the functioning of business; and she added, 'Yet if we had to point to one single notion which is calculated to damage our industrial performance, to prevent us competing effectively in the world and ultimately to undermine the basis of a free and diverse society, it is the idea that profit is somehow wrong.'

It is hardly surprising that with views like these so many of Margaret Thatcher's initial successes came abroad. For in the United States and Germany – where she was a huge success at the Christian Democrat conference in 1976 – reverence for choice, for free enterprise and for profits has survived more successfully than in Britain. Regarded all too frequently as an impossibly wild-eyed radical in her own country, she was not infrequently accepted abroad as one of the few British politicians who spoke straightforward good sense.

This was not, of course, the case in China, which she visited in the spring of 1977, though it was very much the case on her immediately subsequent trip to Japan. The visit to China was partly a matter of curiosity, partly in order to broaden her experience, but most of all the consequence of a feeling that her hosts' views on Russia had an affinity with her own. But, unlike so many foreign visitors, she did not fall for the country, nor suppose its achievements – such as they are – to represent a better or superior kind of socialism. Without transgressing the boundaries of politeness, she made it clear in several brief speeches that she had little time for the Communist Chinese way of life; but that she saw no difficulty in cooperating with the Chinese on matters of common interest, though within limits. With that they seemed well content.

As has been increasingly the case in foreign countries, the Chinese received her with the honours due to a head of government rather than with the courtesy required by the presence of an Opposition leader. In very large part this has been due to an unbelievably spectacular run of by-election successes, culminating in the capture of the mining constituency of Ashfield, legendarily a Labour stronghold. As has been mentioned in Chapter 4 these by-election successes and victories have demonstrated several characteristics unique in the British experience, the most important of which is a steady switch of support from Labour to Conservative, whereas hitherto the commonest thing has been for the supporters of a ruling party to see their people abstain when they are going through a bad patch.

In any event, the total command Margaret Thatcher had over her Party as she entered 1977, her increased confidence in debate, and her often spectacular receptions abroad were buttressed usefully by this undeniable and unprecedented electoral success. Steadily, and in complete accordance with the scheme of peaks and troughs she had mapped out for herself so soon after her election, she began to switch gear.

In March 1977 she was to speak at a meeting of the Zurich Economic Society. In many respects this would be the most important speech she had ever made. From this platform Churchill had made the speech which is graven on the hearts of all supporters, and all the founders, of the European Economic Community. It is certainly the most prestigious platform available to a European politician. In the audience would be some of Britain's international creditors, and many connections of absent creditors. In the austere surroundings of Zurich, men on whose judgement the fate of the pound would rest in the days following her election as Prime Minister, fastened their eyes on her.

She prepared herself with her customary care, but most of her advice for this great occasion she drew, not from the Conservative Research Department, still thought to be to some degree doubtful about the high advocacy of radical Conservatism and capitalism which had been the hallmark of her style and policy, but from the Centre for Policy Studies, her own and Joseph's creation. When she rose the change of gear was apparent. She abandoned neither the castigations nor the savagery of the past two years, but there was a new theme:

Had I spoken to you last year, I should have expressed faith in our nation and civilisation and its capacity for survival. But today, I can offer you more than faith. I bring you optimism rooted in present day experience.

The lessons of the by-elections had not been lost.

I have reason to believe that the tide is beginning to turn against collectivism, socialism, statism, dirigism, whatever you call it. And this turn is rooted in a revulsion against the sour fruit of socialist experience. It is becoming increasingly obvious to many people who were intellectual socialists that socialism has failed to fulfil its promises, both in its more extreme forms in the Communist world, and in its compromise versions.

She had discovered a quotation from James Callaghan, dating from 1960, praising the economic systems of Eastern Europe, and she harried it as would a dog a bone. She was relaxed and witty. She scorned the professed Labour belief in a mixed economy – 'as in a cocktail, it's the mix that counts'. She discoursed at length and in erudite fashion on the history of both socialism and capitalism, and she insisted that beneath the surface of the free enterprise economy lay the bedrock of the only viable ethical system. Choice was what she advocated, and 'Choice is the essence of ethics: if there were no choice, there would be no ethics, no good, no evil; good and evil have meaning only in so far as man is free to choose.' She offered a hardened and unsusceptible audience her vision of a new renaissance and then, just when she had established herself on a new level as a speaker and reached a different height as a politician, she, as always, returned to her roots, quoting Kipling:

> So when the world is asleep, and there seems no hope of waking
> Out of some long, bad dream that makes her mutter and moan,
> Suddenly, all men arise to the noise of fetters breaking,
> And everyone smiles at his neighbour, and tells him his soul is his
> own.

The audience rose. She smiled. She could, in truth, justly claim to have changed everything in her two years.

Chapter eight
The Victory

In mid-morning of 16 March 1976 Margaret Thatcher's secretary brought her the news that Harold Wilson had resigned as Prime Minister. For half an hour or so her office was in a buzz of anticipation and excitement. Only a few days previously – on 10 March – the government had been defeated in an important parliamentary vote on public expenditure, not least because of the abstention of thirty-seven Labour backbenchers. Lord George-Brown, a former Labour Foreign Secretary, had, on 2 March, resigned from the Party in open disgust. The pound was falling steadily on the international money markets. On 4 March the Labour majority in a by-election at Coventry had been halved; and on 11 March the Tories had retained the seats of Wirral and Carshalton, with swings of 13.8 and 8.4 per cent respectively. For half an hour or so, then, she was able to relish the prospect of electoral battle with a discredited minority government, evidently no longer possessing the will to go on; and in political circumstances which seemed to show that government to be bereft of all real authority.

What nobody on the Conservative side considered in that half hour was what turned out to be the truth, that Wilson had merely resigned as Prime Minister, and invited Labour to choose a successor: he was not planning to go to the country. To this day few could claim with any certainty that they understood his motives. To be sure, the situation was bad and he had seemed, for a long time, a tired man. But previously he had always relished difficult political circumstances, and in the 1964 parliament had markedly increased an already high reputation for tactical skill by his conduct of the affairs of a government enjoying only a miniscule majority. Perhaps the simple truth is – as he asserted himself – that he had long planned to go around this time and seek, after more than a decade at the top, the solace of a quiet political life on the backbenches.

By noon, therefore, Margaret Thatcher knew that her initial hopes were to be disappointed – unless, of course, Wilson's successor decided to seek an instant, or at least early, mandate. There was a certain measure of precedence for such a move, for it was widely remembered that in 1955 Sir Anthony Eden, on succeeding Winston Churchill, had gone to the country early and greatly increased his party's majority. On the other hand, the Tory government of 1955 was in much better shape at the time of decision than the Labour government in 1976. Still, Mrs Thatcher had been Leader of the Opposition for little more than a year: much could be made of her inexperience, not only in general, but in particular. And a fresh Labour face at the helm might well, many Tories thought, enjoy a considerable advantage over her. Moreover – so the same people believed – the state of the economy was likely to get worse rather than better, and so a new Labour leader might well be best advised to cut and run to the polls.

All these matters were brooded over and discussed in Tory circles as the morning wore on. A scratch meeting of those members of the Shadow Cabinet who were available was called to consider the auguries, and to await news of which – and how many – Labour hats would be in the ring. There was Roy Jenkins, the Home Secretary, and leader in effect of the so-called social democratic wing of the Labour Party. There was Michael Foot, at the opposite end of Labour's political spectrum, an eloquent purveyor of fundamental Socialism. There was the (somewhat battered) figure of the Chancellor, Dennis Healey. There was Anthony Crosland, Secretary of State for the Environment, and leading theoretician of social democracy, and Anthony Wedgwood-Benn, the former Lord Stansgate who now called himself Tony Benn and was the principal exponent of ideas to be found on the wilder shores of Socialism. And there was James Callaghan, the Labour Foreign Secretary and former Chancellor of the Exchequer. When the available members of the Shadow Cabinet converged, most of the betting – including that of Airey Neave, the grand master of Mrs Thatcher's own campaign for the leadership – was on Jenkins, with the Chairman of the Conservative Party, Lord Thorneycroft, for Callaghan. There were two accurate pieces of prophecy that morning. First, Thorneycroft said that if Callaghan emerged the victor he would sooner or later seek to shore up his parliamentary position by making an accomodation with the Liberals: this was duly done the following year. Then, sitting with Mrs Thatcher while she watched the midday television news bringing information about the candidates for the Labour succession, I asked her who she thought they would be wise to pick. 'Callaghan,' she said, 'would be hardest to beat.' She may well have recalled that judgement in the last week of the eventual general election campaign as, according to the opinion polls, her early lead slipped away, and the polls continually recorded a clean and increasing lead over her by the Prime Minister in public esteem.

Callaghan was duly elected Labour's leader on 5 April. From the very beginning he set himself to make the most of two advantages. In spite of a dismal period as Chancellor of the Exchequer in the middle sixties, he possessed an assuring and avuncular image, and this made a sharp contrast to both the novelty and the radicalism of his rival; in addition, he had not expected to be Prime Minister. He declared, therefore, that if the increasingly turbulent Labour Party did not follow his line he would be perfectly happy, either with or without an election defeat, to retire to his Sussex farm. The usefulness of this second position gradually declined as time went by, for it quickly became evident that the new Prime Minister did not sit at all loose to power: he loved it, and was most reluctant to put his possession of it in jeopardy. This became most clear during the September following his appointment as Prime Minister when the Labour Party chose as its National Youth Officer a young Trotskyist named Andrew Bevan, over repeated and angry expostulations and threats from the Prime Minister. And the point was underlined in a far more dramatic and conclusive fashion when, in October 1978, in spite of widespread expectations – even a widespread conviction – throughout the country that he would take advantage of a considerable improvement in Labour's position in the opinion polls to go to the country, he put off an election.

By this time his position was parlous in the extreme. Through the steady erosion of by-election defeats – with swings of, sometimes, more than twenty per cent against him – his government had been reduced to a minority position in the House of Commons. They survived only because of fairly constant support from the minority parties. Indeed, in 1977, the Liberals entered into a formal pact to support the government in return for consultation about its measures. In general the Nationalists, Scottish and Welsh, preferred Labour to the Tories: not least because, whereas Callaghan and his colleagues were pressing on with schemes for the creation of assemblies in Scotland and Wales to which a substantial amount of Westminster's power would be devolved, Mrs Thatcher was in the process of reversing her predecessor's commitment to just such a measure of devolution. Finally, even the Ulster Unionists (who, during most of their existence had taken the Tory whip) were, under the effective leadership of the former Tory, Enoch Powell, allying themselves with the government and exploiting their ability to influence the balance of power in Parliament to gain concessions to their point of view. They succeeded, in the end, in one of their most important aims: to procure for Ulster an increased parliamentary representation in Westminster, though it is right to add that the Tories also voted for this measure.

It was thus the case that, put forth her best efforts as she would, Margaret Thatcher was continually faced with an effective government majority in the Commons. This effective majority was not shaken even by some terrifying events, the most dramatic of which occurred on 28 September 1976 when the Chancellor, Denis Healey, on his way to important international conferences in Hong Kong and Manila, was forced to turn back at London airport to deal with a precipitate and catastrophic run on the pound. Subsequently, he procured a loan of some £2300m from the International Monetary Fund, but only at the cost of abandoning many of Labour's most treasured projects, and imposing tight restrictions on public spending. But the government survived.

Thus, the three and a bit years of the Callaghan Prime Ministership were intensely frustrating for his challenger. From time to time, of course, and on individual measures, sufficient numbers of the minority parties did vote with the Opposition and one or two remarkable triumphs were scored. But, as she put it herself, the tenacity with which Callaghan clung to office was worthy of a better cause. And during all that time, of course – with the brief exception of the autumn of 1978 – the Tories enjoyed a steady advantage in the opinion polls and continuing success in by-elections.

In seeking to overthrow the government, however, she was seriously inhibited by one self-denying ordinance: she would not enter into any form of arrangement with the minority parties. Again and again, even during the life of their pact with Labour, the Liberals insisted that they were, in principle, as willing to work with the Conservatives as with Labour. Their object, they insisted, was to restrain the immoderate tendencies of both the major parties, and to press forward towards a reform of the British electoral system which, through the introduction of proportional representation, would make the number of seats they won in a general election more commensurate with the number of votes they normally polled. To Margaret Thatcher, however, proportional representation is anathema. But, then, Labour managed to find Liberal allies without committing the Prime Minister to any reform of the electoral system; the Leader of the Opposition would not wheel or deal.

There were a number of her colleagues who, at least in private, seriously doubted the wisdom of her intransigence on this point. A small but not insignificant group of Tories came together in an organization to promote the adoption of proportional representation. By this means, they argued – though it is not easy to follow the reasoning – the Left would be permanently excluded from influence at the centre of British politics. Naturally, this was meat and drink to David Steel, the Liberal Leader. But in spite of blandishments from him Mrs Thatcher remained immovable.

There was a more substantial body of opinion in her Party which sought a reconciliation with the Ulster Unionists. One supporter of such an idea, indeed, was John Biggs-Davison, for some time her junior spokesman on Northern Ireland. There were, to be sure, some important obstacles to such a scheme. Enoch Powell was set against it partly, most Conservatives believed, out of malice towards his former Party, but also for the important reason that Powell believed firmly in dealing with government and could make Labour pay for the support of his group in tight votes. Then, too, Powell enjoyed particularly close relations with Michael Foot, the deputy leader of the Labour Party and, during this period, Leader of the House of Commons, with responsibility for getting the government's legislation through that chamber. However, within the Unionist ranks there was frequently evidence of a considerable degree of uneasiness with the tactics thus supported by Powell and by James Molyneux, the group's official leader. After all, there was little sympathy among Unionists for Socialism: they are, to a man, natural Tories. Again, however, the Leader of the Conservative Party would not budge.

The firmness of her resistance to all schemes for alliance with the smaller parties became evident in the days preceding the vote of confidence which eventually, in March 1979, saw the defeat of the government and the beginning of the election campaign. Official Unionist leaders from Ulster, not members of the House of Commons but enjoying at least a theoretical authority over their colleagues who were, visited London on what amounted to a shopping trip, inviting the leadership of the major parties to bid for their support. Airey Neave, the Conservative Shadow Secretary of State for Northern Ireland and Head of the Thatcher Private Office, had spent long and patient hours restoring civility to relations with the Ulster leaders, particularly Harry West. As the crucial vote approached it was obviously tempting in the extreme to try to ensure that the Ulsterman would march in the Tory lobby by at least hinting that their province and their movement would see better days under a Thatcher government. But Neave was flint-like, even going to the lengths of allowing the press to be informed that West had been sent away empty-handed.

Her resolute independence over the four years she spent as Leader of the Opposition thus gave a convenient focus on her conduct of affairs. There were those prepared to complain that she was too stiff-necked by half. Such views were the more readily held because of the poor state of Conservative morale at the time of the leadership election. The two defeats of 1974 had left the Party exhausted, shocked and even embittered. There was little enough confidence in the prospects for Tory revival. There was almost none, for instance, in the belief that a future Tory government would be able to work effectively with – or against – the trade unions. It seemed to many, therefore, politic at least to explore the possibilities of co-operation with others. But the Leader would have none of it. She aimed resolutely for an overall majority for herself and her Party, though there were many, in the press as well as within the Party, who were convinced that the 1974 elections had ushered in what might well be a long period of indecisive elections and so-called 'hung' parliaments.

Because of these differences, there was a separateness in authority about her which colleagues found unexpected. While it is true that the Conservative Party traditionally affords to its leaders a deference which parties differently constituted might regard as slavish, and while the Leader is the *fons et origo* of policy, it was expected from the beginning that she would prove a less dominating chief than her predecessors, and certainly than Edward Heath. There were a number of reasons for this belief. Her sex was one, and her relative inexperience another. There was also the fact that immediately after her election there arose in several important sections of the Party a feeling of distinct unease in the face of her clearly radical impulses. As Mr Keith Waterhouse was to put it in the *Daily Mirror* at the outset of the election campaign, it was not so much – at least on the surface – that there was opposition to her because she was a woman as that there was opposition to her kind of woman.

Some of the difficulties which she faced and, ultimately, surmounted can be illustrated from the story of the evolution of immigration policy. In 1962 the Conservatives, in the person of the then Home Secretary, R.A. Butler, had been the first Party to introduce measures restricting coloured (essentially, New Commonwealth) immigration into Britain. Though the Labour Opposition had fiercely resisted the Butler measure they did not, on coming to power in 1964, seek to repeal it. Indeed in 1968 they had, through the medium of their Home Secretary, James Callaghan, somewhat tightened up the Conservative measure, particularly as applied to holders of British passports coming from countries formerly in the British empire. To these provisions was added, during the life of the Heath government, a further Conservative measure in 1971.

But the evolution of Party attitudes on the subject that had taken place, particularly over the period since 1968, led to growing concern, fuelled by a prolonged and emotive campaign by Enoch Powell, who had been dismissed from the Conservative Front Bench by Edward Heath in 1968 as a consequence of one of his speeches on immigration. By 1975 it was widely held that the 1971 act had been shown to be ineffective. In consequence, and as part of the overall review of policy which she initiated as soon as she became Leader, Margaret Thatcher charged her deputy leader and Shadow Home Secretary, William Whitelaw, with the production of new proposals for further curbing immigration.

It was widely, if inaccurately, believed that there were sharp differences between the Leader and her deputy on the subject. In fact, as I learned from frequent conversations on the matter with Whitelaw (before 1970 I was the desk officer responsible for policy in immigration at the Conservative Research Department), he was quite as hawkish (to use the modish term) on the subject as she. And that a further curb or series of curbs on immigration was common ground in the Shadow Cabinet was shown in the Campaign Guide published in 1977.

The problem was, however, precisely what steps could be taken to achieve the desired end without excessive inhumanity, especially to the dependants of immigrants already in Britain who were planning to follow later. In the larger general picture, moreover, there was considerable, if somewhat vague, support for the oft-canvassed idea of a British nationality act, such as most other countries possess, and which would lay down, once and for all, who was entitled to reside in the United Kingdom.

Whitelaw and his team worked on all these subjects. But before their report was completed – and quite some time before the Shadow Cabinet had had an opportunity to consider the subject – trouble began. There was a series of clearly inspired leaks to the press from the proceedings of the All-Party Select Committee on Immigration and Race Relations. The majority of the committee, it seemed, shared the Conservative apprehension about the level of immigration. Then, from a Tory source – not Whitelaw himself – came largely accurate accounts of what the Opposition was planning. These revelations flustered Whitelaw, and his palpable disorientation was taken by a number of journalists to mean that he in fact differed on the matter from his Leader.

Then, on 30 January 1978, Mrs Thatcher appeared on television. In itself, this was a slightly odd occasion. During the leadership campaign Granada TV filmed a report on her efforts which she and her family much liked. In a casual moment she had undertaken, if elected, to give the producer an exclusive interview. By 1978 he was in charge of a local area current affairs show, not nationally networked, and he sought to reclaim his rain check. However, the interview she did was seen by the Granada people to be of much wider interest and significance than they had expected. Her permission to put the film out on the network was sought and granted. What had seized Granada's attention was the passage about immigration in which, having commented on a native fear of being 'swamped' by coloured immigrants, she added, 'We are not in politics to ignore people's worries: we are in politics to deal with them.'

These comparatively innocuous remarks created a sensation. Unfortunately, moreover, Whitelaw had not been informed about the interview, and his consequent and very evident embarrassment strengthened rumours of a breach between them. It was widely believed that she had perpetrated a serious gaffe, and even suggested that she did not have the authority so to pronounce on policy without having discussed the matter with the Shadow Cabinet.

On the other hand, there was a solid body of opinion, consisting not just of those who were concerned about immigration but of others as well, which defended her behaviour stoutly. All that happened, ran their argument, was that Margaret was asked a question which she answered without flannelling. That, they went on, is what makes her different from other politicians, and a good thing, too. Whatever the merits or demerits of the argument, she showed no sign either of perturbation in the face of hostile press coverage or, for that matter, of in any way diluting the immigration policy she adopted.

Though the question of immigration policy is an extremely serious one, the *contretemps* over her Granada interview is not of itself terribly important. I have described it at some length in order to illustrate and highlight the way in which judgement about her leadership was beginning to develop and her reaction to it. By the time a general election eventually came, there was a certain amount of unanimity at least in the press about her nature and character. It was widely accepted, for example, that she was an unusually straight-forward and down-to-earth politician and, essentially, an unusually honest one. It was felt by many, however, that her lack of discretion in such episodes as the immigration dispute indicated a naïvety undesirable in a leading politician and potential prime minister. Journalists who had met her, even if they were not of her persuasion, inclined to be favourable. Indeed, there were many tributes to her private charm. Her public image, however, remained a somewhat frosty one. She was thought of as tough, if not actually a little wild. Her stinging denunciations of Socialism, her (some thought) all too frequent attempts to bring the government down on a vote of confidence – one such effort led to the Lib-Lab pact – and her abrasiveness in political argument, all constituted a phenomenon unfamiliar in British politics: that of the politician as ideologue.

Yet there were highly important areas of policy and tactics where she showed a quite exceptional ability for quiet diplomacy. Of these, easily the most sensitive was the question of devolution for Scotland and Wales. She inherited a difficult policy position, and one that was at odds with her essential instincts, for she had the gravest reservations about the whole idea of setting up semi-independent assemblies in Scotland and Wales.

The middle years of the sixties saw the development of a great vogue for participation politics, accompanied by a steady rise in the influence of the Scottish National Party. In 1967 Edward Heath had set up a Scottish Policy Group, and in May 1968, following its report, Margaret Thatcher proposed to the Scottish Tory conference that there should be an elected Scottish Assembly. This policy statement rapidly became known as the Declaration of Perth. It was followed, in August 1968, by a Conservative commission under Sir Alec Douglas-Home charged with working out the details of the proposal. Not to be outdone, the Wilson government appointed a Royal Commission on the constitution in April 1969.

In March 1970 the Scottish Constitutional Committee proposed a directly elected assembly, and both the major Party manifestos adopted this proposal for the general election of June 1970. In

October 1973 the Royal Commission also recommended an
assembly, and the Conservative manifesto for the general election of
February 1974 repeated the June 1970 pledge – which had not been
implemented because of the delays occasioned by local government
reforms. Not only, therefore, was Margaret Thatcher saddled in
1975 with a commitment which she distrusted, but it was one to
which the Party, and particularly the Scottish section of the Party
(though there were notable exceptions) had made repeated
obeisance. Indeed, it was so powerfully supported by some sections
of Scottish Tory opinion that its abandonment would have invited a
most serious split.

Her first test was the Scottish Party conference in May 1975.
Despite the urgings of some of her advisers, she declined to abandon
the Perth commitment. However, she did reject suggestions for her
speech made by her Scottish Shadow Ministers, and inserted a
powerful peroration stressing above all the Tory commitment to
union, rather than the desirability or necessity of providing the Scots
with more control over their own affairs. This – a highly important
shift of emphasis – indicated to those willing to see it that the retreat
from the devolution commitment had begun.

Her conduct from then to the referendum in Scotland and Wales
in 1979 was a fascinating exercise in political skill. True, she lost her
entire Scottish Office team when she decided to oppose legislation
providing for devolution introduced by the government. After
spending most of a day endeavouring to persuade her colleagues to
change their minds about resignation, she none the less indicated the
state of her own mind by appointing as Shadow Secretary of State for
Scotland Teddy Taylor, the notoriously anti-devolution member for
Glasgow Cathcart. She did not, however, entrust him with the full
and undivided responsibility for managing the Tory campaign on
devolution, giving that task first to Whitelaw and later to Francis
Pym who had been Heath's chief whip and, subsequently and
briefly, Secretary of State for Northern Ireland. In this extremely
delicate position Pym proved himself, it is universally agreed, to be a
politician of exceptional skill, so much so that by the time of the
general election he had become favourite to succeed her should
disaster befall her.

On the issue of devolution she demonstrated her possession of a quality not normally associated with her even by her admirers: the quality of exceptional patience. In general, the Tory Party in Parliament sought the alliance of Labour members themselves opposed to devolution, most notably Tam Dalyell and George Cunningham. The latter was the author of an amendment to the government's bill which subsequently proved to be the means of wrecking devolution. The Conservatives supported him in his argument that a simple majority for devolution in the referendum would not suffice to set up the assembly, and required instead an ample plurality of those voting and high percentage of the previous average Scottish general election turnout. during these debates she took special care not to wound the susceptibilities of Labour's anti-devolution measures, standing down both herself and Taylor from a number of debates in deference to the antipathy she and he attracted from some Socialist MPs. In the event, she then found herself strong enough to advocate a 'no' vote in the referendum, in which appeal, to her great pleasure, she was joined by the doyen of the party in Scotland, Lord Home. Although, then, the devolutionists did gain a majority on the day, it was insufficient to give them their hearts' desire. She ended the campaign in very much better shape in the matter of commitments on Scottish policy than she had begun it – and in very much better shape than the government as well.

The gradually emerging pattern of her leadership, indeed, demonstrated her determination eventually to take office burdened with as few policy commitments as possible. Her success in this regard has had something of the flavour of paradox. It is clear that no British political leader of modern times has so distinct and identifiable an ideological image. Her libertarian capitalistic attitudes are known to and recognized by all. Likewise her right-wing stand on matters such as immigration and law and order have made a successfully deep impression on the public mind. Yet, the more one examines the policy baggage which she has acquired in the course of her journey the more one realizes how successfully she has resisted the giving of hostages to fortune. Devolution is not her only success in this regard.

And it was her triumph over devolution, rather than her successful deployment of economic arguments such as have in recent years become the staple of British political argument, and more even than the wretched winter of industrial strife which preceded the election, that brought about the fall of the Callaghan government.

After the referendum débâcle Callaghan faced a particularly serious parliamentary situation, with a growing number of critics within his own Party beginning loudly to deplore his refusal to go the country at the moment when the polls had favoured him, in October 1978. For, in spite of the referendum result a pro-devolution parliamentary option remained open to him. He was required, by his own legislation, and following the referendum, to lay before the House orders for the repeal of the devolution acts. But he could, of course, invite the House to vote those orders down and still proceed with an assembly – at least in Scotland where, in contrast to Wales, a majority had supported devolution.

This the Scottish National Party, which had been of continual parliamentary use to him following the demise of the Lib-Lab pact, insisted he should do. It was an impossible course in practice, for there was no chance of obtaining a majority for the proposal. However, it had certain merits. For one thing, it was something he had done before when, as Home Secretary in the Wilson government, he had used the then substantial Labour majority to vote down the proposals of the Boundary Commission for revising British constituencies in such a way as, it was thought, to favour the Conservatives. For another, such a move, even if it was unsuccessful, might at least placate the SNP, who could be assured that the Prime Minister had at least done his best to keep his word to them. However, demoralized by the referendum, and rudderless in practice, the Callaghan government seemed incapable of effective decision-making. The hour of its fall was at hand.

The Conservatives had more than once failed to defeat the government in crucial votes. Margaret Thatcher was, therefore, exceptionally cautious in preparing the way for another vote of confidence. This time, however, the omens were very much better than the previous spring, when her attempt to defeat Callaghan had merely produced the pact. For on this occasion, with a confidence that seemed remarkable given his Party's by-election results (and, in the event of the election, unjustified), David Steel announced a firm intention of voting against the government and thus seeking an early election. He was joined by the SNP, furious at their failure, and blind to the dangers a general election would pose for them. As Callaghan observed in the confidence debate, minority support for the Tories on this occasion was the first recorded instance of turkeys voting for an early Christmas: the Nationalists, in the event, lost nine of their eleven seats, and the Liberals saw their former Leader, Jeremy Thorpe, their economic spokesman, John Pardoe, and their defence spokesman, Emlyn Hooson, go down to defeat – Hooson in a seat that had been Liberal for a century.

As the day of the vote – Wednesday, 28 March – approached, frantic efforts were made by ministers to shore up their crumbling positions. The two Welsh Nationalist members (one of whom was to lose his seat in the election) were placated by an offer of a bill compensating quarry workers suffering from dust disease. Major efforts were again made with the Ulster Unionists, and the suggestion of large-scale financial help for Northern Ireland was dangled before them. On this occasion, however, all but two Unionists stood firm with the Opposition, in spite of the fact that Airey Neave had refused to make any extra promises to them.

Came the night of the 28th. All day the tide of speculation ebbed and flowed, and by early evening Margaret Thatcher had begun to wonder if she had not made a serious blunder, for the expectations of victory were so high that defeat might have been a bad blow to morale. True, there was not much dignity about the government's scramble for survival. Special attempts were made, for example, to persuade the Independent Irish Republic member, Frank Maguire, to vote with them: in the event Maguire, who rarely bothers to attend Westminster, came over to (as he put it) 'abstain in person'.

It was evident that the vote would be exceptionally close. As the calculations became more and more intense it began to be believed that Callaghan would survive, probably by a single vote. Apprehension mounted on the Conservative benches. A Labour teller came through from the division lobbies and gave a thumbs-up sign to his colleagues. Mrs Thatcher was shattered, turning to Whitelaw, beside her on the bench, and repeating, 'I'm sorry. Oh, I'm sorry.' But, a moment later gloom shifted to the other side of the House as the Conservative teller, Spencer Le Marchant, advanced to the Speaker's chair and announced victory, by a single vote, for the Tories. The following day the Prime Minister announced that the general election would take place on 3 May.

But, on Friday the naturally jubilant Conservatives – and, indeed, the whole body of politicians – were plunged into gloom by the murder by terrorists of Airey Neave. It was an almost unimaginable personal blow to Margaret Thatcher, and the extent of the shock was clear to millions of television viewers who saw her reaction to the news on an early evening television programme. Neave had become, in the four years of her leadership, almost a father to her. I discussed in an earlier chapter his skill in managing her campaign for the leadership, but it is important to remember how stout a support he was to her as Head of her Private Office, a constant counsellor completely unaffected by the passing crises of quotidian politics, and a subtle master of his profession.

The Thatcher plan was to fight an exceptionally low-key campaign, and to expose her personality far more than her policies. Since the Prime Minister planned to do much the same thing in his own campaign, the weeks of the struggle presented an undistinguished, not to say drab, spectacle. But it was her conviction, and the conviction of her advisers, that the essential object of their operation was to enable as many people as possible to see and even meet the candidate, so that the private warmth of her personality would overcome potentially dangerous public hostility to the chill of her political persona.

To be sure, her campaign was not on one or two specific policies. At its heart was a proposal drastically to reduce taxation and to move rapidly towards the creation of a free market economy. But it could be argued – and many commentators did argue – that Callaghan had the best of her in discussion of such proposals. Particularly during the second week of the campaign, as the Conservative lead in the polls shortened, it began to appear possible that the Prime Minister would pull off a famous victory, and that the almost incredible career of Mrs Thatcher would come to an end. As she said herself, 'I'll only be given the chance to win or lose *one*. If we win, I'll have a chance of another.'

If that remark implied a certain nervousness about her prospects, such was not apparent during the campaign itself. She made very few speeches, and only one – at Cardiff, deep in Callaghan territory – that might justly be called major or philosophical. But she criss-crossed the country in a seemingly endless series of constituency visits – in the American phrase, pressing the flesh. She was followed wherever she went by a truly amazing caravan of journalists and cameramen, including, it sometimes seemed, every foreign reporter in town, for the fascination of the first woman leader of a major Western party spread well beyond British shores. And, despite a slight failure in her voice towards the end of the second week, she never faltered. Trim, unflappable, elegant, she took all the intensely personalized campaigning with a smile, accompanied everywhere by her equally calm, but somewhat protective husband. So good did Denis Thatcher turn out to be at the business of politics that Frank Johnson was moved to say, in the *Daily Telegraph*, 'From Norfolk until the end in the South London marginals yesterday afternoon he fought a campaign conspicuous for its dignity, candour, laconic humour. . . . For these reasons my vote for Man of the Match goes to Denis Thatcher. The only thing which can stop him reaching Number 10 tomorrow is his wife.'

But that eventuality did not occur. The even tenor of her fight went right on to the end. If it did not provide opportunities for more than rather frivolous copy, and if in consequence it was intellectually the reverse of stimulating, her campaign was more remarkable than any since Harold Macmillan's in 1959 for the way it proceeded exactly according to plan, unruffled and undisturbed by accident, blunder or outside events.

And that was also paradoxical. For few were in doubt that a victory for her would produce one of the most markedly radical prime ministers of recent times – one absolutely set on transforming the nature of the society she was elected to govern. From a welfare state, with social provision coming more and more from government, she had always made it clear that her object was to create an essentially free enterprise economy: '. . . you have constantly to assert that people have a moral responsibility which they must accept. Moral in the widest sense of the term. Moral responsibility for their own actions. We must exorcise the idea that if you do something wrong it is not your fault but the fault of society around.'

It is, of course, conceivable that she will fail in her task. The problems that beset her, not of failure only, but of ingrained social habit, are formidable. On the other hand, anyone who considers what she has achieved so far, and from such an unremarkable beginning, would be brave indeed to argue that she will not achieve what she has now set herself to do. Whatever else happens, Margaret Thatcher's Britain will be a bracing and challenging place in which to live.

THE HILLS IS LONELY

Lillian Beckwith

When Lillian Beckwith advertised for a quiet, secluded place in the country, she received the following unorthodox description of the attractions of life on an isolated Hebridean croft:

'Surely it's that quiet here even the sheeps themselves on the hills is lonely and as to the sea it's that near I use it myself every day for the refusals . . .'

Intrigued by her would-be landlady's letter and spurred on by the sceptism of her friends, Lillian Beckwith replied in the affirmative. THE HILLS IS LONELY is the hilarious and enchanting story of the extremely unusual rest cure that followed.

65p

LILLIAN BECKWITH'S HEBRIDEAN COOKBOOK

Lillian Beckwith's stories of her life as a crofter on the Hebridean island of Bruach have delighted her millions of readers over the years. Now she has collected together the many traditional recipes that she learnt in her Bruach kitchen.

Ranging from the simple, delicious dishes of Hebridean fare to her own versions of universal favourites, LILLIAN BECKWITH'S HEBRIDEAN COOKBOOK contains unusual and original recipes for every occasion and budget.

80p

THOMAS THE FISH

Diana Morgan

When the giant Goliath Copper Mining Company decide to develop the beautiful valley above the village of Llangoch, they don't anticipate any difficulties that a few pounds won't smooth away.

But then the villagers are quite unlike anybody the American company executives have ever encountered. Olwen the Post, Glyn the Bank, Jenkins the Co-op and Tommy the Phantom Rapist lead the would-be developers a merry dance.

And the greatest schemer of them all is Thomas the Fish, a wily old poacher grown rich on his ill-gotten gains, who vows to drive the foreigners from his valley . . .

'A gem of a book' *Derby Evening Telegraph*

70p

HEDINGHAM HARVEST

Geoffrey Robinson

For years Geoffrey Robinson has recorded his family's accounts of village life in Lincolnshire. Based on these memories, *Hedingham Harvest* is a cheerful, affectionate and often hilarious chronicle of life and love in a Victorian village.

'A delightfully lively, graphic and captivating chronicle of village life' *Sunday Express*

'Marvellous . . . unique of its kind' *Guardian*

85p

CLARA REEVE
Leonie Hargrave

Clara Reeve – the neglected orphan of a noble family who, by a strange twist of fate, inherits the fortune intended for her cousin Niles.

Niles, Conte de Visconti – his soft sinister charm draws Clara into marriage – and a web of deception and depravity stretching from the moors of Cumberland to the glittering salons of Venice.

Manfredo – the sinister valet whose strange amusements involve Niles in passions and intrigues that Clara scarcely understands.

Fear and jealousy, money and property, rank and power – innocent, captivating Clara is caught in the web of these magnificent obsessions. And she must suffer bewildering changes in fortune before this enthralling novel reaches a horrifying resolution high on the slopes of Vesuvius.

'Enthralling . . . on the scale of *Gone with the Wind' Sunday Times*

'Crammed with suspense and excitement . . . elegance and power . . . I don't remember such a good period thriller since *Rebecca* so long ago!' *Sir John Gielgud*

'A nightmare vision of Victorian sexuality . . . rich . . . entertaining . . . splendidly wrought' *New York Times Book Review*

80p

A BREATH OF BORDER AIR

Lavinia Derwent

'Looking back, I often wonder if any of it was real . . .'

Lavinia Derwent, well known as a best-selling author of children's books, and as a television personality, memorably portrays a childhood spent on a lonely farm in the Scottish Border country.

Hers was an enchanted world of adventure: a world of wayward but endearing farm animals, and of local characters like Jock-the-Herd . . . and Lavinia's closest friend, Jessie, who never failed to temper her earthy wisdom with a rare sense of humour.

'A love of a book' *Glasgow Herald*

60p

ANOTHER BREATH OF BORDER AIR

Lavinia Derwent

Lavinia Derwent takes us back to the magical world of a childhood spent on an isolated Border country farm that she so memorably captured in her first bestselling book – A BREATH OF BORDER AIR.

Now surrounded by colourful and often hilarious local characters like Jock-the-Herd, Auld Baldy-Heid and her old friend Jessie, Lavinia experiences the thrilling moments of growing up – her graduation to the Big School, her first visit to Edinburgh and the excitement of crossing the Border to England for a seaside holiday. And, above all she still enjoys the everyday excitements of life on the farm.

'Lavinia Derwent has the rare power to bring the past alive'
Sunday Times

70p

DESTROYER

Ewart Brookes

'The best book on the subject I have ever read' Douglas Reeman

'Seek out and attack the enemy'

The motto of those who serve in destroyers sums up the magnificent history of this fighting ship.

Destroyer is the story of a breed of ship that has inspired more loyalty among the men who sailed and fought in them, provided more stories of gallantry, high adventure and hard-fought action than any other in recent naval history.

'A thrilling account of the role of a brave breed of fighting ship in two World Wars' *Evening News*

75p

HOW TO ORDER

If you would like to order any of the books advertised in these pages, send purchase price plus 8p postage per book to Arrow Books, Book Service by Post, P.O. Box 29, Douglas, Isle of Man. Customers outside the UK should send purchase price plus 10p postage per book.

Whilst every effort is made to keep prices down and to keep popular books in print, Arrow Books cannot guarantee that prices will be the same as those advertised here or that the books will be available.